Pierre Franey's
Cooking in America

Pierre Franey's Cooking in America

PIERRE FRANEY AND RICHARD FLASTE

Illustrations by Lauren Jarrett

 ALFRED A. KNOPF   NEW YORK   1994

THIS IS A BORZOI BOOK
PUBLISHED BY ALFRED A. KNOPF, INC.

Copyright © 1992 by Pierre Franey and Richard Flaste
Illustrations copyright © 1992 by Lauren Jarrett

All rights reserved under International and Pan-American Copyright
Conventions. Published in the United States by Alfred A. Knopf, Inc.,
New York, and simultaneously in Canada by Random House of Canada
Limited, Toronto. Distributed by Random House, Inc., New York.

ISBN 0-679-75288-9
LC 91-23227

Manufactured in the United States of America

Published April 6, 1992

First Paperback Edition, August 1994

For Betty and Dale

Contents

Introduction   x i

CATTLE COUNTRY: BEEF   3

A GLANCE TOWARD SPAIN   2 1

COOKING WITH CHILDREN   3 5

THE CAJUN LIFE   5 1

A CRAB FEAST   7 7

HONEY   9 1

WEST INDIAN COOKING IN AMERICA   1 0 7

PRAISE THE PIG   1 2 1

THE OLD FAMILIES AND THE NEW BREED   1 3 5

EVEN THE HUMBLE POTATO . . .   1 5 9

THE TROUT HARVEST   1 7 5

MADE IN AMERICA: RICE   1 8 5

SAY CHEESE   1 9 7

THE BIG CATCH   211

STRAWBERRIES AND ARTICHOKES   227

AMERICA'S BIRD: TURKEY   245

SALMON SPLENDOR   261

BEYOND SAN JUAN   277

THE LENTIL LAND   293

IN THE GROVES   307

THE FOOD AND WINE OF NAPA VALLEY   321

SPA CUISINE   339

THE RISKIEST FRUIT: CHERRIES   351

Vegetable Side Dishes, Salads, Sauces and Stocks   367

Afterword: The Studio Set   379

Index   381

In a book designed to accompany a television series, it is always difficult to determine how much influence the video people had on the book and vice versa. A great many of the people who helped and guided us are already cited in the course of the narrative. In addition, here are some of the indispensable people on the television side: Charles Pinsky, the producer and director of the show, was the ringmaster. The executive producer was John T. Potthast. Michel Roux of Carillon Importers was the show's benefactor.

The technical staff varied, but traveling with us to handle camera, audio and lighting on most trips were Jeff Cirbes, Steve Mason and Bob Benedetti; at other times we were joined by Harry Vaughn, Tim Pugh, Frank Leung, Marlene Rodman and Ray Kawata. Behind-the-scenes chefs were Lauren Jarrett (also this book's illustrator) and Maurice Bertrand; food coordinators were Carol Carpenter and Faith Durgin. The associate producer was Anne de Ravel; coordinating producer was Margaret Sullivan; assistant producers and directors were John Alan Spoler, Natalie Seltz, Donna Hunt and Frank Batavick; public-information directors were Sharon Philippart and Dorothy Fuchs. In fact, the entire Maryland Public Television studio staff was, as usual, extraordinarily skillful and diligent.

The book itself was encouraged and refined by a good friend of long standing, its editor, Jonathan Segal.

Introduction

As we began our journey through America, we—those of us working on this book and the television show that it accompanies—knew the objectives. The idea was to search out and celebrate the nation's spectacular food. That meant we needed to talk to Americans everywhere about what they cook and eat. And we needed to visit the most productive fields and streams to see the wellspring of the nation's bounty with our own eyes. Still, as we tried to imagine just what we would discover out there in Alaska or Florida or Iowa, it was, of course, impossible to really know until we made the trip.

Who could have guessed what the sky would be like over the Pacific, from the vantage point of a strawberry field reaching right to the sea? How could we have anticipated the awesome beauty of the Nevada high desert where, in the first light of day, cowboys still gallop and shout, a million miles from civilization? And the roar of the airboat as it glided through the bayou. . . . Who could have completely imagined the experience ahead of time?

But what impressed me most—and I think everyone in our group would agree—was the intensity and the love that Americans bring to the production and cooking of food. Potatoes, for instance, are literally babied as they come out of the ground, moved along on padded conveying machinery so that they won't bruise. And wherever harvesttime beckons, there are Americans working from dawn to dark to bring in the treasure. Sometimes they start long before dawn. At 2 A.M. on a chilly June day, a 58-foot boat equipped with a seining net will make its way out of the harbor at Ketchikan, Alaska, toward some spot in the black, choppy water where whole schools of fish will be captured before they reach their spawning streams. And as the sun is setting in El Campo, Texas, after a steamy day in midsummer, the

combines are still plying the rice fields, gathering a food staple that will go to feed Americans and people in much of the rest of the world, too.

Everywhere, in fact, we discovered that food we took for granted was really a stunning part of the American adventure. A region of Washington and Idaho called the Palouse (a French-derived term alluding to green lawns) produces virtually all of the nation's lentils. Ordinarily, we think of lentils as a drab-looking product. But the journey to the Palouse—the expansive terrain and the warm people—was such a beautiful experience that lentils will never look the same to us again.

Everything out there in the food-producing areas poses risks and rewards. The most dramatic and unfortunate example was presented to us by the cherries we saw near Yakima, Washington. No sooner had we learned how fragile the crop was, how rain during the harvest could fill the cherries with water and make them burst, ruining the whole crop—no sooner had we learned that when the rains came. We were out of Yakima just a few days when we heard of the devastation.

The family farm is certainly not what it used to be, as big business has absorbed so many of the smaller operations in the quest for greater and greater efficiency. But we can testify to this: Lots of family farms are still functioning well, relying on the most dedicated workers of all, the members of the family itself. In so many of these places, we might see a grandparent driving a combine, a niece or a grandson driving a truck. The advantage on the farms—as it was with the Montauk waterman who takes his children out to sea just as his great-grandparents took him with them as they worked—is that their food-producing wisdom and intense affection for the earth survive, passed on from generation to generation. The family-run farm preserves individuality. It allows for the sort of independence that inspires a citrus grower in Florida to produce the oranges that will earn the paycheck, but also an uncommon, unprofitable tangerine, the Royal Lee, just because he admires it so much—"the food of the gods," he calls it.

As for the restaurants, there were excellent ones where you might imagine they'd be: Fullers in Seattle, Tra Vigne in the Napa Valley of California, Pierpoint in Baltimore and The River Café in New York City. But we also had a terrific time in Moscow, Idaho, meeting a young chef who runs a whimsical restaurant called Café Spudnik. And we ate wonderfully well in a poor section of San Juan, Puerto Rico, at a little restaurant called Casita Blanca. Some of the best restaurants we visited demonstrated how very aware they were of the need to foster and protect the flavors and customs of their region—and that made these establishments shine all the more.

Often we toured an area's markets. Each, from New Orleans, Louisiana, to Madison, Wisconsin, is different in its own way. But surprisingly, they were all very much alike, too. The market in Ponce, Puerto Rico, and the legendary Pike Place in Seattle are both bursting with color and life, crowded and joyous. All of these markets are significant contributors to the thrust in this country away from overly processed foods and toward fresh ingredients.

The amazing thing is the lengths that people will go to keep those foods fresh. All across America, right now and on their way toward a market near you, are trucks and planes bearing California's fresh artichokes, perhaps, or fresh trout from Idaho. Seen this way, the whole country is a blur of food whisking hither and yon at high speed so that it is still fresh when it reaches you—even if that means driving straight through from one coast to the other.

This book tells the story of our experiences: who we met, what we did and what we learned. Even though it closely parallels the television series of the same name, it is capable of standing alone. The book contains the recipes for the dishes that we demonstrate on television, of course, but it also presents many more that were suggested by the regions we visited or by the particular foods we chose for our focus. The book, like the show, does not visit everywhere in America. But in creating it we saw the big picture; we saw the American heart.

Pierre Franey's
Cooking in America

Cattle Country: Beef

America is supposed to be a place where the old ways die easy. But time and again, as we whisked across the country with our motley band of TV people, we found the past alive and well and living somewhere beautiful. This site in northern Nevada, in particular, on the high desert—a flat plain 5,200 feet above sea level, flanked by soft, undulating hills—is a bastion of old-time ranching. This is a part of the country where the cowboys wear big dusty rimmed hats and follow the cattle on horseback. It's a place of high, cloudless skies. The nights are frigid, and during the day wind gusts burst across the plain with a ruthless disregard for people, animals, tents and the fragile foliage.

On the IL Ranch, where we'd arrived after some 14 hours of travel by jet, truck and single-engine Cessna, there are 500,000 acres of land for grazing cattle. The terrain is moistened by a mere 8 or 10 inches of rain a year and yields so little food for the animals that each cow needs about 100 acres a year to survive. In this magnificent but harsh environment, the cowboys seem happy, even jubilant in their escape from the civilized world, and the cattle appear content enough, roaming the great distances on their own until the cowboys come hooting and hollering on horseback to move them to new pasture.

Each of the eight cowboys in the group we joined owns his own tepee. When we arrived we were not afforded any special luxury. We were given sleeping bags and sent off to bed either in tepees or a couple of large tents (that were no match for the wind, which ripped their sides free). As dark fell, two of the video crew wandered off, unfurled their sleeping bags beneath the sky and settled in right there, on the unsheltered ground. All of us awoke early. Although it was already mid-June, the temperature had plunged into the 30's.

But none of us was up and roaming about as early as the people in the cook tent.

At 3:30 A.M., the gas lanterns were lit and Bernie Bainbridge, the cook, was already starting the coffee. That's standard breakfast fare out here, along with scrambled eggs. Later in the day, the cowboys will be fed mostly beef, in the form of steaks and roasts. On Sundays, they get chicken prepared one way or another. Bernie bakes hundreds of cookies a week, too. The cook tent was attached to a genuine chuck wagon, which the ranchers use to haul their stove, water and provisions. By 4:30 A.M the cook tent—a structure glowing in the still-dark morning—was full of cowboys, already wearing their hats, drinking coffee and laughing at each other's wisecracks.

Sure, it is possible to have a central headquarters and go out after the cattle in trucks everyday, even transporting them by truck when necessary. Many ranches do that. On a ranch as big as this, however, Bob Rebholtz, who supervises the ranch, wants his people to follow the cattle as they move, set up branding pens on the location and brand them there. He also wants to give his sophisticated genetic breeding methods a chance to work. When a new breed of cattle is introduced to the herd, it is intended to alter the nature of this vast gene pool in a very specific way. But the tool for doing that is nature, which is allowed to take its course. Gradually the characteristics of the new cattle will be seen to emerge throughout the herd. It's a system that requires freely roaming cattle in a natural environment.

Also, Bill Russell, an old-time cowhand with a brush mustache and wearing a black hat and checked shirt, explained that the cowboys just liked horses. For one thing they're more reliable than trucks. When it does rain, he said, "trucks get stuck in the mud. Horses don't. Horses always start."

The chuck wagon is the enduring symbol of old-style ranching because it is the traveling hearth that accompanies cowboys when they roam the land. If you're going to follow the cattle over hundreds of miles, staying with them for five days in one place, then pushing them 40 miles or so to another feeding ground, one piece of equipment is indispensable, the chuck wagon. It has to be there, wherever "there" is, for breakfast, lunch and dinner. This is hungry work in the heat and the dust.

It seems like such a hard life, but not a single cowboy conceded that it was difficult. One, Roger Fisher, who had been running cows for 20 years, was just glad to be away from people, he told us one evening. "Town is all right," he said, the flickering light in the tent dancing around his face and glinting on his glasses, "but not for long." Another of the cowboys, David Slover, had badly wanted to be a cowboy all his life. But his family back in Connecticut wasn't so pleased with the prospect. So to satisfy them, he went to college, Colorado State, but—and this was so sly of him—he majored in range ecology. And, lo and behold, he found himself out here in the middle of nowhere as a genuine buckaroo, learning "when to do stuff and when not to do stuff." And these men do call themselves buckaroos. It's a term—as Bill Maupin, the ranch's general manager, explained it to us—that connotes special pride in rope and saddle and horse.

As the light came up, soft and slow, burning away the chill in the air, we could see the cowboys getting their saddles and bridles in order, practicing tossing their ropes, gabbing about the kind of tobacco they were chewing. The tepees that had been invisible in the dark came clear again, pointing upward across the landscape like so many little pyramids.

Bill Maupin called out the names of the buckaroos, and they in turn called out the names of the horses they had chosen for the day . . . Flash, Popcorn, Doc, Yo-Yo. Each cowboy has a week's supply of horses and it's up to him to know the one that's likely to be sufficiently rested on a given day. Then Bill and one of the other cowboys race into a large pen, separate out the designated horses and in a group they trot over to the waiting buckaroos. Steady now, all lined up side by side in a makeshift corral, the horses stand, almost tranquilly, poised for the saddle.

Then it's off into the desert. And how these young men love their work! They shout and carry on as they head out to round up the calves for branding. They fan out over a vast area and, riding this way and that, maneuver the cows and calves toward a branding pen. The idea is to keep the young ones with their mothers and cut the bulls away from the herd so they don't interfere.

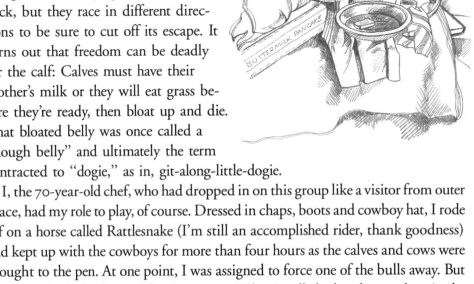

When a calf pulls away from the group, two cowboys gallop off to get it back, but they race in different directions to be sure to cut off its escape. It turns out that freedom can be deadly for the calf: Calves must have their mother's milk or they will eat grass before they're ready, then bloat up and die. That bloated belly was once called a "dough belly" and ultimately the term contracted to "dogie," as in, git-along-little-dogie.

I, the 70-year-old chef, who had dropped in on this group like a visitor from outer space, had my role to play, of course. Dressed in chaps, boots and cowboy hat, I rode off on a horse called Rattlesnake (I'm still an accomplished rider, thank goodness) and kept up with the cowboys for more than four hours as the calves and cows were brought to the pen. At one point, I was assigned to force one of the bulls away. But that was mostly for fun and for the camera. What I really had to do, out there in the brilliant sun and the wind, was cook some steak, lean but tender sirloin, followed by a dessert of strawberries Romanoff (see recipe, page 236).

I am an unfaltering admirer of beef and veal, even in a time when red meat has lost some of its popularity. It seems to me that these days those meats can be just about as lean as you want them to be. And they have, throughout all the centuries of culinary history, provided some of the best eating known to man. I am not going to reject them now.

In this case, speaking of culinary history, I was determined to prepare one of the most traditional of all sauces, even there on the wind-swept open range: a béarnaise. Now, you might think such a fancy sauce was going to be met with hoots of derision. But it wasn't. It's true, I may have been aided by the wine we brought. Cowboys don't drink on the range, ordinarily. They wait until they get their four days off, and then this particular group heads for a place called Elko, where they drink everything in sight. But now the wine was a treat, permitted under the unusual circumstances of our presence. Anyway, it loosened them up a bit. They thought it was hilarious when a gust of wind blew my hat away during a taping session.

I cooked the steaks over a charcoal fire in a crude pit, with the help of Bernie who turned them for me and with the help of the wind, which spread the salt quite evenly, thank you. Meanwhile, I whisked together the egg yolks, butter and seasonings required for the béarnaise. When I served these hardened cowboys their steaks with sauce, it was a great triumph. Bill Maupin invited me to sign on as a cook. I told him I'd consider it—when I retire. One of the cowboys, a veteran buckaroo, looked up at me from a glistening, clean plate—and he said, almost timidly, "Pierre, could you give me the recipe." I explained how to cook the sauce as best I could, but I think I made it sound too difficult, urging him to watch the eggs ever so carefully so they wouldn't turn out scrambled; I issued several other warnings, too. His eyes glazed over. But I know he loved the food.

I just wish I could have been a fly on the wall of that cook tent the next morning, listening to the cowboys talk about us. Laughter, for sure. But I do believe they sort of liked us.

That Béarnaise in the Desert

This is dedicated to the cowboy who wanted to know more about béarnaise out there in the desert. At the time I didn't have the written recipe with me, now I do.

It's not so hard to make, really, but I think many people are scared away because they think it is. A béarnaise is sort of a flavored hollandaise, and both are versions of cooked mayonnaise. The difference is that in mayonnaise, you ask the egg yolk to incorporate vegetable oil for the purpose of creating a creamy emulsion. In hollandaise and béarnaise, the combination is primarily butter and egg yolk.

When we used the béarnaise for steak, it was the absolutely perfect application of this sauce. But it is also magnificent with broiled fish or poached eggs.

BÉARNAISE SAUCE

1 cup butter
2 tablespoons red wine vinegar
salt and freshly ground pepper
    to taste
2 tablespoons finely chopped
    shallots

3 teaspoons chopped fresh
    tarragon or 1$^1/_2$ teaspoons
    dried
2 egg yolks
1 tablespoon water
1 tablespoon cold butter

1. Place the 1 cup butter in a saucepan and let it melt gradually over low heat.

2. Meanwhile, combine in a saucepan the vinegar, pepper, shallots, 2 teaspoons of the fresh tarragon or 1 teaspoon dried. Cook over low heat until the vinegar has evaporated. Allow the saucepan to cool briefly.

3. Add the egg yolks and the water to the shallot mixture. Start beating vigorously with a wire whisk. Place over low heat and continue beating rapidly until the yolks start to thicken. Take care that they do not

overheat or they will scramble. Beat in the 1 tablespoon cold butter and remove from the heat.

4. Tilt the pan with the hot melted butter and add the golden clear liquid spoonful by spoonful to the egg yolk mixture, beating rapidly with the whisk. Continue beating until all the golden liquid is added. Discard the thin milky liquid that settles on the bottom of the pan.

5. Line another saucepan with cheesecloth and scrape the sauce into it. Squeeze the sauce through the cheesecloth and into the pan. Beat in the remaining 1 teaspoon chopped tarragon and salt and pepper to taste.

Beef is cooked everywhere in America, of course, but nowhere is it better prepared than at the New York City restaurant Les Halles by the chef Jean-Michel Diot. Les Halles is meant to evoke the butcher shops of Paris and part of the establishment is in fact given over to a boucherie, *which sells a variety of marvelous meats. But the remainder of the place is a bistro boasting zesty beef dishes. One of them, cooked for us by Jean-Michel while I looked on, is this immensely flavorful braised beef.*

Braised Beef with Red Wine

Marinade

2 tablespoons coarsely chopped shallots

6 cloves garlic, crushed

1 cup sliced carrots

1 bouquet garni, consisting of 6 parsley sprigs, 2 sprigs fresh thyme, 4 sprigs fresh sage, green of 1 leek, 1 bay leaf, all tied with string

2 tablespoons olive oil

1 tablespoon crushed peppercorns

8 coriander seeds

1 bottle dry red wine, such as Côte du Rhône

2 tablesppons balsamic vinegar

2 tablespoons Grand Marnier

1 small onion, studded with 1 whole clove

salt to taste

1 6-pound shoulder of beef, trimmed and oven ready

In a bowl combine all the marinade ingredients, except the beef, and blend well. Add the meat, cover and marinate in the refrigerator for 12 hours.

The Braise

1/2 cup diced salt pork

2 tablespoons olive oil

6 shallots, peeled and cut in half

3 tablespoons flour

2 cups fresh or canned beef broth

3 anchovy fillets, finely chopped

2 orange peel strips about 1/2 inch wide

12 baby carrots, scraped

3 leeks, washed well and cut into large pieces

12 pearl onions, peeled

12 dry chestnuts, peeled

4 celery stalks, cut into 1-inch pieces

1. Preheat oven to 325°.

2. Drain the meat and pat it dry, reserving the marinade, the vegetables, and the bouquet garni.

3. Heat the salt pork in a heavy Dutch oven or casserole. Cook, stirring, until the fat is rendered. Scoop out the cooked salt pork and reserve. Discard the fat. Add the olive oil and the meat to the Dutch oven or casserole and brown well on all sides. Remove the meat and set aside.

4. Add the shallots. Cook and stir until golden brown. Add the flour and blend it in well. Add the reserved salt pork, marinade, and bouquet garni and the beef broth. Blend well. Add the meat, and season to taste, cover, bring to a simmer, and place in the oven for 2 hours.

5. Discard the clove-studded onion and bouquet garni. Strain the cooking liquid. Discard the solids and return liquid to the pot. Add the anchovies, orange peels, carrots, leeks, pearl onions, chestnuts and celery. Return to the oven and braise for 1 hour or until done. Remove from the oven and skim the fat.

6. Slice the meat and serve with the vegetables and the braising liquid.

Yield: 10 to 12 servings

This skewered beef is going to be better over charcoal than done in the broiler. But it can be cooked either way with success. The real secret of the dish is the marinade, which is tart-sweet and a bit exotic.

Beef Brochettes with Red Peppers and Coriander

1½ pounds lean beef, such as fillet or sirloin

2 red onions, about ½ pound

2 medium sweet red peppers

2 tablespoons fresh lemon juice

2 tablespoons coriander seeds

1 teaspoon chopped garlic

¼ teaspoon hot red pepper flakes

½ teaspoon ground cumin

4 sprigs fresh thyme or 1 teaspoon dried

¼ cup dry red wine

2 tablespoons honey

2 tablespoons Dijon mustard

4 tablespoons coarsely chopped fresh coriander

salt and freshly ground pepper to taste

1. Preheat a charcoal grill until it is very hot or an oven broiler to 500°. If wooden skewers are used, soak them in cold water until ready. Cut the beef into 1-inch cubes. There should be 24 cubes.

2. Peel and cut the onions into 24 1-inch cubes.

3. Cut away and discard the pepper cores. Remove the seeds. Cut the peppers into 16 equal pieces.

4. Combine the meat, the onions, the peppers, and all the remaining ingredients in a bowl. Blend well and marinate for 15 minutes.

5. Drain the meat and thread equal portions of meat, onions and peppers on each skewer. Reserve the marinade for basting.

6. If the brochettes are to be cooked under the broiler, arrange them on a rack about 4 inches from the source of heat, leaving the door slightly ajar. Cook about 4

minutes for rare, basting and turning often. If the brochettes are cooked on a grill, place them on the grill and cook 4 minutes for rare, basting them often while turning. Serve with the marinade if desired.

Yield: 4 servings

❧ *How I love hamburgers! I've cooked them countless ways. These days I almost always choose lean meat (but it can't be so lean that it won't hold its shape). Too many people, when they're forming the patties, handle the meat too much, causing it to lose its texture. So pay particular attention to the instruction requiring you to slap it around as little as possible. Of course, in America, ketchup is the most common topping for hamburgers. In the next two recipes, I offer a couple of very different ways to serve them. The first, with capers, is sharp and subtle at the same time. The second one employs goat cheese, which is becoming increasingly popular in this country.*

Broiled Chopped Sirloin with Capers

1 1/2 pounds freshly chopped sirloin
salt and freshly ground pepper to
   taste
1 tablespoon butter
1/4 pound mushrooms, thinly sliced
1 tablespoon finely chopped shallots

2 tablespoons red wine vinegar
2 tablespoons capers
1/2 cup sour cream
1 tablespoon vegetable oil
2 tablespoons finely chopped fresh
   dill or coriander

1. Form 4 hamburgers, each about 3 inches in diameter and about 3/4 inch thick. (Do not handle the meat more than necessary or the texture will be ruined.)

2. Preheat outdoor grill or oven broiler to high.

3. Meanwhile, heat the butter in a skillet. Add the mushrooms, cook and stir them over high heat until lightly browned. Add the shallots and cook 15 seconds. Add the vinegar and capers and cook and stir briefly. Add the sour cream, salt and pepper to taste and bring to a simmer. Keep warm but do not let the sauce boil.

4. Sprinkle the meat with salt and pepper to taste. Brush with oil. Place the hamburgers 3 inches from the source of heat. Broil the meat for 3 minutes, then turn and broil for 3 minutes longer or to the desired degree of doneness.

5. Transfer the hamburgers to warm serving plates and pour the sauce over them. Garnish the tops with the chopped dill or coriander.

Yield: 4 servings

Chopped Steak with Goat Cheese

1¹/₂ pounds freshly chopped lean
   round steak
¹/₂ teaspoon chili powder
¹/₂ teaspoon coarsely ground black
   pepper
salt to taste

¹/₄ pound goat cheese of your
   choice, crumbled, at room
   temperature
2 tablespoons chopped fresh chives
   or parsley

1. Form 4 hamburgers, each about 3 inches in diameter and ³/₄ inch thick. (Do not handle the meat more than necessary or the texture will be ruined.)

2. Blend together the chili powder, black pepper and salt. Sprinkle the mixture over both sides of the patties.

3. Heat a black cast-iron skillet until hot. Add the hamburgers and cook over high heat 3 or 4 minutes on each side, or to the desired degree of doneness.

4. Transfer the patties to a warm heatproof serving plate. Place 1 ounce of goat cheese in the center of each patty and run under a preheated broiler for about 30 seconds. Top the hamburgers with chopped chives. Serve immediately.

Yield: 4 servings

And then there's that wonderful thing called a meat loaf. In France, when I make a meat loaf it often contains veal, pork or chicken, or sometimes a combination of all three. In the United States beef is more common by far, so that's what I've employed but with a couple twists of my own.

Meat Loaf with Herbs

1 tablespoon butter

4 tablespoons finely chopped onions

1 teaspoon minced garlic

2 pounds ground beef

1 1/2 cups fine, fresh bread crumbs

1/4 teaspoon freshly grated nutmeg

1/8 teaspoon Tabasco sauce

1/4 teaspoon ground cumin

salt and freshly ground pepper to taste

4 tablespoons chopped fresh herbs, such as parsley, dill, or coriander, or a combination of several herbs

1/2 cup plain yogurt, drained in cheesecloth or strainer

1. Preheat oven to 425°.

2. Heat the butter in a small skillet. Add the onions and garlic and cook until the onions are wilted. Cool briefly.

3. In a bowl combine the veal, bread crumbs, nutmeg, Tabasco, cumin, salt and pepper to taste. Add the onion mixture and herbs of choice. Stir in the yogurt and blend well. Pack the mixture into a loaf pan, about 9 1/4 by 5 1/4 by 2 3/4 inches. Smooth over the top with a spatula.

4. Place the loaf pan in a baking dish and pour boiling water around the pan to a depth of about 1 1/2 inches. Bake for 45 minutes.

5. Remove from water bath and let rest in a warm place for about 15 minutes before serving. Serve the loaf with the natural juices.

Yield: 4 servings

Note: For an unusual effect, pack half of the meat into the loaf pan and then brush a whole zucchini with olive oil, roll it in chopped herbs and position it on the meat so it runs lengthwise, almost from end to end, in the pan. Finish by packing the rest of the meat over it.

If you haven't used it before, the oxtail in this pot roast may strike you as an unusual ingredient. But it is really quite traditional in certain beef dishes. In making a beef stock, for instance, the addition of oxtail means more flavor as well as a slightly more gelatinous texture. Both of those bonuses will be apparent here, too.

Pot Roast and Oxtail in Red Wine

1 3¹/₂-pound boneless bottom round
2 pounds oxtail, cut into 2-inch lengths, with most of the fat removed
salt and freshly ground pepper to taste
1 tablespoon corn or peanut oil
2 large white onions, cut into 1-inch cubes (about 2 cups)
1 tablespoon finely chopped garlic
1 pound small mushrooms

1 tablespoon flour
2 cups dry red wine, such as Burgundy, Cabernet or dry California wine
1 cup fresh or canned beef broth
1 bay leaf
2 sprigs fresh rosemary or 1 teaspoon dried
2 sprigs fresh thyme or 1 teaspoon dried
2 whole cloves

1. Preheat oven to 350°.

2. Sprinkle the beef and the oxtail on all sides with salt and pepper to taste. Heat the oil in a deep Dutch oven or heavy casserole, add the meat and brown it on all sides for about 10 minutes.

3. Scatter the onions, garlic and mushrooms around the meat. Stir and cook over medium-high heat until wilted, about 5 minutes. Drain off all the fat and sprinkle the flour over the onions and mushrooms. Stir for about 1 minute. Do not burn the flour.

4. Add the wine, beef broth, bay leaf, rosemary, thyme, cloves, and salt and pepper to taste. Bring to a simmer, stirring and scraping the bottom of the pan. Cover tightly and bake for 2 hours or until well braised.

5. Remove the bay leaf and rosemary and thyme sprigs. If sauce is too reduced, add a little water. Slice the roast and serve it hot with the sauce and oxtails.

Yield: 6 to 8 servings

Note: This can be accompanied by mashed potatoes, buttered noodles, parsley potatoes, carrots or turnips or a combination of the last three.

The braised beef with red wine earlier in this section takes a long time to cook because the cut of meat is relatively tough. This recipe calls for the tender fillet and is easy to put together fast. You get a lot of payback for not much work.

Roast Fillet of Beef with Madeira Mushroom Sauce

1 center-cut fillet of beef, well trimmed and tied, about 1³/4 pounds

salt and freshly ground pepper to taste

1 tablespoon olive oil

1¹/2 cups finely sliced mushrooms

2 tablespoons finely chopped shallots

¹/2 cup Madeira wine

¹/2 cup fresh or canned beef stock

1 teaspoon tomato paste

2 tablespoons butter

1 tablespoon finely chopped parsley

1. Preheat oven to 450°.

2. Sprinkle meat on all sides with salt and pepper to taste. Rub with the olive oil.

3. Place beef in a small shallow roasting pan and put pan on bottom rack of the oven. Bake for 25 minutes for rare, turning and basting once or twice as it roasts.

4. Transfer meat to a warm platter and cover loosely with foil to keep it warm.

5. Pour off fat from pan. Place pan on top of stove and add the mushrooms, salt and pepper. Cook, stirring, over medium heat until lightly browned. Add the shallots, cook briefly, stirring, and add the Madeira. Cook, stirring and scraping the bottom of the pan to dissolve the browned particles that cling to the bottom until reduced by half. Add the stock, tomato paste and any juices that have accumulated around the fillet. Cook over high heat for about 5 minutes or until the sauce is reduced to ³/4 cup. Swirl in the butter and add the parsley.

6. Transfer the fillet to a warm serving platter, slice it on the diagonal and serve with the sauce.

Yield: 4 to 6 servings

A Glance Toward Spain

SAN JUAN, PUERTO RICO

At first, you laugh. In order to enter the Casita Blanca, a tidy little white restaurant in a poor neighborhood of San Juan, you have to pass through a door flanked by barnyard animals. The sentinels on one side are two goats bleating in their wire cages. On the other side are roosters (mercifully keeping their thoughts to themselves on the day we were there). The idea, I suppose, is to affirm the down-to-earth authenticity of the place. The floral oilcloths on each table inside do that, too. So does the gigantic quenepa tree that grows up from the patio in the back and reaches out over the raucous street.

But the fact is that at Casita Blanca, a sterling San Juan success story, the food alone might be enough to make the point, as it sings out its heritage. The *tostones* (double-fried plantain slices) are crisp and light; the *bacalaitos* (codfish fritters) bring forth the full flavor of the fish embedded in batter. The *pasteles* (spicy meat wrapped in plantain leaves) are beautiful as they arrive at the table. The sugar offered with the coffee is a bottle of molasses, cinnamon and rum.

Needless to say, we didn't discover Casita Blanca. At lunch time, here in the impoverished barrio, there is the sudden arrival of a stream of well-dressed bankers, lawyers and office workers of every stripe. Women in pearls. Men in ties. Many of them have traveled some distance. They take their noontime meal as the goats bleat and a guitarist croons. The place is packed inside and out, the bar is jumping, a line quickly forms on the street.

Casita Blanca is owned by a young man named Jesús Pérez who grew up nearby in a poor family, his father working as a maintenance man while his mother cooked for a large family. Jesús went off to work on a Cunard liner as a waiter, tried his hand as a cook in Italy, came home to wait tables in San Juan. When he learned that the little white house owned by Doña Cachaon and her 13 sons since 1922 was up for sale, he made an offer. "The minute I learned this house was available, I said, 'Mama, let's go. Get your best friends over here and let's start cooking.'"

His mother recruited the women she knew to be the best cooks in the neighborhood, elderly women who'd been cooking for big, poor families just as she had been doing, and now she sent them off to work for her son. That was just a few years ago. Today, Casita Blanca is a shining star of the neighborhood and of San Juan.

It was one of Jesús's mother's friends, Celeste Morla, who taught me to make a *mofongo* (a fried, mashed plantain) and to do it the authentic way, cooking the plantain first and then, using a pestle, mashing it in a mortar along with garlic and oil. I didn't have her feel for it initially, failing to make the *mofongo* fine enough, but I certainly did enjoy myself.

This bustling restaurant was evidence of a point our guide to the culinary world of San Juan had been trying to make as emphatically as she could. Giovanna Huyke—known simply as Giovanna to all the people who watch her daily cooking show on Puerto Rican television—told us that the islanders were working to overcome an inferiority complex about their cooking. This was the familiar syndrome: The people would go to the States, and everything there seemed superior, she said, and they would come home hiding who they were, culinarily speaking, even from each other.

"Once we were ashamed of rice and beans," she said. "If a kid ate it for dinner, he might love it, but he wouldn't tell people about it the next day."

Unlike many of the other neighboring islands, Puerto Rico looks to Spain more than Africa or France for its culinary roots. But Puerto Rican cooking is a cuisine designed to make food go as far as it will; so it is a less expensive version of the more elegant Spanish traditions. For instance, Giovanna describes *arroz con pollo,* chicken and rice, as a kind of poor man's *paella* (leaving out as it does the profusion of seafood and many other ingredients). Understandably, this approach to cooking must have seemed like an emblem of poverty, something to be secreted away. "Now we're trying to change that," Giovanna told us. "We're not afraid to serve guests old-fashioned home-cooked meals. We feel pride in our red beans. We take our basic *mofongo* and use it as a base for creative dishes."

And many Puerto Ricans today have other sources of pride: They revel in the fine array of astonishing produce available on the island. We saw a lot of it for ourselves when Giovanna met us at a market—the Plaza del Mercado in the San Juan area of Santurce—where wheelbarrows groaned beneath the burden of fresh vegetables and the colors were dizzying. Some of the more than 20 species of banana available on the island were hanging so thickly they seemed to cage in the men selling them. There were piles of coriander and of tiny green peas. She pointed out the stalls selling garlic, peppers and onions, ingredients that, taken together, usually form the "*sofrito*" that is the base for much Puerto Rican cooking the way a *mirepoix* (a combination of diced carrot, onion and celery) shows up so often in French cooking.

Giovanna's mission is to spread the pride, and from what we saw with our own eyes—an elegant shrimp-stuffed *mofongo* at a restaurant called Criollísimo, for instance—her evangelism is working, even in restaurants where one is greeted by a maître d' instead of a goat.

Plantain Smashing

Tostones *are the deep-fried slices of plantain that we had every-where in San Juan.* Tostones *experts we met bought their plan-tains green and did not let them ripen. They peeled them with a sharp knife drawn in one deft stroke along each of the flat sides. To do this and get the fruit out without nick-ing it takes practice—something on the order of 40 years from what I can tell. Don't be afraid to use your fingers, too. But, in any event, you don't have to do it perfectly. Just free the fruit and then cut it into slices of about 1½ inches in length.*

Most of the time the slices are cut on the diagonal because that will yield a flatter, longer tostone. *The plantain slices are fried twice, the first time at about 330 degrees for 5 minutes or so. Then they are taken out of the fat, drained and flattened to a thickness of about ¼ inch, using just about anything that works (a flat-surfaced meat pounder is a good idea; one fellow we met was actually using one of those old pre-electric clothes irons). Once they are smashed down, the plantains are returned to the oil to cook for a half-minute or so more until the* tostone *is an even golden color. You'll find that, like everything else in this procedure, learning to flatten these things correctly takes practice. The first time you're likely to hit it too hard, smashing it to smithereens—or you might be too timid. But the knack comes quickly.*

If you slice the plantain straight down, instead of on the diagonal, it will not be as elongated after you hit it, but it will tend to puff up during the second frying (this reminded me of the way certain fried potatoes— pommes soufflées, they're called—often behave). The straight-cut method makes the tostone *lighter, to my mind, and also provides the opportunity to cut into the cooked tostone horizontally and fill it like pita bread with, say, a bit of crab meat.*

~ Arroz con pollo, *the classic chicken and rice dish of Puerto Rico, is a wonderful, satisfying combination of ingredients, a kind of Puerto Rican soul food. In my version, I've tried to remain reasonably authentic, and so you'll see that it contains elements of the basic* sofrito *that is the basis for many Puerto Rican dishes. Usually, a* sofrito *contains onions, garlic, peppers and sometimes bits of ham. All of which are added in step 4. (The truth is, as far as I can tell, that the* sofrito *can come in many variations.)*

Arroz Con Pollo

1   3¹/₂-pound chicken, cut into 10 serving pieces

salt and freshly ground pepper to taste

2   teaspoons ground cumin

2   teaspoons freshly chopped oregano or 1 teaspoon dried and crumbled

2   tablespoons olive oil

¹/₂   cup finely chopped onions

1   tablespoon finely chopped garlic

1   large sweet green pepper, cored, seeded and cut into 1-inch cubes

¹/₄   pound boneless smoked ham, cut into ¹/₄-inch cubes

1¹/₂   cups canned crushed tomatoes

4   ripe plum tomatoes, peeled and cut into small cubes

¹/₂   teaspoon saffron threads

1   bay leaf

3   cups fresh or canned chicken broth

2   cups converted or long-grain rice

1   tablespoon drained capers

12   green olives stuffed with pimientos

1   10-ounce package frozen or fresh green peas

¹/₂   cup grated Parmesan cheese

1   6¹/₂-ounce can fancy pimientos, cut into 8 long strips

4   tablespoons coarsely chopped fresh coriander

1. Preheat oven to 375°.

2. Season the chicken with salt, pepper, cumin and oregano.

3. Heat the olive oil in a skillet over medium-high heat. Add the chicken pieces and brown on all sides. Remove the pieces to a baking dish, set aside and keep warm.

4. To the skillet add the onions, garlic, green pepper and the ham. Sauté until onions are wilted. Add the crushed tomatoes, tomato cubes, saffron, bay leaf and the

chicken broth. Bring to a boil while scraping the bottom to loosen the particles. Add the rice, capers, olives, chicken. Stir, cover tightly, place in the oven and bake for 20 minutes.

5. Uncover and stir in the peas and the Parmesan cheese. Arrange the strips of pimiento on top and bake for 5 minutes in the oven. Uncover. Remove the bay leaf and serve with the chopped coriander sprinkled on top.

Yield: 6 servings

❧ *Rice and beans are such a Puerto Rican staple that sometimes you'll find them served almost as the main dish with the beef or poultry on the side. I include here a recipe for cooking kidney beans, which can also be served as a side dish without the rice.*

Rice and Beans

2 tablespoons olive oil	1 cup drained and cooked or
4 tablespoons finely chopped onion	canned red beans (recipe To
1 teaspoon finely chopped garlic	Cook Dried Beans follows)
1 cup converted or long-grain rice	$^1/_8$ teaspoon Tabasco sauce
1$^1/_2$ cups water	salt and freshly ground pepper to
2 tablespoons tomato paste	taste
2 teaspoons chopped fresh oregano or 1 dried	

1. In a saucepan combine the oil, onion, garlic. Cook and stir over medium heat until wilted. Add the rice, water, tomato paste, oregano, the beans, Tabasco, salt and pepper. Blend well.

2. Bring to a boil, cover tightly and simmer for 20 minutes. Remove from the heat and toss gently with a fork to fluff.

Yield: 6 servings

To Cook Dried Beans

1 pound dried kidney beans
2 cups chopped onions
1 clove garlic, peeled

1 bay leaf
salt and freshly ground pepper to
   taste

   Bring 2 quarts salted water to a boil, add the beans, onions, garlic and bay leaf. Simmer for 1¹/₂ hours or until the beans are soft and not mushy. Remove the bay leaf and drain. Add salt and pepper to taste.

Yield: 6 servings

   Another recipe for cooked beans uses some of the typical Puerto Rican seasonings in it, but will also be familiar to cooks more firmly rooted in the French.

Kidney Bean and Sweet Pepper Salad

1 pound dried kidney beans or any
   other dried bean of choice
2 cups chopped onions
1 bay leaf
1 tablespoon Dijon-style mustard
2 tablespoons red wine vinegar
¹/₂ teaspoon ground cumin
salt and freshly ground pepper to
   taste

6 tablespoons vegetable or corn oil
1 tablespoon finely chopped garlic
1 sweet red pepper, cored, seeded
   and cut into ¹/₄-inch cubes
1 sweet green pepper, cored, seeded
   and cut into ¹/₄-inch cubes
2 tablespoons chopped fresh
   tarragon or other fresh herb

1. Bring 2 quarts of salted water to a boil, add the beans, 1 cup of the chopped onions, bay leaf and simmer for 1¹/₂ hours or until beans are soft but not mushy. Let cool, remove the bay leaf and drain.

2. In a salad bowl combine the mustard, vinegar, cumin, salt and pepper and the oil. Blend well with a wire whisk. Add the beans, the remaining onions, the garlic, red and green peppers, chopped tarragon. Toss and blend well.

Yield: 6 servings or more

This is the salad we had at an elegant San Juan restaurant called Criollísimo. Octopus is readily available in Puerto Rico and is often caught by hand. A diver swims to an octopus hideout, pokes around with a pole and, when the octopus emerges, the diver grabs it with his hands.

Octopus Salad

1 octopus, about 3 pounds, cleaned for cooking
1 tablespoon coarsely chopped garlic
salt and freshly ground pepper to taste
6 tablespoons olive oil
2 tablespoons vinegar
$^{1}/_{2}$ cup chopped fresh coriander
1 teaspoon dried oregano
$1^{1}/_{2}$ cups coarsely chopped onions

$^{3}/_{4}$ cup coarsely chopped sweet green pepper, seeds removed
$^{3}/_{4}$ cup coarsely chopped sweet red pepper, seeds removed
$^{1}/_{4}$ cup fresh lemon juice
4 tablespoons capers
$^{1}/_{2}$ cup small green pitted olives
$2^{1}/_{2}$ cups coarsely sliced iceberg lettuce

1. Boil the octopus in 1 gallon of salted water for 3 hours or until tender. Cool. Pull off the skin with hands and a paring knife.

2. Cut the octopus into $^{1}/_{2}$-inch lengths.

3. Place garlic, salt and pepper in a mortar or mixing bowl and mash them together. Add oil and vinegar and blend. Place the octopus in the bowl and toss.

4. Add $^{1}/_{4}$ cup of the coriander and the remaining ingredients. Check for seasoning. Toss.

5. Garnish with the remaining coriander.

Yield: 4 servings

❧ *Here is one of the surprises of our visit to San Juan. I had long been familiar with many codfish preparations but not this one. And it's quite a treat. In San Juan, the codfish batter is usually plunged into hot oil in a deep fryer. I've chosen to use less oil and a nonstick pan.*

Codfish Fritters (Bacalaitos Fritos)

$^1/_2$ pound dried skinless boneless
   salted codfish fillets
$^1/_2$ cup flour
$^1/_2$ cup water
1 teaspoon baking powder

1 teaspoon finely chopped garlic
salt if necessary and freshly ground
   pepper to taste
$^1/_3$ cup vegetable oil for frying

1. Soak the codfish in cold water for about 3 to 4 hours, changing the water 3 times. Place the fish in a saucepan and cover with water. Bring to a simmer and remove immediately from the heat. Drain well and let cool. Shred the fish to a fine texture.

2. In a bowl make a batter by combining the flour, water, baking powder and garlic. Add salt if necessary and black pepper. Blend with a wire whisk to a smooth texture. The batter should be very thin. Add the shredded fish and mix thoroughly.

3. Heat 2 tablespoons of oil in a large nonstick skillet over medium heat. Using a large spoon drop about 2 tablespoons of batter into the oil to form a thin fritter. Be sure to leave spaces in between the fritters. Cook until lightly browned; turn the fritters over to brown second side. Remove and drain on absorbent paper. Continue cooking, adding more oil if necessary until all the batter is used.

Yield: about 36 fritters

≫ Mofongo, *a fried, mashed plantain, is a ubiquitous starch side dish in San Juan, the way mashed potatoes show up all over the mainland. The Puerto Ricans make it as they have for generations, using a mortar and pestle. Preparing it this way has a nice down-to-earth feel to it, and is a bit muscular, giving you the same sort of satisfaction you might get from making mayonnaise with a whisk rather than in a blender. But I've also tried blending* mofongo *in a food processor with some additional seasoning and, to tell you the truth, liked the result just about as much. Both methods are offered here.*

Mofongo

2 green plantains
salt to taste
2 cups vegetable oil for frying

2 teaspoons chopped garlic
2 tablespoons olive oil

1. Peel the plantains by making 4 incisions lengthwise in the skin. Peel off, using the knife and your fingers.

2. Cut the plantains on the diagonal into 1-inch slices. Place in salted water to soak for 15 minutes. Drain well.

3. Heat the 2 cups vegetable oil to 350° in a fryer or skillet. Add the plantains and fry at 300° for about 15 minutes or until done but not brown. Remove and drain on absorbent paper.

4. In a mortar crush 1 teaspoon of the garlic and add 1 tablespoon of the olive oil. Add half of the plantain slices and crush together. Mix well.

5. Repeat with the remaining ingredients. Serve warm.

Yield: 4 servings

Mofongo (Food Processor Method)

2 green plantains
salt to taste
2 cups vegetable oil for frying
3 tablespoons olive oil

2 cloves garlic
1/8 teaspoon hot red pepper flakes
4 tablespoons freshly chopped
    coriander or parsley

1. Peel the plantains by making 4 incisions lengthwise in the skin. Peel off, using the knife and your fingers.

2. Cut the plantains on the diagonal into 1-inch slices. Place in salted water to soak for 15 minutes. Drain well.

3. Heat the 2 cups vegetable oil to 350° in a fryer or skillet. Add the plantains and fry at 300° for about 15 minutes or until done but not brown. Remove and drain on absorbent paper.

4. In the container of a food processor combine the plantains, 2 tablespoons of the olive oil, garlic, pepper flakes. Blend to a semicoarse texture.

5. To serve hot, heat the remaining 1 tablespoon of the olive oil in a nonstick skillet. Add the blended plantains and the coriander. Toss for 1 minute, and serve immediately.

Yield: 4 servings

🌱 *Most of the time we were in Puerto Rico, the cooks used the green, unripe plantains. But when I found myself with a bunch of ripened ones (they turn black), I decided to try sautéing them in a simple fashion and was very pleased with the result.*

Sautéed Ripe Plantains

4 ripe plantains, about 2 pounds
2 tablespoons olive oil
2 teaspoons chopped garlic

$1/4$ teaspoon hot red pepper flakes
2 tablespoons coarsely chopped
   fresh coriander

1. Peel the plantains. Slice them into $1/4$-inch-thick rounds.

2. In a nonstick skillet large enough hold the slices in one layer, heat the olive oil over medium-high heat. Sauté the plantains for 2 minutes.

3. Add the garlic, pepper flakes and coriander. Sauté briefly. Be sure not to burn the garlic. Serve immediately.

Yield: 4 servings

Cooking with Children

I am a grandfather now, and like every grandfather I have ever met I am absolutely enchanted by children. Even children I encounter for the first time draw me to them, and I put my arms around them; with luck we become friends very quickly, laughing about silly things. Whenever I get the opportunity, I invite kids to join me in the kitchen and pitch in. Cooking with kids has always been one of the truly joyful experiences of my life.

I learned from my own children and grandchildren that, given the chance, cooking is one of those adult-and-child activities that really works. The adult instructs, explicitly and by example, and the kid pays attention, tries hard and learns. One of the most popular television shows I ever made—during my PBS-TV series called "Cuisine Rapide"—came about serendipitously when my grandson Nicolas, then not yet three years old, wandered onto the set. We kept the cameras rolling during the creation of a chocolate mousse. Nicolas ignored the camera entirely and became my sous chef, more eager, in fact, than a few I can think of. There are actually moments during that show when it's hard to tell who's in charge, so deft and assured was my young Nicolas with his whisk. For the new show, I brought Nicolas back for an encore. This time it was a plum tart. He helped roll the dough and position the plums. He also proved adept at breading the chicken breasts presented later in this chapter.

When I found myself here in Disney World, the magnetism of children was all around me. For an adult who truly loves children and wants to be among them, there is no place on earth better than this. It was here, too, that I met the amiable executive chef for Disney World, Johnny Rivers. Together we worked on some dishes guaranteed to please children who might wish to join in preparing them.

The two settings for our food preparation were Chef Mickey's Village Restaurant

(a pleasant place in a Disney shopping area) and the deck of an elaborately designed stationary riverboat called the *Empress Lilly*. Both places are very likely to induce a playful mood in anyone, even in the dourest adult. (We met one couple, Edward Cushman and his wife, Kathryn, from Pittsburgh, who have no children of their own and simply come to Disney World to watch: "We all become kids again," Edward said.)

While we were there, in one of several restaurants on the *Empress Lilly*, the main show was a parade of Disney characters visiting the tables at breakfast. They arrived after a sort of warm-up MC got the crowd going: "You guys can scream and shout and toss your sisters in the air," he yelled, as the laughter rose in anticipation of the arrival of the characters. (Some sisters seemed more likely to throw their brothers in the air, but never mind.) At Chef Mickey's restaurant there is a big Mickey character in a toque who, according to the Disney World people, oversees the restaurant.

Well, whoever was in charge, it was Johnny and I who did the cooking (assisted winsomely, part of the time, by Juliette Pinsky, the four-year-old daughter of my show's producer). There was, for instance, a yogurt drink that can be prepared by any kid old enough to use a blender. Mexican fajitas was another of the dishes—the fun here is that everyone at the dinner table gets to make his or her own by spooning the cooked ingredients into soft tortilla shells. And there was a salmon lasagne whose construction was certainly within the capability of kids of many ages, even if the oven part might best be left to an adult.

The whole experience put me in mind of the kinds of things I've always found kids like to do most: Obviously, anything that involves blending various ingredients with a whisk or spatula or bare hands is a good idea. This is especially true of tarts and pies, where the kids get to mess around with raw dough. Any chocolate concoction at all is going to be a big hit. In my own family, my daughters Diane and Claudia, cooking with their children often, have had particular success with mousses, simple cakes, pancakes and breads.

All of this is more than good family fun, of course. Kids need to get the feel of real food early on. They need to get their hands into the raw ingredients and then witness what happens when those ingredients are combined and transformed into wonderful foods. This is an important way to teach kids—without belaboring the pedagogical intent—that the preparation of food is a creative process with great rewards beyond the mere elimination of hunger. How else are they ever to learn that those paper-wrapped hamburgers hurled over the fast-food counters of America aren't the real thing? Those of us who love to cook have to keep that love alive in the coming generations.

But when cooking with kids, remember this: Be patient. Don't pull a whisk out of a kid's hand just because the blending is going a bit too slowly or imperfectly; anyway, in cooking, perfection comes only now and then, under the best of circumstances.

I think I was, in fact, patient most of the time with my son Jacques and pressured him as little as I could. He grew up to be a waiter and then a cook, a culinary businessman (studying the business in college) and a wine merchant. Now, he is off on his own life's journey. But I will remember always the sense of him as a teenager, standing there off to the side of the kitchen, confidently chopping the parsley as I went about my job. Hardly a word passed between us; no need for talk, really. We were father and son in the same kitchen, working away.

Safety

One of the things parents must keep in mind is the level of maturity of their own children. Rarely is a child younger than 10 ready to deal with heat, for instance, and 10 is probably too young for a child to use a knife. It's up to you to work closely with your child and through common sense and vigilance decide what that particular child is ready to do. As you work together, pass along a few good cooking tips:

Respect knives. Always work so that the blade is directed away from the hand.

Do not leave a spoon in a hot pan where it will become too hot to touch.

Turn pan handles toward the middle of the stove (so a pan won't be accidentally knocked over) and be sure the handle isn't over the heat of a neighboring burner.

Remember that steam can burn and lids must be removed carefully (this is especially so in microwave cooking where the careless removal of plastic wrap has caused many a burn).

Use dry pot holders, since wet ones transmit heat.

Keep fingers and hair away from the moving parts of any kitchen machine.

There are a lot of other warnings I could pass along here, but you get the point. Most important, a child should never be permitted to work in the kitchen alone until a parent is absolutely confident that he or she can handle it.

For older children, with a demonstrated ability to focus on the task at hand, the making of crepes can be tremendously enjoyable. My granddaughter Noelle, just 11 years old, has managed to master it. To make a good crepe, one has to have the dexterity to swirl the batter about the pan so that each crepe is thin and round. Then comes the eating, and covered with raspberry sauce, these crepes are the perfect reward for all that earnest concentration.

Crepes with Strawberry Filling and Raspberry Sauce

The Crepes

2 large eggs	2 teaspoons sugar
1 cup flour	$1/2$ teaspoon pure vanilla extract
pinch salt	4 tablespoons butter
1 cup milk	Strawberry Filling (recipe follows)
$1/4$ cup water	Raspberry Sauce (recipe follows)

1. Place the eggs, flour and salt in a bowl and start beating and blending with a wire whisk. Add the milk and water, stirring. Add the sugar and the vanilla extract.

2. Melt 2 tablespoons of the butter in a 7- or 8-inch Teflon pan. Pour the melted butter into the crepe batter. Blend well.

3. Place a fine sieve into a bowl and pour the batter into the sieve. Strain the batter, pushing any solids through with a rubber spatula.

4. Melt the remaining 2 tablespoons butter and use this to brush the pan each time or as necessary before making a crepe.

5. Brush the pan lightly with the butter and place it on the stove. When the pan is hot but not burning, add 2 tablespoons batter (it is preferable to use a small ladle with a two-tablespoon capacity). Swirl it around neatly to completely cover the bottom of the pan. Let cook over moderately high heat about 30 to 40 seconds or until lightly browned on the bottom. Turn the crepe and cook the second side only about 15 seconds. Turn the crepe out onto a sheet of wax paper.

6. Continue making crepes, brushing the pan lightly as necessary to prevent sticking, until all the batter is used. As the crepes are made turn them out, edges slightly overlapping onto the wax paper.

7. To serve, place about 1 tablespoon strawberry filling in each crepe, spreading it with the back of a spoon. Roll the crepe up and ladle a small amount of the raspberry sauce over it.

Yield: 16 to 18 crepes

Strawberry Filling

1 pint fresh strawberries, hulled and $^{1}/_{4}$ cup strawberry jam
   sliced thin

Place sliced berries and jam in a small saucepan and cook over medium heat for 2 minutes. Let cool. Set the filling aside.

Raspberry Sauce

1 10-ounce package frozen $^{1}/_{4}$ cup sugar
   raspberries, thawed

Combine raspberries with their juice and the sugar in the container of a food processor and blend well until smooth. If desired, push through a sieve to remove the seeds. Set aside.

Kids of just about any age are good at moving chicken breasts from one component of the breading batter to the next. My grandson Nicolas has been helping his mother, Claudia, for years. The mess that ensues, sticky hands and flour-covered work area, can't be beat. But then, alas, comes clean-up time.

Breaded Chicken Breasts

4 skinless boneless chicken breasts, about 1¹/₂ pounds in all
¹/₄ cup flour for dredging
salt and freshly ground pepper to taste
1 large egg
2 tablespoons water

1 cup fresh bread crumbs
¹/₄ cup freshly grated Parmesan cheese
¹/₄ teaspoon grated nutmeg
3 tablespoons olive oil
1 tablespoon butter
seeded lemon slices for garnish

1. Place the breasts, one at a time, between 2 sheets of plastic wrap and pound them lightly with a flat mallet or the bottom of a heavy skillet. The pounding should make them even in thickness but not too thin.

2. Dredge the breasts on both sides with flour and season with salt and pepper.

3. Beat the egg with the water in a shallow dish. Season with salt and pepper. Dip the breasts on all sides into the egg mixture, removing the excess with the fingers.

4. Combine the bread crumbs, Parmesan cheese and nutmeg in a plate. Dip the breasts, one at a time, into the bread crumb mixture. Press on the sides lightly with a spatula to help the crumbs adhere.

5. Heat the oil and the butter in a nonstick skillet large enough to hold the breasts in one layer. Cook over medium heat for about 3 to 5 minutes until golden brown on one side. Turn and cook about 3 to 5 minutes on the second side until lightly browned. Remove and serve hot with the lemon slices as garnish.

Yield: 4 servings

This is a truly simple tart to prepare, but everything about it is enjoyable, from the preparation of the dough, to the forming of the crust and, finally, the eating. My grandson, Nicolas, has been helping with tarts since he was three.

French Plum Tart

1½ cups plus 2 tablespoons all-purpose flour

10 tablespoons cold butter, cut into small pieces

3 tablespoons cold water

6 tablespoons sugar

2½ pounds fresh plums

1. Combine the 1½ cups flour, 8 tablespoons of the butter, the water and 1 tablespoon of the sugar in the container of a food processor and blend until the mixture forms a ball, in perhaps 30 seconds.

2. Using a floured rolling pin, roll out the dough into a round 13 inches in diameter and ¼ inch thick.

3. Pick up the dough by rolling it onto the pin. Then unroll it over a 10½-inch black tart pan with a removable bottom. Press the dough gently into the pan, gathering it toward the wall of the pan to thicken the sides of the shell. Trim off the excess dough. Place the pan in the refrigerator for 10 to 15 minutes to allow the dough to relax.

4. Preheat oven to 375°.

5. Split the plums in half and remove the pits. With a paring knife score each half 3 times.

6. Blend the remaining 2 tablespoons flour with 2 tablespoons of the sugar. Sprinkle the tart shell evenly with the flour and sugar mixture. Place the halved plums, skin side up, in the shell, forming a circular pattern. Sprinkle the plums with the remaining 3 tablespoons sugar and dot the remaining 2 tablespoons butter, cut into small pieces, over all.

7. Place the tart pan on a baking sheet and bake on the bottom rack of the oven for about 45 minutes or until done.

Yield: 8 servings

❧ *My daughter Diane has always found this pancake to be a special favorite for cooking with her children, especially Larissa, who is 13. It's unusual because it is baked and puts on something of a show as it bubbles and rises.*

Diane's Pancake

½ cup flour
½ cup milk
2 large eggs, beaten
pinch freshly grated nutmeg

4 tablespoons butter
2 tablespoons confectioners' sugar
juice of ½ lemon

1. Preheat oven to 425°.

2. In a bowl combine the flour, milk, eggs and nutmeg. Beat with a wire whisk until smooth.

3. Melt the butter in a 12-inch cast-iron skillet or nonstick skillet with a metal handle. When the pan is hot, pour in the batter. Bake 15 to 20 minutes. The batter will form large bubbles, rise and turn golden brown. Remove from the oven and sprinkle with the sugar and lemon juice. Serve at once.

Yield: 4 servings

There's a lot of kneading and punching going on in the following recipe, making it an ideal baking project to undertake with children of just about any age.

Raisin Brioches

$^1/_2$ cup warm water
$^1/_2$ cup warm milk
$^1/_4$ cup sugar
1 teaspoon salt
2 packages fast-acting (RapidRise) yeast
1 cup large egg yolks (about 12 yolks)

$^1/_2$ cup butter, melted and cooled, plus 1 tablespoon butter, melted
$4^1/_2$ cups bread flour
$^3/_4$ cup golden raisins
eggwash made by beating 1 egg yolk with 1 tablespoon water

1. In the container of a food processor combine the water, milk, sugar, salt, yeast, the 1 cup egg yolks and the $^1/_2$ cup melted butter. Process 1 minute, scraping down the sides of the bowl. Add 4 cups of the flour, one cup at a time, turning machine on and off between additions.

2. Remove dough from bowl and place on floured counter. (Dough will be soft and sticky.) Add the remaining $^1/_2$ cup flour and raisins and knead until they are well blended. Shape dough and place in a buttered bowl and brush surface with the remaining 1 tablespoon melted butter. Cover and let rise until double in size, about 1 hour.

3. Punch down dough, knead lightly and shape into 2 flattened balls of equal size. Place balls in 2 buttered 8-cup brioche pans or any pans of suitable size. Cover and let dough rise until double in size, about 45 minutes.

4. Preheat oven to 350°.

5. Bake the brioches for about 20 minutes. Brush the tops of the brioches with the eggwash the last 10 minutes of baking time. Let cool in pans.

Yield: 8 to 10 servings

At Disney World and in Mexican restaurants the sautéed meat and vegetables in the fajitas are usually served in sizzling hot cast-iron pans that are brought to the table, one for each serving. If you happen to have those pans or want to buy them, cook the chicken only part of the way before bringing it out on the heated pans, since it will continue to cook. In adapting this recipe a bit, I thought it made sense to simplify things and prepare the chicken completely in a sauté pan. If you're cooking with children, it's probably best not to make everything from scratch in this case, anyway. You'll notice that some of the ingredients—the salsa, guacamole and tortillas—will have to be purchased from specialty stores or supermarkets with good specialty sections.

Chicken Fajitas

The Marinade

¹/₄ cup Worcestershire sauce
¹/₄ cup Kikkoman steak sauce
¹/₂ cup white vinegar
1 tablespoon finely chopped garlic

1 tablespoon fresh lemon juice
salt and freshly ground pepper to taste
2 tablespoons ground cumin

In a bowl combine well all the marinade ingredients.

Yield: 1¹/₂ cups

The Fajitas

1¹/₂ pounds skinless boneless chicken breasts, sliced into 1-inch strips
2 tablespoons vegetable oil
1 large sweet green pepper, cored, seeded and sliced
1 sweet red pepper, cored, seeded and sliced
1 medium Spanish onion, sliced
1 small head iceberg lettuce, shredded

1 tomato, finely chopped
1 cup shredded Cheddar cheese
1 cup guacamole
1 cup sour cream
1 cup mild salsa
16 6-inch flour tortilla shells, warmed in oven just before serving

1. Place the chicken strips in a bowl and add the marinade. Cover and refrigerate. Allow to stand at least 1 hour or overnight.

2. In a sauté pan heat the vegetable oil, add the chicken strips, the green pepper, red pepper and onion and cook, tossing, for about 6 or 7 minutes or until the chicken is done.

3. Place the lettuce, tomato, Cheddar cheese, guacamole, sour cream and salsa in separate bowls on the table. Allow each person to assemble fajitas individually, spooning some of the chicken and vegetables into the tortilla shell, then adding the remaining ingredients.

Yield: 4 servings

✻   *This salmon lasagne is adapted from one prepared at Walt Disney World and is served with a sauce that is richer than many of the other dishes we saw there. Obviously, to spare the calories, you can substitute a good tomato sauce of your own choosing.*

Individual Salmon Lasagne

4 lasagne noodles
1 cup ricotta cheese
1/2 cup shredded mozzarella cheese
1 large egg
2 teaspoons chopped parsley
salt and freshly ground pepper to
    taste

4 skinless salmon fillets, 4 ounces
    each
4 slices provolone cheese
Pine Nut Spinach Sauce (recipe
    follows)

1. Preheat oven to 350°.

2. In 2 quarts of boiling water cook the lasagne noodles until al dente. Drain and set aside.

3. In a bowl combine the ricotta, mozzarella, egg and parsley. Season with salt and pepper.

4. For each lasagne, spread 1 of the noodles out on a work surface and place a salmon fillet in the center. Top each fillet with 2 tablespoons of the cheese mixture

and fold one end of the pasta over the mixture. Spoon 2 more tablespoons of the cheese mixture on top and fold the other end of the pasta over. Top each lasagne with a slice of provolone.

5. Place the lasagne in a greased baking pan and bake for 15 to 20 minutes or until the cheese is browned.

6. To serve, pour $^1/_2$ cup of the pine nut spinach sauce on each plate and arrange the lasagne on the sauce.

Yield: 4 servings

Pine Nut Spinach Sauce

3 strips bacon, chopped
2 tablespoons toasted pine nuts
$^3/_4$ cup cooked spinach, chopped
$^1/_2$ cup chopped onions
$1^1/_2$ tablespoons flour

3 cups heavy cream
$^1/_2$ cup dry white wine
$^1/_8$ teaspoon freshly grated nutmeg
salt and freshly ground pepper to
    taste

1. In a sauté pan cook the bacon, pine nuts, spinach and onions until the onions are wilted. Drain off most of the fat.

2. Add the flour and cook briefly, stirring. Add the cream, stir and simmer for about 5 minutes. Add the wine, nutmeg, salt and pepper to taste. Keep the sauce warm over low heat.

The Cajun Life

The flat-bottomed airboat, its propeller roaring behind us, bounced and swerved and shimmied through the bayou. Here we were racing across the wetlands of Louisiana, an area rich with so many images that it was hard to absorb them all at once. That speeding moment felt much like our whole experience of the Cajun countryside: so much to see, to taste and to learn. And we were moving fast. Three television shows would be shot here among marvelous, down-to-earth people. Certainly the moment in the sun when that airboat pulled up to a dock in front of a neatly kept trappers' cabin in the bayou was one of the most brilliant images of all.

As we arrived with a roar, there was a crawfish boil and a Cajun party ready to go. The crawfish, a staple and a source of joy in these parts, is about three to six inches long and resembles a small lobster. It flourishes in the fresh water here and is also farmed nearby, often on the same mud and low-water fields employed for rice-growing. It is the star of one of the signal Cajun dishes, crawfish *étouffée*.

On this glorious day, 150 pounds of crawfish, along with corn and potatoes, were dumped into a propane-heated tank full of simmering seasoned water. And when they were done they were hauled onto the weathered porch of the cabin. There, unceremoniously, the crawfish and vegetables were arrayed in great red heaps, about a half dozen piles of them, on a long picnic table. They were devoured while, to our immense pleasure, a Cajun musical group called the Basin Brothers fiddled and strummed and sang the folk songs of the Acadian people—the French forebears of the Cajuns who fled persecution in Nova Scotia during the eighteenth century. An egret lofted skyward just in front of us. In the shimmering distance, we could see large ships gliding along the Intracoastal Waterway that cuts through the wetlands on its way to Texas.

It was Cajun, all right. Beautiful. Exuberant. Flavors burst from food served up

in portions that were more than ample and supremely fresh. But nothing fancy here. New Orleans was two and one half hours away by car (more than that when you realize you had to take a boat to get to the car). We were among country people now.

Well, mostly country. One of the people with us was our host, Paul McIlhenny, whose family guides the Tabasco producing company on nearby Avery Island. Paul, a big man of few pretensions, a man who likes a joke and relishes the outdoors, manages to move easily between country and city. He was eager to show us his Tabasco plant, and tell us the story of that nearly miraculous hot pepper sauce. And we did have a fine time walking among the oak barrels where the pepper mash ferments, watching the efficient workers as they liquefied the peppers with vinegar. At tour's end we could see the familiar red bottles streaming along a conveyor belt on their way to all the world.

I have always cooked with Tabasco sauce and most cooks I know use it, too. But it turns out that in much of Louisiana people cook with it less than you might think, preferring to see it on the table (and it is nearly everywhere), so that they can turn up the heat of a dish to suit their own taste.

Paul was also eager to whisk us here and there in Cajun country to be sure we got a feel for it in the time we had allotted. He took us, for instance, to a nearly rustic seafood restaurant in Abbeville, Dupuy's, established in 1887. It's a restaurant that leases thousands of acres of sea floor from the state so that it can harvest its own oysters in great quantity. The challenge of shucking all the oysters they sell at this place—raw, broiled, in stews—would be more daunting than it is were it not for a remarkable man.

His name is Andy Phares. At least that's his name now. He used to be Trung Van Ding, a frightened Vietnamese immigrant without a job. When Jack Phares, one of the proprietors of Dupuy's, took him in and got him going as an oyster shucker, it turned out that he had an awe-inspiring talent for this sort of work. Now he's a champion—plaques on the wall attest to that—who shucks 24 oysters in under two minutes. In an acrobatic show of dexterity, he grabs each oyster, flips it into position, pops it open with his knife and cuts the flesh loose. He is now known as Andy Phares because, on the day he became a naturalized citizen, he called Jack Phares from the Customs House. "He asked me," Jack recalls, "if he could take my name, and I said I'd be proud if he would." (I should tell you that in a moment of folly I put myself up against Andy in shucking oysters; he was faster, but I think I might have done just a little better in the competition if somebody weren't slipping the tougher oysters my way.)

The oysters and the crawfish offered us only a narrow window into Cajun life. The view broadened explosively when we were in Lafayette and nearby Opelousas, the inland heart of the Cajun experience. Although Lafayette is a town of some size, the general area is typified more by its rural, close-to-the-earth feeling. Driving through it, you'll notice store after store selling freshly made *boudin,* the French word for sausage that appears on signs all across the area. And it's in this region that Paul Prudhomme—the chef who did more than anybody else to bring the cooking of this part of Louisiana to the attention of the rest of the world—was born and raised. Although he eventually

Turtle Soup 3⁰⁰
Cajun Jambalaya 3⁰⁰
Crawfish Big Marnou 3⁵⁰

opened K-Paul's in New Orleans, it was in Opelousas that one could see the great reverence and pride people felt for him.

We were at the St. Landry Parish Heritage Festival in Opelousas, a dizzying profusion of food stalls—everything from alligator hush puppies to turtle soup, to deep-fried turkey, the whole bird fried at once! And people were dancing in the streets to music cascading down the courthouse steps. Everywhere, they were munching on the fried pork rind called crackling. A young mother pushing her perfectly dressed toddler along in a stroller could be heard soothing the child: "Don't worry, honey, I'm going to get you some cracklin' in a minute, O.K.?"

And then Prudhomme, the hometown hero, moved through the crowds, as if he were an emperor, or maybe Huey Long. "There he is, there he is," one man called out to his wife. People stopped to shake his hand and chat. Paul never turned them away and refused to be rushed. He spoke to each one about their families or food or whatever, and later he gave a demonstration of some of his own cooking techniques. He has an evangelist's fervor about the food of the region. He believes that Cajun cooking is a more complex eating experience than it might seem, a cuisine of many-layered flavors. That's why he so often likes to use black, red and white peppers all in one dish, to keep a kind of orchestrated pepper-popping going on continuously so that the dish doesn't grow boring while you eat it. He also employs the "holy trinity" of Cajun cooking—celery, green peppers and onions—all the time. But they don't grow dull, either, he says, because their proportions and the methods for cooking them can be varied almost infinitely.

We had another opportunity to learn about Cajun cooking back at Marsh House, the guest quarters, on Avery Island. There the McIlhenny family cook, Eula Mae Doré, took us through some of the classics of the region. She made a gumbo, of course: the Cajun soup that is sometimes thickened with filé, an herb of ground sassafras. She cooked jambalaya, a rice dish that usually combines meats or seafood and tomatoes. Very frequently there's ham or sausage in a jambalaya as well, a fact that is evidently linked to its name: *Jambon* is French for ham. According to the "Acadian Dictionary," the "ya" is African for rice, suggesting the strong African influence that has joined with that of the French and other groups here in creating the exciting fare that comes from this corner of the world. Eula prepared an okra dish for us, too (again, the African influence). And then there were little pecan tarts.

As dusk settled over the subtropical greenery of Avery Island, it was possible to unwind a bit by just walking and looking. The deer came close, to check us out. The egrets settled in for the night.

The Strength of Iron

Good cooks like to say that they can make do under any conditions. But most of them, myself included, would rather not be forced to be so inventive. We'd rather have the right equipment and the perfect ingredients. In Cajun cooking, cast-iron pots offer an immense advantage. Cast iron works better than any other material for some cooking chores. It distributes heat very well, evenly and intensely. There are no hot spots. So it is perfect for the kind of slow cooking that is part of the Cajun "smothering" technique. You'll notice that some of the recipes in this chapter urge you to employ a cast-iron Dutch oven for the purpose. Because it can get so hot when left on the fire for an extended period, cast iron is also the ideal material for searing and browning meat. One drawback to cooking with cast iron you might want to keep in mind is that it is not as responsive as steel or copper: When you turn down the heat, cast iron tends to retain it longer than the other materials.

As for ingredients in Cajun and Creole cooking, some of them are found more readily in Louisiana than anywhere else. I'm thinking specifically of the tasso, a kind of smoked pork, and the sassafras-derived seasoning called filé powder. If you mean to get serious about cooking in this style, you'll want to have access to Louisianan products. Here are three sources:

K-Paul's Louisiana Mail Order
824 Distributors Row
Post Office Box 23342
Harahan, LA 70183-0342

Phone: (800) 4KPAULS

Savoie's Food Products
581 Highway 742
Opelousas, LA 70570

Phone: (318) 942-7241
Fax: (318) 948-9571

Old New Orleans French
Market Seafood Company
1101 North Peters Street
New Orleans, LA 70116

Phone: (504) 522-8911
(Ask for Keith Bernard)

Patrick Mould is the well-respected chef of the Hub City Diner in Lafayette, Louisiana, the heart of Cajun country. It's a charming restaurant with a jukebox playing early rock songs, an old-fashioned soda fountain, and hand-painted signs evoking the mom-and-apple-pie days. Patrick grew up in Louisiana and has a good feeling for its heritage, as his crispy catfish dish, modified slightly by us, will testify.

Patrick's Catfish

1 tablespoon peanut oil

1/4 cup finely chopped onion

1/2 cup finely chopped celery

1/2 cup finely chopped sweet green pepper

1 tablespoon minced garlic

1 cup Basic Shrimp Stock (page 378) or bottled clam juice

1/2 cup dry white wine

salt and freshly ground pepper to taste

1/2 teaspoon paprika

1/2 teaspoon Tabasco sauce

1 tablespoon cornstarch or arrowroot

2 tablespoons water

1/2 pound very small shrimp, cooked

3 tablespoons chopped scallions in all, reserving 2 tablespoons for garnish

1 tablespoon chopped parsley

vegetable oil for deep frying

2 eggs

1/2 cup buttermilk

2 tablespoons Creole Seafood Seasoning (page 145)

3 cups flour

4 skinless catfish fillets, 7 to 9 ounces each

1. In a saucepan heat the peanut oil over medium heat. Add the onion, celery and green pepper and cook for 1 minute, stirring, until wilted.

2. Add the garlic and sauté for 1 minute. Don't burn the garlic.

3. Add the shrimp stock, white wine, salt and pepper to taste, paprika and Tabasco. Bring to a boil and simmer for 5 minutes.

4. Blend the cornstarch with the water and add to the vegetable mixture, stirring until thickened. Add the cooked shrimp, the 1 tablespoon scallions and parsley. Blend, set aside and keep warm.

5. Heat the oil to 350° for deep frying.

6. In a bowl beat the eggs lightly, and add the buttermilk and 1 tablespoon of the seafood seasoning. Blend well.

7. Blend the flour with the remaining 1 tablespoon seafood seasoning.

8. Dredge each fillet in the seasoned flour, then dip it in the egg batter. Dredge again in the flour and pat the coating gently to be sure it adheres.

9. Place the fish fillets in the hot oil and fry until golden brown, about 3 or 4 minutes. If the fillet floats to the surface before it is browned, turn it with tongs to brown evenly.

10. Place a fillet in the center of each plate and pour the sauce around it. Garnish with the remaining scallions. Serve with Creole Rice (page 195).

Yield: 4 servings

The legendary Louisianan musician, Stanley "Buckwheat" Dural, Jr. (his band is known as Buckwheat Zydeco), contends that the African-American influence on the region's cooking has too often been ignored. The black-inspired cuisine, he maintains, isn't properly called Cajun but rather Creole—and, in fact, the blacks of southwestern Louisiana refer to themselves as Creole. We visited his farm for a satisfying crawfish étouffée created by Buckwheat's wife, Bernite. In deference to Buckwheat's viewpoint, I've dubbed this dish "à la Creole."

Bernite's Crawfish Etouffée à la Creole

$^1/_3$ cup vegetable oil
2 cups coarsely chopped onions
2 cups coarsely chopped celery
$1^1/_2$ cups chopped seeded sweet
    green peppers
4 tablespoons chopped garlic
1 tablespoon cayenne
salt and freshly ground pepper to
    taste

2 pounds mushrooms, sliced
5 pounds cleaned crawfish tails,
    with their fat
$^1/_2$ cup flour, cornstarch or
    arrowroot
$^3/_4$ cup water
2 tablespoons filé powder (optional)

1. In a large heavy cast-iron Dutch oven or heavy saucepan heat the vegetable oil, add the onions, celery, green peppers, garlic, cayenne and salt and pepper to taste. Cook, stirring, over medium heat for 15 minutes. Add the mushrooms, cook and stir for 15 minutes. Most of the moisture in the vegetables will be gone. (It is very important to cook and stir often and to cook slowly.)

2. Add the crawfish tails, rinsing each container well with $^1/_4$ cup water to remove the fat and add the water to the pot. Add 2 more cups water. Bring to a boil and simmer for 15 minutes.

3. Combine the flour and the $^3/_4$ cup water, and mix well until smooth. Add to the crawfish mixture, blending well with a wooden spoon while cooking. Bring to a boil and simmer for 10 minutes.

4. Add the filé powder, if desired, and simmer for 5 minutes. Serve over Creole Rice (page 195).

Yield: 12 to 15 servings

Note: This dish should be well seasoned. Check often while cooking.

＊ *The following shrimp dish comes directly from Paul Prudhomme, the Cajun master. It employs one of his typical seasoning mixtures, which is meant to play the various peppers like a calliope. The recipe has been adapted from* Chef Paul Prudhomme's Louisiana Kitchen.

Paul's Barbequed Shrimp

2 dozen large shrimp with heads
   and shells (about 1 pound)

Seasoning Mix

1 teaspoon ground red pepper
   (preferably cayenne)

1 teaspoon freshly ground black pepper

$^1/_2$ teaspoon salt

$^1/_2$ teaspoon crushed red pepper

$^1/_2$ teaspoon dried thyme leaves

$^1/_2$ teaspoon dried rosemary leaves,
   crushed

$^1/_8$ teaspoon dried oregano

$^1/_2$ cup (1 stick) plus 5 tablespoons
   unsalted butter, in all

$1^1/_2$ teaspoons minced garlic

1 teaspoon Worcestershire sauce

$^1/_2$ cup Basic Shrimp Stock (page
   378) or $^1/_2$ cup strong fresh
   chicken broth

$^1/_4$ cup beer at room temperature

1. Rinse the shrimp in cold water and drain well. Then pinch off and discard the portion of the head from the eyes forward (including the eyes, but not the

protruding long spine above the eyes). Leave attached as much as possible of the orange shrimp fat from the head. Set the shrimp aside.

2. In a small bowl combine all the seasoning mix ingredients.

3. In a large skillet melt the 1 stick butter and combine with the garlic, Worcestershire and seasoning mix over high heat. Add the shrimp. Cook for 2 minutes, shaking the pan in a back-and-forth motion. Add the remaining 5 tablespoons butter and the stock. Cook and shake the pan for 2 minutes. Add the beer and cook and shake the pan 1 minute more. Remove from heat.

4. Serve immediately in bowls with lots of French bread on the side, or on a platter with cooked rice mounded in the middle and the shrimp and sauce surrounding it.

Yield: 2 to 4 servings

When it came time to grill shrimp in the television studio for one of the Louisiana segments, I took my inspiration from Prudhomme but gave it my own twist: So here you have spicy shrimp with an herbed butter sauce.

Grilled Shrimp with Herbed Butter

24 jumbo shrimp, about 2 pounds, shelled and deveined
1/4 teaspoon hot red pepper flakes
salt and freshly ground black pepper to taste
4 tablespoons Dijon mustard

2 tablespoons olive oil
2 tablespoons lemon juice
1 tablespoon chopped fresh thyme or 1 teaspoon dried
Herbed Butter Sauce (recipe follows)

1. Preheat outdoor grill or oven broiler to high.

2. In a bowl combine all the ingredients, except the butter sauce. Blend well.

3. Arrange 6 shrimp on each of 4 skewers. Brush sides with oil.

4. Place the shrimp on the grill or under the broiler about 4 inches from the heat source. Cook for about 2 minutes and turn. Continue grilling for about 2 minutes more. Serve with the butter sauce.

Yield: 4 servings

Herbed Butter Sauce

1/4 cup minced shallots
3/4 cup dry white wine
1/4 cup heavy cream
8 tablespoons unsalted butter
salt and freshly ground white pepper to taste

2 tablespoons finely chopped basil
2 tablespoons finely chopped fresh chervil leaves
2 tablespoons finely chopped fresh chives

1. Combine the shallots and wine in a heavy saucepan. Cook over medium-high heat until the wine has evaporated.

2. Add the cream and reduce by half. Add the butter quickly, one tablespoon at a time, whisking constantly. Remove the saucepan from the heat and stir in the salt and pepper and herbs.

❧ *In Louisiana, the cooks like deep-fried seafood as much as any cooks anywhere in the country. Here's an interesting combination of fried shrimp and squid that has a bit of bite to it (especially if you choose to be liberal with the Tabasco in the sauce).*

Fried Shrimp and Squid

1 pound medium raw shrimp, peeled and deveined

1 pound squid, cleaned
vegetable oil for frying

The Batter
1 cup all-purpose flour
salt and freshly ground white pepper to taste
3 large eggs, separated

2 cups beer at room temperature
1 tablespoon vegetable oil for batter
2 teaspoons curry powder

The Sauce
2 teaspoons finely chopped garlic
1 tablespoon Dijon mustard
Tabasco sauce to taste
1 teaspoon wine vinegar

1 cup olive oil
$^1/_4$ cup chopped fresh basil or any other fresh herb

1. To make the batter, place the flour and salt and pepper in a bowl. Add 2 of the egg yolks. Beat with a whisk, then blend in the beer, vegetable oil and curry powder. Cover and let stand.

2. In another bowl beat the egg whites until they form soft peaks. Fold them into the batter using a rubber spatula. Cover the mixture and let stand until needed.

3. To prepare the sauce, place the remaining egg yolk in a third bowl with the garlic, mustard, Tabasco, salt and pepper to taste. Blend well. Add the olive oil in a thin stream while beating vigorously. When the mixture is thick and smooth, stir in the chopped basil. Cover and refrigerate until shrimp and squid are ready to serve.

4. Cut the squid into $^1/_4$-inch rounds. Slice the tentacles into bite-sized pieces.

5. Heat the vegetable oil for frying to 360° in a deep fryer. Place the shrimp and squid in the batter and stir to coat well. Fry them in batches. Drop the shrimp and squid pieces into the oil a few at a time without crowding them. Fry and stir until crisp and lightly golden, about 1 minute for each batch. Remove the shrimp and squid and drain on a paper towel. Keep warm, continue cooking in batches until all the pieces are done. Serve immediately with the sauce.

Yield: 4 to 6 servings

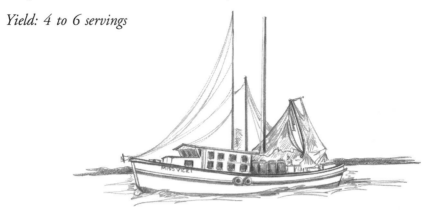

  We ate so many oysters while we were in the Louisiana countryside—especially at that restaurant called Dupuy's in Abbeville—that I wanted to include here my favorite dressing for raw oysters (and clams).

Mignonette Sauce for Oysters and Clams on the Half Shell

$^1/_2$ cup red wine vinegar
4 tablespoons finely chopped
  shallots

1 tablespoon white peppercorns,
  freshly and finely crushed
salt to taste

Combine all ingredients and serve. The sauce may be kept refrigerated in a tightly closed jar.

Yield: $^3/_4$ cup

If the mignonette is my favorite dressing, the following cocktail sauce is a close second and extremely popular among my guests.

Cocktail Sauce for Clams and Oysters

$^{1}/_{2}$ cup ketchup
4 tablespoons fresh lemon juice
$^{1}/_{2}$ cup finely chopped celery
2 tablespoons freshly grated
   horseradish

$^{1}/_{2}$ teaspoon Tabasco sauce
$^{1}/_{4}$ teaspoon Worcestershire sauce

Combine all ingredients and serve. The sauce may be kept refrigerated in a tightly closed jar.

Yield: $^{3}/_{4}$ cup

Eula Mae Doré, the cook on Avery Island, is a skilled woman whose every move reflects generations of handed-down Cajun tradition. The next three recipes are dishes she prepared while we were guests there. She made a chicken and sausage gumbo for us at Marsh House; I prepared a shrimp gumbo of my own at home and have appended that recipe to this chapter as well.

Cajun Potato Salad

2 pounds potatoes, about 6
6 hard-cooked eggs
2 cups Mayonnaise (page 377)
1 sweet green pepper, cored, seeded
   and chopped

2 sweet pickles, chopped
$^{1}/_{2}$ cup coarsely chopped celery
salt and freshly ground pepper to
   taste
Tabasco sauce to taste

1. Boil the potatoes until tender, about 20 minutes. Let cool, peel and cut into $^{1}/_{4}$-inch cubes.

2. Peel the eggs and separate the whites from the yolks. Chop the whites and set aside. In a bowl blend the yolks with the mayonnaise and force the mixture through a strainer.

3. In a large bowl gently combine all the ingredients. If the salad is not sharp enough, add 1 teaspoon of vinegar and blend well.

Yield: 6 to 8 servings

Pork Jambalaya

3 pounds boneless pork loin, most
    of the fat removed, cut into $^1/_4$-
    inch slices
salt and freshly ground pepper to
    taste
5 cloves garlic, peeled
1 pound pork sausage, cut into
    slices $^1/_4$ inch thick
1 cup coarsely chopped onions
$^3/_4$ cup coarsely chopped seeded
    green pepper

$^3/_4$ cup coarsely chopped seeded
    sweet red pepper
$^1/_2$ cup coarsely chopped celery
$1^1/_2$ cups peeled cubed tomatoes
3 cups water
Tabasco sauce to taste
3 cups long-grain rice, washed and
    drained to remove starch
$^1/_2$ cup coarsely chopped scallions

1. Sprinkle the pork with salt and pepper. Place the pork in a preheated heavy skillet and cook, covered, over low heat for 15 minutes until tender. Turn and stir the slices often. Pour off the fat.

2. Add the garlic, sausage, onions, green and red peppers and celery. Cook, stirring constantly, for 5 to 7 minutes, until the vegetables are wilted. Scrape the bottom of the pan often.

3. Add the tomatoes and cook until almost all the liquid is gone but the mixture is still moist. When the garlic is tender, crush it with a fork and blend it in.

4. Stir in the water, bring it to a boil and simmer, covered, for $^1/_2$ hour.

5. Add the Tabasco and the rice. Cover and simmer for 30 minutes, stirring occasionally. Garnish with scallions and serve.

Yield: 6 to 8 servings

Eula's Chicken and Sausage Gumbo

1 6-pound hen, cut into 10 to 12 serving pieces
2 pounds smoked sausage, such as Louisiana tasso or kielbasa, cut into 1-inch slices
1/2 cup vegetable oil
3/4 cup flour
1 cup coarsely chopped onions
3/4 cup coarsely chopped seeded green pepper
1/2 cup coarsely chopped celery
5 cloves garlic, peeled
2 quarts fresh or canned chicken stock
1/4 cup chopped parsley
3/4 cup chopped scallions

1. In a nonstick pan brown the hen pieces on both sides and set aside.

2. In a large saucepan cover the sausages with water, bring to a boil, drain and set aside.

3. In a large heavy pot such as a cast-iron Dutch oven heat the vegetable oil and blend in the flour, stirring constantly to prevent the flour from burning. As the flour thickens and darkens, look for a dark reddish mahogany color, after about 5 minutes.

4. Add the onions, green pepper, celery and garlic. Cook, stirring, for 3 or 4 minutes.

5. Add the stock, bring to a boil and simmer for 5 minutes.

6. Add the hen pieces and sausages. Cover and simmer for 1 to 1 1/2 hours, skimming the fat frequently. When it is soft, crush the garlic with the back of a spoon and stir it in.

7. Stir in the parsley and scallions and serve in soup bowls.

Yield: 12 to 14 servings

Paul Prudhomme isn't the only one in the family who can cook, as you might imagine. In fact his sister Enola has fans as avid for her cooking as Paul has for his. We visited her fine restaurant, Prudhomme's Cajun Cafe near Carencro, Louisiana, and observed as she prepared these pirogues. The pirogue is a bayou boat, and both she and Paul are fond of carving eggplants into that shape and then filling them beautifully.

Enola's Eggplant Pirogues

2 1-pound eggplants, peeled and
   halved lengthwise

salt to taste

$^1/_2$ teaspoon garlic powder

$^1/_4$ teaspoon paprika

$^1/_4$ teaspoon cayenne

$^1/_8$ teaspoon crumbled dried basil

$^1/_8$ teaspoon crumbled dried thyme

$^1/_8$ teaspoon black pepper

$^1/_2$ cup dry bread crumbs

vegetable oil for deep frying

2 tablespoons unsalted butter

$^1/_2$ pound fresh crawfish tail meat
   or frozen meat, thawed

1 cup small shrimp, shelled and
   deveined

1 cup thinly sliced mushrooms

$^1/_2$ cup lump crab meat

$^1/_2$ cup chopped scallions

$1^1/_2$ cups heavy cream

1. With a spoon scoop the flesh out of the eggplant halves, leaving a $^1/_2$-inch shell. Finely chop the flesh and set aside.

2. In a small bowl combine the salt, garlic powder, paprika, cayenne, basil, thyme and black pepper. Blend well. Sprinkle a scant $^1/_2$ teaspoon of the seasoning over each eggplant half and divide the bread crumbs among the eggplant halves, patting them on.

3. Pour enough oil into a large deep skillet to reach a depth of 2 inches. Heat the oil to 375°. Fry the eggplants in two batches for 8 to 10 minutes or until golden. Drain on paper towels. Keep warm.

4. In another skillet melt the butter and in it cook the eggplant flesh, crawfish, shrimp, mushrooms, crab meat and the scallions, stirring, for 10 minutes. Add the

cream and cook for another 5 to 10 minutes, until the mixture is thickened. Season with salt and black pepper to taste.

5. Arrange an eggplant half on each of 4 plates and spoon filling into them.

Yield: 4 servings

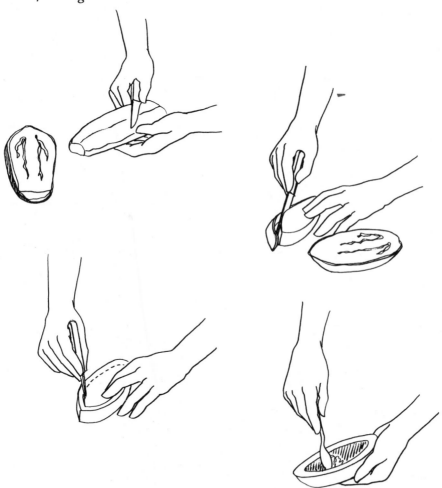

To create a true pirogue, cut the eggplant in half and peel it with a paring knife. In long, smooth strokes, carve each eggplant half into the shape of a boat, tapered at both ends. With the point of the knife, make an incision inside the boat that follows the contour of the pirogue. Finish by scooping out the well with a spoon.

For many years now I have cooked with Tabasco sauce—one of Louisiana's gifts to the rest of us—to give sparkle to a dish. It is particularly pleasant when combined with the natural bite of a yogurt dish.

Shrimp with Yogurt and Tabasco Sauce

1¹/₂ pounds raw shrimp with the shells

1 cup plain yogurt

¹/₂ teaspoon Tabasco sauce

1 tablespoon finely chopped garlic

1 teaspoon ground turmeric

1 teaspoon caraway seeds

¹/₂ cup finely chopped fresh coriander

¹/₂ teaspoon ground cumin

salt to taste

2 tablespoons mustard oil (sold in Asian markets) or vegetable oil

¹/₂ pound small white mushrooms

1. Shell and devein the shrimp, rinse well and drain. Pat dry.

2. Combine the yogurt, Tabasco, garlic, turmeric, caraway seeds, ¹/₄ cup of the coriander, the cumin and salt. Add the shrimp, and blend well. Cover and refrigerate until ready to use.

3. Heat the oil in a large nonstick skillet. Add the mushrooms, salt to taste and cook, stirring, for 2 minutes. Add the shrimp mixture and cook gently, stirring, until the shrimp changes color, about 2 or 3 minutes. Do not overcook. Serve hot, garnished with remaining coriander. Accompany with Creole Rice (page 195).

Yield: 4 servings

❧ Shrimp and crab meat go hand in hand throughout Louisiana and this salad, given heat by the jalapeño, reminds me of some salads we had there.

Shrimp and Crab Meat Salad with Jalapeño Pepper

1 pound medium shrimp
salt and freshly ground pepper to
    taste
6 whole allspice
$^1/_2$ pound fresh crab meat,
    preferably lump
1 cup Mayonnaise (page 377)
juice of 1 lime
2 jalapeño peppers, chopped (about
    1 tablespoon)
$^1/_4$ cup finely chopped loosely
    packed fresh coriander or parsley

$^1/_4$ cup chopped scallions
16 large firm unblemished spinach
    leaves, trimmed of the top stem,
    rinsed well and patted dry
16 trimmed endive or radicchio
    leaves
1 head Boston lettuce, cut into bite-
    sized pieces
4 sprigs coriander for garnish

1. Put the shrimp in a saucepan and add salt and pepper to taste and the allspice. Add cold water to barely cover and bring to a boil. Remove from heat and let the shrimp stand until they are at room temperature. Shell and devein and set aside.

2. Pick over the crab meat to remove bits of shell and cartilage.

3. Combine the mayonnaise, lime juice, jalapeños, coriander, scallions, salt and pepper to taste in a large bowl. Add the shrimp and crab meat and toss lightly to blend without breaking the lumps.

4. Arrange 4 spinach leaves on 4 individual serving plates. (Dinner plates are recommended.) Arrange alternately the radicchio or endive between the spinach leaves.

5. Arrange equal portions of Boston lettuce leaves in the center of each serving.

6. Spoon equal portions of the shrimp and crab meat salad over the center of each plate. Garnish with the coriander sprigs. Serve chilled.

Yield: 4 servings

A classic shrimp dish is this shrimp Creole. You'll notice that it uses the "holy trinity" of Cajun cooking—onions, celery and green pepper—along with my own predilection for sprinkling in some Tabasco during the cooking.

Shrimp Creole

1 pound medium shrimp
3 tablespoons olive oil
$3/4$ cup coarsely chopped onions
1 cup coarsely chopped celery
2 sweet green peppers, cored, seeded and coarsely chopped
1 sweet red pepper, cored, seeded and coarsely chopped
3 cloves garlic, minced
2 cups canned tomatoes, preferably crushed Italian tomatoes

1 sprig fresh thyme or $1/2$ teaspoon dried
1 bay leaf
Tabasco sauce to taste
$1/2$ teaspoon grated lemon rind
salt and freshly ground pepper to taste
2 tablespoons finely chopped parsley
juice of $1/2$ lemon

1. Shell and devein the shrimp. Rinse them, pat dry and set aside.

2. Heat the olive oil in a saucepan and add the onions. Cook, stirring, until wilted. Add the celery, green and red peppers and garlic. Cook briefly, stirring. The vegetables must remain crisp.

3. Add the tomatoes, thyme, bay leaf, Tabasco, lemon rind, and salt and pepper to taste. Simmer for 10 minutes, uncovered.

4. Add the shrimp and cover. Cook 3 to 5 minutes, no longer. Remove bay leaf and thyme. Add the chopped parsley, lemon juice and, if desired, more Tabasco to taste. Serve with rice of your choice.

Yield: 2 to 4 servings

I call this a shrimp gumbo to distinguish it from the chicken and sausage one earlier in the chapter, but as you see it also includes sausage and pork.

Shrimp Gumbo

3 tablespoons olive oil

1 pound kielbasa sausage or *andouille,* cut into ¼-inch-thick slices

½ pound tasso (Louisiana's smoked pork, or substitute other smoked pork), cut into ¼-inch cubes

2 tablespoons finely chopped garlic

½ cup chopped onions

½ cup chopped scallions

1½ cups finely chopped seeded sweet green peppers

1½ cups chopped celery

2 pounds fresh okra, thinly sliced or 2 10-ounce packages frozen

2 cups cored cubed plum tomatoes

2 bay leaves

5 cups Basic Shrimp Stock (page 378) or bottled clam juice

1 teaspoon Tabasco sauce

1 tablespoon Worcestershire sauce

salt and freshly ground pepper to taste

4 tablespoons all-purpose flour

5 pounds raw shrimp, shelled and deveined

12 lemon slices

1. Heat 1 tablespoon of the oil in a cast-iron Dutch oven. Add the sausages and tasso, and cook over high heat, stirring often, until lightly browned. Transfer the meat to a bowl and set aside. Pour off the fat.

2. Add the garlic, onions, scallions, green peppers and celery to the Dutch oven. Cook, stirring, until the vegetables are wilted. Add the okra and cook until the vegetables become fairly dry, about 5 or 6 minutes.

3. Stir in the tomatoes, bay leaves, 4 cups of the shrimp stock, Tabasco, Worcestershire sauce, salt and pepper and the tasso and sausages. Bring to a boil and simmer for about 15 minutes.

4. Heat the remaining 2 tablespoons oil in a small frying pan. Add the flour and cook, stirring constantly, with a wooden spatula until the flour is brown but not burned. Stir in the remaining 1 cup shrimp stock with a wire whisk. Bring to a boil. Stir mixture into the vegetables and cook for 10 minutes.

5. Add the shrimp and the lemon slices and bring to a boil. Cook for 3 minutes, stirring occasionally. Serve with Creole Rice (page 195).

Yield: 10 servings

A Crab Feast

When a crab frees itself from its shell there is some similarity to a chick doing it, but this is more startling. The crab does it backwards, as if it had gotten itself cornered and now had to punch its way out, retreating very slowly. The effort seems so great as it goes on for 10 or 15 minutes. Finally, the arduous fight is over, the whole crab has extricated itself, claws last, from the old shell. For the crab, it is almost a rebirth because it is now much larger than before. Its soft shell will, if left in the water, be hard in two days. Crabs usually like to molt in private, hiding somewhere to do it. But on one midsummer day I was able to observe this act of renewal and growth close at hand. I was standing over a wooden tub containing a bunch of crabs, when one of them began to molt, and the slow battle commenced. When the crab had finally freed itself, I called out, bravo!

I was there to witness it thanks to a Chesapeake waterman named Albert "Bo Bo" Merritt who regularly brings his crabs ashore at Crisfield, where he holds them until they molt and then sells them to the John T. Handy Company whose headquarters are just a few steps away. (Handy describes itself as the world's largest soft-shell crab processor and obtains its crabs from 250 independent watermen; the company's crabs are available fresh May through September and frozen year round.)

Bo Bo, 35 years old, has been a waterman most of his life. He says he began crabbing at the age of 13 when he'd go out on the bay with his uncle. These days he heads out alone in the predawn hours, about 4 or 4:30. His only companion is his dog, Roxy, a Chesapeake retriever with a tight wiry coat and big feet meant for swimming. His 28-foot boat is powered by a 340-horsepower Pontiac V-8, so that he can make it back fast if the weather changes. It's a lonely life, he concedes, "but not too bad as long as I've got the dog."

HANDY SOFT SHELL CRABS

He explained how he could tell whether a crab was about to molt. The clue is a color change—a change so subtle that only experts can really detect it—in one of its swim fins. White means two weeks or so until molting, pink means one week and red means less than two days to go.

The Chesapeake is North America's largest estuary, with the Atlantic to the east and, to the west, four great rivers: the Potomac, York, James and Susquehanna. Estuaries are well-defined places. To be a good estuary, a prodigious birthplace for sea creatures, a body of salt water has to be enclosed at one end, but fed by at least one freshwater source. The estuary should be shallow enough to be warmed by sunlight and it should have protective marshlands around it. The Chesapeake, despite the perils of urban growth on its banks, manages to be extraordinarily productive even now. It produces oysters, clams, striped bass and, of course, crabs in tremendous volume. Although soft-shell crabs are found from New Jersey to Florida, we can thank the Chesapeake for 80 percent of the total. Crisfield has been one of the nation's crab centers for more than a hundred years. In 1873, the first soft-shell crabs were shipped from this place.

A soft-shell crab is a blue crab that has just molted (even after one day in the bay, its soft shell will show signs of definite hardening). The blue crab sheds as many as 23 times during a lifespan that, in the natural course of things, will run three years. Many of the crabs are trapped in pots, which are simply wire-mesh cages with funnels at the bottom to allow the crab entry as it seeks out the bait in a compartment in the middle of the trap. Other funnels lead to the upper portion of the cage. Crabs tend to flee upward, as William W. Warner explains in his book *Beautiful Swimmers*, and once a crab is in the upper portion of a pot, he writes, it "is pretty much confused and may be safely considered caught."

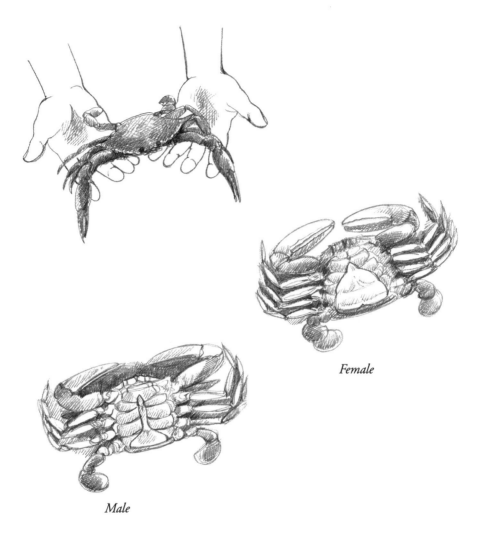

Female

Male

I didn't get to go out on a crabbing boat during our brief visit to Crisfield. In Alaska, though, I'd participated in pulling in some Dungeness crabs. The trapping is more or less the same in both places. But one of the practices used by the watermen of the Chesapeake to trap soft-shell females is unusual. It's called Jimmy potting, and it takes advantage of a powerful urge to mate. For crabs to copulate, a female must be soft shelled and the male hard shelled. In Jimmy potting, large Jimmies, or males, are placed in pots. The avid females come after them. Two or three males can lure as many as 20 or 30 amorous she-crabs into a trap.

A Cooperative Creature

Soft-shell crabs give the cook a hand. Not only do the crabs remove themselves from their shells but they pretty much clean themselves in the process. The crab doesn't eat for three days during the process, purging itself of waste, one reason that you can eat nearly the whole thing without thinking twice. You do have to trim the crab, though, to remove the head and the less edible apron. This can be done by the seafood shop, of course, but it is easy enough to do at home, and, for the sake of freshness, I do prefer to do it myself. Here's how:

Trimming Soft-Shell Crab

1. Remove the eyes.

2. Cut off apron.

3. Remove gills.

4. Remove skin.

The restaurant we chose to visit for a soft-shell crab feast was Pierpoint in an up-and-coming neighborhood near the harbor of ever-changing Baltimore. There, Nancy Longo, a young and vivacious chef, runs a small, narrow restaurant with marble-top tables that seems to draw everybody from Baltimore's baseball stars to its politicians. Since the simplest—and some would say best—way to serve soft-shell crabs is just to sauté them, that's what she did. But then she put her mind to adding some color to the production and demonstrated her own lively presentation, employing two different salsas and charred corn. Here's an adaptation of what she did. If green tomatoes are not available, you may want to try it with the red tomato salsa alone.

Pierpoint's Soft-Shell Crabs with Salsa and Corn Salad

Green Tomato Salsa (recipe follows)
Red Tomato Salsa (recipe follows)
Charred Corn Salad with Mustard
   Vinaigrette (recipe follows)
8 medium soft-shell crabs, trimmed
   for cooking (see illustration, page
   82)

$^1/_2$ cup milk
1 cup all-purpose flour
$^1/_8$ teaspoon cayenne
salt and freshly ground pepper to
   taste
2 tablespoons vegetable oil

1. Prepare the salsas and corn salad and set aside.

2. Place the crabs in a shallow platter and add the milk. Turn the crabs to coat them.

3. On a flat dish combine the flour, cayenne and salt and black pepper. Dredge each crab in the flour. Shake off the excess.

4. Heat the oil in a nonstick frying pan. Cook the crabs in batches, as many at a time as will fit in the pan in one layer. Sauté for about 3 minutes on each side, or until golden brown.

5. To serve, place a portion of the corn salad in the middle of each plate and a serving of the green salsa on one side and the red on the other. Place one crab on top of each salsa, leaving the corn uncovered.

Yield: 4 servings

Green Tomato Salsa

6 green tomatoes, chopped
$1/3$ cup cider vinegar
$1/4$ cup olive oil
$1^1/2$ teaspoons Old Bay Seasoning

juice of 1 lime
$1/2$ teaspoon celery salt
$1/2$ teaspoon chopped garlic

Combine all the ingredients in a bowl and blend well.

Yield: 3 cups

Red Tomato Salsa

6 tomatoes, peeled and chopped
$1/2$ red onion, diced
1 teaspoon finely chopped parsley
$1/4$ cup olive oil
juice of 3 lemons

1 teaspoon chopped garlic
1 teaspoon chopped fresh coriander
3 tablespoons red wine vinegar
pinch cayenne
2 teaspoons ground cumin

Combine all the ingredients in a bowl and blend well.

Yield: 3 cups

Charred Corn Salad with Mustard Vinaigrette

4 ears fresh corn
3 tablespoons Dijon mustard
juice of $1/2$ lemon
3 tablespoons cider vinegar
$1/4$ teaspoon cracked mustard seed

1 teaspoon chopped garlic
1 teaspoon chopped shallots
$1/2$ teaspoon sugar
$1/2$ cup olive oil

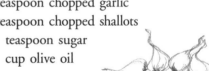

1. Preheat charcoal grill or broiler.

2. Grill the corn until it starts to char, turning the ears so that they cook evenly. Be sure the corn doesn't burn. Allow to cool and with a knife remove the kernels from the cobs and reserve in a bowl.

3. To make the vinaigrette, place the mustard, lemon juice, vinegar, mustard seed, garlic, shallots and sugar in a bowl and blend well with a wire whisk. Add the olive oil slowly, whisking well.

4. Pour the vinaigrette over the corn and combine the salad.

Yield: 2 cups

My friend Ed Giobbi is an artist first, I suppose, but he is also a terrific gardener and cook and cookbook writer. In particular, he has a genuine feel for homey Italian dishes. I learned to use soft-shell crabs in pasta from Ed. It's an unusual dish but quite beautiful.

Soft-Shell Crabs and Pasta à la Giobbi

4 tablespoons olive oil

12 small soft-shell crabs, 1 pound 12 ounces in all, trimmed for cooking (see illustration, page 82)

salt and freshly ground pepper to taste

1/4 teaspoon hot red pepper flakes, or to taste

1 cup coarsely chopped onions

2 tablespoons finely chopped garlic

3 cups cut into 1/2-inch cubes peeled ripe plum tomatoes

2 teaspoons chopped fresh oregano or 1 teaspoon dried

1 cup dry white wine

2 tablespoons tomato paste

2 small zucchini, about 1/2 pound in all, ends trimmed and sliced into rounds 1/4 inch thick

1 pound bow-tie pasta

1/2 cup reserved cooking liquid from pasta

1/2 cup coarsely chopped fresh basil or, if not available, 4 tablespoons coarsely chopped Italian parsley

2 tablespoons butter

1. In a very large saucepan heat the olive oil. Add the crabs and sprinkle them with salt and pepper and red pepper flakes. Sauté over high heat for about 1 minute on each side. Do not brown.

2. Add the onions, garlic, tomatoes and oregano. Cook until the onions are wilted. Add the wine, tomato paste and zucchini. Stir well, bring to a boil and cover. Simmer for 10 minutes.

3. Meanwhile, bring 3 quarts of salted water to a boil. Add the pasta and cook until al dente. Drain, reserving 1/2 cup of the cooking liquid.

4. With a slotted spoon remove the crabs from the sauce and, on a large platter or cutting board, cut them in half.

5. To the pasta, add the sauce, reserved cooking liquid and the crabs with all the juices from the platter. Stir and bring back to a boil. Add the basil and butter. Toss well and serve hot.

Yield: 6 servings

This dish of crab meat and ham on toast, with its rich and smooth cream sauce, is meant to be an elegant lunch. I've specified Alaska's Dungeness crab here, but king crab will serve as well.

Dungeness Crab with Smithfield Ham on Toast

1 pound Dungeness crab meat or
  other lump crab meat
2 tablespoons butter
2 tablespoons finely chopped
  shallots
5 tablespoons dry sherry
1/2 cup heavy cream
1/2 cup half-and-half

1 teaspoon Worcestershire sauce
1 egg yolk, lightly beaten
freshly ground pepper to taste
4 slices toast
8 thin slices Smithfield ham or
  prosciutto
lemon wedges for garnish

1. Pick over the crab to remove any traces of shell or cartilage. Drain well.

2. Heat 1 tablespoon of the butter in a nonstick heavy skillet and add the shallots. Cook, stirring, until wilted. Add 3 tablespoons of the sherry and cook to reduce the liquid by about half.

3. Add the cream, half-and-half and Worcestershire sauce and cook about 5 minutes over high heat.

4. Meanwhile, in a nonstick skillet heat the remaining 1 tablespoon butter and add the crab meat. Add the remaining 2 tablespoons sherry, heat thoroughly and remove from the heat.

5. Add $^1/_4$ cup of the hot cream mixture to the egg yolk and stir to blend. Return this mixture to the cream, and add the pepper, stirring rapidly. Remove from the heat.

6. Spoon and scrape the sauce over the crab meat.

7. Preheat the broiler. Prepare the toast and keep it warm.

8. Heat the ham under the broiler, and place the slices on the toast. Top with the crab meat in cream sauce. Garnish with lemon wedges. A good accompaniment is Parslied Cucumbers (page 374).

Yield: 4 servings

❧ *Although crab meat can be purchased year round, the time we think of it most is in the summer, often in salads. Here's another summertime approach, omelettes served at room temperature with a chilled crab filling. It was a favorite in the old days, especially with the Duchess of Windsor, at New York's Le Pavillon restaurant.*

Cold Crab Meat Omelettes with Spicy Mayonnaise

8 large eggs
2 tablespoons chopped fresh parsley
1 tablespoon chopped fresh tarragon
1 tablespoon chopped fresh chives
1/4 cup heavy cream
3/4 cup peeled and seeded ripe plum tomatoes, cut into 1/4-inch cubes

salt and freshly ground pepper to taste
2 tablespoons butter
Chili Sauce Mayonnaise (recipe follows)
parsley sprigs for garnish

1. Break the eggs into a bowl, and beat lightly with a fork. Add the parsley, tarragon, chives, cream, tomatoes and salt and pepper to taste. Beat well.

2. Using a small omelette pan or a 7-inch nonstick pan, heat about 1/2 teaspoon of the butter. Add about 1/3 cup of the egg mixture. Let cook until firm and lightly browned on the bottom. Stir quickly with a fork until the omelette starts to set. When set, slip a large pancake turner under the omelette and flip it quickly. Let cook about 5 seconds. (Remember: You want to produce a flat omelette, not the typical folded one.) Slide the omelette onto a sheet of wax paper. Continue making omelettes until all the egg mixture is used. There should be 8 omelettes to be served at room temperature.

3. When ready to serve, place a portion of the chili sauce mayonnaise in the center of each omelette. Fold the omelette over, and garnish with the parsley sprigs. Serve with the remaining mayonnaise on the side.

Yield: 4 to 8 servings

Chili Sauce Mayonnaise

1 whole egg
1 teaspoon Dijon mustard
1/2 teaspoon Worcestershire sauce
1 teaspoon red wine vinegar
salt and freshly ground pepper to taste
1 cup vegetable or peanut oil
2 tablespoons bottled chili sauce
2 tablespoons finely chopped parsley

2 tablespoons finely chopped shallots
1 pound Dungeness crab meat or other lump crab meat, picked over and all traces of shell or cartilage removed
juice of 1/2 lemon

1. To make the mayonnaise sauce, break the egg into a bowl. Add the mustard, Worcestershire sauce, vinegar and salt and pepper to taste. Beat with a wire whisk.

2. Gradually add the oil, beating constantly until thickened. Add the chili sauce, parsley and shallots and blend well. Set aside.

3. Place the crab meat in a bowl and add half the mayonnaise sauce. (There should be just enough sauce to bind the crab meat thoroughly.) Sprinkle with the lemon juice. Check for seasoning and keep cold. Serve the remaining mayonnaise with the omelettes.

Yield: 1 1/2 cups

Honey

I arrived in Turlock, a smallish city 100 miles east of San Francisco, in the middle of the night, so it was only in the first light of morning that I could get any idea at all about where this leg of my American exploration had taken me. As dawn came up and I and my television team hit the road, what we saw was an agricultural area dotted with housing developments and dominated by wide expanses of extraordinarily productive farmland.

Cherry trees were in glorious bloom. There were stubby kiwi plants, not yet doing much. We sped by the almond trees that are a major source of income here and, of course, some grapevines. We were on our way toward the sweetest produce of all, honey, and a farm run since the early days of the Great Depression by the Beekman family—now the brothers Bruce and Bob along with their 82-year-old parents Jack and Laura Belle. When we reached the farm, a mere five acres (and most of that taken up by walnut trees), we were in no way prepared for the surprises the day would hold.

I already knew a great deal about honey. Or thought I did. I carried with me indelible childhood memories of the bees on neighboring farms in Burgundy. And I have cooked with honey all my life, using it as a glaze, or in a syrup or a barbecue sauce. Like everyone else, I have taken honey in my tea and thanked providence for it. I have sipped honey wine, and thanked providence again.

But my appreciation for honey, the bees that make it and the beekeepers who manage the process expanded many times over in this one day at the Beekman farm. When we arrived in the early light, a flatbed truck loaded with crates, each containing a colony of bees—112 of them on that one truck—was poised to pull out. It was cool and the bees were quieter now than they would be later when the sun would warm them into activity. But you could still see a few guardian bees slipping out of their boxes to reconnoiter in the commotion. Bob Beekman was preparing to take these bee colonies to a nearby flowering mountainside where he would release them for nourishment—not to produce honey for human consumption this time— but just to keep them fat and healthy for the work that lay ahead.

Surprise number one: The bees are almost never kept on the farm, but are continually carted off to natural fields and orchards and other agricultural areas that may be hundreds of miles away, where they gather nectar and pollen. That's why the bee farm itself can be as small as it is; they're rarely home. Another surprise: Because the bees are left to their own devices for weeks on end, sometimes in virtually untended fields, bee rustling is an ongoing problem; thieves come after dark in their pickup trucks, load up the night-cooled and quiet bees as they rest in their hives, and take off. No one has yet learned how to brand a bee.

There is no way that a bee farmer can be everywhere at once. Each of them is not just a producer of honey but also a sort of foreman overseeing millions of tiny migrant workers at many locations. Bee colonies are rented to farms all up and down the state to boost natural pollination and increase the farmer's yield. While we were there, the bees were pollinating cherries. At other times it might have been almonds, kiwis or melons. Natural pollination by bees—a process in which the bee, while foraging for food, picks up the male pollen and inadvertently deposits it on the female organ of another flower, fertilizing it—has, of course, been going on for millennia. But now it's big business. To pollinate California's 360,000 acres of almonds alone, bee farms must supply 750,000 colonies of bees. "There just aren't enough bees in the wild," Bruce Beekman explained, "to pollinate all these trees and give us the production we need." The bees are also rented to pollinate the plants— alfalfa is one—that supply food for the animals we eat. By one calculation, a third of everything Americans eat is either directly or indirectly the result of the work of these astonishing insects.

To give us a firsthand look at colonies of bees doing their best, Bruce led us to a cherry orchard some 30 miles away. Bruce is a quiet guy, very steady, just the sort of fellow I'd choose to lead me into a swarm of bees. He donned the beekeeper's familiar white jump suit and netted headgear. No fool, I did too. Sealed tight, we strolled through a cherry orchard in bloom, a canopy of pink flowers stretching into the distance.

Bruce's bees were everywhere, flapping their wings 11,400 times a minute to create a buzzing racket, as they moved from blossom to blossom. The same sort of boxed hives that Bob had taken to the mountainside earlier could be seen here. Each bee out among the blossoms knew exactly which hive was hers (the workers are all undeveloped females) and would return to it regularly, burdened with little spots of pollen on her legs; the nectar to produce honey was mostly carried in an internal sac, a specialized stomach, for delivery to the hive. At my request, Bruce opened one of the crates and quieted the bees with a couple of puffs of smoke from a can-like contraption (the smoke seems to take just enough of the aggression out of them). The scene was startling. There, in the box, were hundreds of bees depositing their loads, preparing to go out again, and in the middle we could see royalty herself, the fat queen.

Back at the Beekman farm, I learned a little more about the process. There, the honey is extracted from the comb—a more strenuous activity than you might think since the bees have sealed their treasure with considerable ingenuity. First a lid of wax needs to be removed from the surface of the comb and even then the viscous gold will not simply pour out. It must be forced out with great energy, either by a manual centrifuge (the old-fashioned way) that spins the honey free, or by machine. The Beekman farm produces 105 tons of honey each year.

Although what we commonly find in stores in the United States is a blend, much of the honey produced on farms has a distinctive flavor and aroma derived from particular floral sources. Some honey is bad stuff. The honey from those cherry trees, for instance, is too bitter and will not be sold. But when the orange trees are in bloom, that's a different story. Orange honey is silken and sweet: "When you open the bottle for the first time," Bruce said, "you get an aromatic blast that makes you think you're in a citrus grove." He likes the mild flavor of clover honey, too, redolent of cinnamon and among the most commonly sold in the United States.

In the "rumpus room" of the Beekman farm, actually a separate cinder-block building containing a single large room for family gatherings, I chatted with Jack and Laura Belle. In 1929 Jack, white-haired now and wearing a string tie, had come to California from upstate New York on a big Harley motorcycle (he calls himself the "first Hells Angel") where he married Laura Belle and started the farm. In those days, Laura Belle would prepare the family's food on a pale green and white woodburning cookstove. The stove is still there, and when called upon it still works beautifully. I decided to give it a try, concocting an orange-honey syrup first and then poaching California figs in it. I call the dish Laura Belle's Honeyed Figs as a way of thanking this family for

being so kind to us, so patient, and for telling us so much we never would have known, if we hadn't met them here in the bee country of Northern California.

Honey Tips

Although much of the honey available to us in the United States is a blend, there are, according to the National Honey Board, 300 distinct types of honey available in the country, each derived from a different floral source. Honey is produced in every state. If your shops have only a limited selection, it makes sense to visit a local beekeeper to see what he has to offer.

In general the darker the honey the stronger the flavor. So dark honey is best in the cooking of dishes that call out for a pronounced honey flavor. The lighter, silkier honey is fine in cooking (as in Laura Belle's Honeyed Figs), but it is also the choice when your mouth is watering for something aromatic and sweet on a muffin or toast.

Caution: Honey is 25 percent sweeter than table sugar. When substituting honey for sugar, it's important to employ proportionately less or you'll ruin the dish. A benefit is that the diminished quantity of this natural sugar means fewer calories in a serving.

Honey is one of the great secret ingredients in American cooking. We have it in ready supply in this country and the quality is often extremely good. It's endlessly useful, in sauces, syrups and baking and should be kept on hand, like mustard. (Don't worry about honey spoiling; it virtually can't, refrigerated or not.) The recipes here are intended to showcase some of its major uses. In the fig recipe below, I might just as well have used sugar—and often have in similar preparations, such as my poached pears—but what a sweet difference the honey makes!

Laura Belle's Honeyed Figs

2 pounds dried or fresh figs
1 cup orange honey
1 cup dry red wine, such as a
   Cabernet or Pinot Noir
1/2 cup water

2 bay leaves
2 sprigs fresh oregano or 1/2
   teaspoon dried
6 tablespoons finely julienned strips
   of orange zest

1. In a shallow, wide saucepan large enough to hold the figs in one layer combine the honey, wine, water, bay leaves, oregano and 2 tablespoons of the orange zest. Bring to a boil and simmer covered for 5 minutes.

2. Add the figs and simmer for 5 minutes. Allow to cool.

3. For each serving reserve 1 whole fig. Cut the others in half lengthwise. On each plate, place a whole fig in the center and arrange about 8 halves in a circle around it. Spoon a little of the syrup over the serving.

4. Garnish with the remaining 4 tablespoons of orange zest.

Yield: 6 to 8 servings

⁂ This sautéed salmon was prepared for me at a little restaurant called Trax, in Turlock, California. The honey-sweetened onions beneath the fish serve as a dramatic textural contrast.

Sautéed Salmon with Honey-Onion Compote

3 cups coarsely sliced red onions
4 tablespoons red wine vinegar
1 1/4 cups California Cabernet
4 tablespoons honey
salt and freshly ground white
   pepper to taste
4 tablespoons butter
1 1/2 cups puréed fresh tomatoes,
   skinned and seeds removed

2 sprigs fresh thyme or 1/2 teaspoon
   dried
1/8 teaspoon cayenne
4 skinless boneless salmon fillets, 6
   ounces each
1/2 cup fine, fresh bread crumbs
2 tablespoons vegetable oil
8 basil leaves for garnish

1. In a saucepan combine the onions, vinegar, wine and honey. Salt and pepper to taste. Cook over medium-high heat, stirring until liquid is mostly evaporated. Remove from heat, add 2 tablespoons of the butter, blend well and keep warm.

2. In a small saucepan combine the tomato, thyme, cayenne and salt and pepper to taste. Bring to a boil and simmer until reduced to 1 cup. Remove from the heat, add the remaining butter, blend well and cover. Keep warm.

3. Sprinkle salmon with salt and pepper. Dredge it in the bread crumbs to coat lightly on both sides. Pat the bread crumbs to be sure they adhere.

4. Heat the vegetable oil in a nonstick skillet large enough to hold all the salmon in one layer. Add the fillets and cook over medium heat until lightly browned, about 3 minutes (for rare), turn and cook for 3 minutes more. Do not overcook.

5. To serve, warm 4 plates. Place a quarter of the sauce in the center of each plate. Over the sauce place evenly divided servings of the onions. Over the onions, for each serving place a single fillet and garnish with 2 basil leaves.

Yield: 4 servings

🐝 *Honey goes particularly well with lamb, especially the less expensive or older cuts, which have strong flavor. It makes the dish smoother and, to my mind, pleasanter.*

Marinated Brochette of Lamb with Honey

1½ pounds skinless boneless loin
   or leg of lamb meat
4 tablespoons fresh lemon juice
4 tablespoons olive oil
½ cup dry red wine
⅓ cup honey
1 tablespoon chopped fresh
   rosemary or 2 teaspoons dried
1 tablespoon finely chopped garlic
2 teaspoons ground cumin
salt and freshly ground pepper to
   taste

2 sweet red peppers, cut into 16
   2-inch squares
2 white onions, cut into 16 2-inch
   squares
1 medium-sized eggplant, cut into
   16 2-inch squares, each ½ inch
   thick
8 tablespoons coarsely chopped
   fresh coriander or parsley for
   garnish

1. Cut the lamb into 16 2-inch cubes.

2. Marinate the lamb for at least 2 hours in the lemon juice, olive oil, wine, honey, rosemary, garlic, cumin, salt and pepper to taste. Blend well and cover with plastic wrap.

3. Preheat oven broiler or charcoal grill.

4. Drain the meat, reserving the marinade. Thread the meat on 4 skewers, alternating with a piece of red pepper, onion and eggplant.

5. Broil under high heat 3 minutes on each side for rare, brushing with the marinade. Garnish with the herbs.

Yield: 4 servings

Note: This marinade and preparation also work well with pork or chicken.

❧ *Because barbecue sauces—and how we love them in this country—are usually attempts to achieve a tart-sweet piquancy, honey is almost always a major player. Here's a sauce that I've designated for Cornish hens, but you should feel free to use it for any meat you like.*

Barbecued Cornish Hens

The Barbecue Sauce

2 tablespoons olive oil
1¹/₂ cups finely chopped onions
2 tablespoons finely chopped garlic
1 28-ounce can crushed tomatoes
1 6-ounce can tomato paste
¹/₂ cup red wine vinegar
¹/₄ cup Worcestershire sauce
1 tablespoon chili powder
1 tablespoon ground coriander
3 tablespoons fresh lemon juice
¹/₄ teaspoon hot red pepper flakes

3 teaspoons Tabasco sauce, or to
  taste
2 tablespoons chopped fresh
  oregano or 1 tablespoon dried
2 teaspoons ground cumin
2 bay leaves
4 sprigs fresh thyme or 1 teaspoon
  dried
1 teaspoon freshly ground pepper
4 tablespoons honey
salt to taste

Heat the oil in a saucepan and add the onions. Cook, stirring, until wilted. Add the garlic and cook briefly. Add the remaining ingredients and bring to a simmer, stirring often, for about 30 minutes. Let cool, and use for basting. This sauce keeps very well when refrigerated.

Yield: 5 cups

The Hens

4 1-pound Cornish hens, split for
  broiling
2 tablespoons vegetable oil
1 teaspoon paprika

1 tablespoon salt
1 tablespoon freshly ground pepper
1¹/₂ cups prepared Barbecue Sauce
  (recipe above)

1. Preheat oven broiler to high or preheat charcoal grill. To facilitate broiling, have the backbone removed from each Cornish hen. Turn the hens skin side down on a

flat surface. Using a sharp knife, carefully split the joint halfway down where the leg and the thigh bone meet. Do not split all the way through.

2. Rub the hen halves with the oil, paprika, salt and pepper. Place the hens on their sides in a shallow baking dish. Arrange the giblets between the hen halves. Let stand 10 minutes.

3. If the oven broiler is used, place the baking dish about 5 inches from the source of heat for 10 minutes, basting with the barbecue sauce. Turn the halves and continue broiling for about the same length of time, basting and turning often, until cooked.

4. If the hens are charcoal broiled, drain them and place them, skin side down, on the grill. When the skin is nicely brown, turn the hens and cook on the other side. Baste the hens, continuing to turn and baste them every 5 minutes for about 15 minutes more or until done. Serve with more barbecue sauce if needed.

Yield: 4 servings

One of my favorite chefs in New York is David Burke, now of The Park Avenue Café. I didn't try this dish until I got back from California's honey country but wanted to include it here to show how marvelously honey combines with other ingredients in yet another barbecue sauce, this one exotic and intended for fish. There are a lot of ingredients here, but David's sauce is easy to prepare. You'll probably have some left over. Store it.

David Burke's Honey-Barbecued Swordfish

The Barbecue Sauce

2¹/₂ cups honey

1 cup rice wine vinegar

¹/₂ cup soy sauce

1 cup ketchup

¹/₂ cup fresh lemon juice

¹/₄ cup Grand Marnier

4 tablespoons vodka

2 cinnamon sticks

5 star anise

3 cloves garlic, minced

1 tablespoon coriander seed

1 teaspoon hot red pepper flakes

1 teaspoon cardamom

1 tablespoon green peppercorns

1 heaping tablespoon chopped fresh ginger

1 teaspoon whole cloves

1 teaspoon mace

¹/₂ cup chopped fresh coriander leaves

Combine all the ingredients in a saucepan. Bring to a boil. Reduce by half. Strain and reserve.

Yield: about 2¹/₂ cups

The Swordfish

6 1-inch swordfish steaks, about 6 to 7 ounces each

6 teaspoons olive oil

coarse or kosher salt and freshly ground pepper to taste

2¹/₂ cups Barbecue Sauce (recipe above)

1. Preheat outdoor grill or broiler.

2. Brush swordfish with oil on both sides. Sprinkle with salt and pepper. Place on grill or in broiler. Cook for 2 to 2$^{1}/_{2}$ minutes on each side, basting with sauce.

3. To serve, spoon a tablespoon of the sauce over each serving of fish.

Yield: 6 servings

༈ *On the Beekman farm in Turlock, they produce honey and also grow walnuts. Lucky family. Honey walnut bread consists of such a natural combination that it practically begs to be baked. It also happens to be one of the breads I have been eating since childhood.*

Honey Walnut Bread

2 envelopes fast-acting (RapidRise) dry yeast

2$^{1}/_{4}$ cups warm water, 90°

3 tablespoons honey

1 cup whole wheat flour

5 cups bread flour

1 tablespoon salt

1$^{1}/_{2}$ cups coarsely chopped walnut halves

4 ice cubes

1. Preheat oven to 400°.

2. Place the chopping blade in the bowl of a food processor. Add the yeast and $^{1}/_{4}$ cup of the warm water and the honey. Mix by turning the chopping blade by hand (turn the stem without touching the sharp blade). Add all the flour, turn on the machine and blend for 5 seconds. Add the salt and blend for 5 seconds more. While the blade rotates, add the remaining 2 cups water. Blend until the batter forms a large ball, about 30 seconds.

3. Flour a board. Knead the dough on it and add the chopped nuts, forming it into a ball. Flour a large mixing bowl and place the ball of dough in it. Cover with a dish towel. Let the dough rise until it is doubled in size (the time required varies with the environmental factors but at room temperature of 75° it will take about 1 hour).

4. Turn the dough onto a lightly floured board and punch it down. Make a new ball. Place it back in the mixing bowl. Sprinkle with flour, cover and let it rise again for 45 minutes to an hour.

5. When the dough rises to almost double again, remove it from the bowl and punch it and shape it to the loaf size desired. This quantity is sufficient for 4 equal round loaves. Place the 4 round loaves on a cookie sheet with space in between for expansion. Cover with a towel and let rise by 50 percent, half as large, again.

6. With a razor blade, diagonally score the surface of each loaf several times. Each incision should be about $^1/_2$ inch deep.

7. Place the cookie sheet in the bottom of the oven and throw the ice cubes onto the oven floor (the ice cubes add steam to produce a thin crisp crust). Bake for 40 minutes or until nicely browned. Transfer the bread to a rack and let cool.

Yield: 4 round loaves

Note: This bread freezes well, wrapped in plastic.

🐝 *In this recipe, the honey works as a flavoring agent in the marinade but at the same time it acts as a glaze, giving the finished pork a handsome gleam.*

Pork Tenderloin with Apples

2 boneless pork tenderloins, about 1³/₄ pounds in all
salt and freshly ground pepper to taste
2 Granny Smith apples
3 tablespoons flour
1 teaspoon ground cumin

1 tablespoon vegetable oil
4 tablespoons finely chopped onions
2 tablespoons red wine vinegar
¹/₂ cup fresh or canned chicken broth
2 tablespoons honey
1 tablespoon tomato paste

1. Sprinkle the tenderloins with salt and pepper to taste. Cut each apple into quarters. Peel the quarters and core them.

2. Dredge the tenderloins in the flour that has been blended with the cumin. Heat the oil over medium-high heat in a heavy skillet and add the tenderloin. Cook, turning the pieces so they brown evenly on all sides, about 5 minutes.

3. Pour off the fat from the pan and add the apples and onions around the meat. Cook and stir for about 3 minutes. Add the vinegar, chicken broth, honey and the tomato paste. Bring to a simmer, stirring, and cover tightly. Cook about 20 minutes.

4. Slice the pork on the diagonal and present the apples with some sauce over each serving.

Yield: 4 servings

If I haven't got you thinking sufficiently about the virtues and pervasiveness of honey yet, let me add a recipe for a familiar dish beloved in this country, although it is Chinese in derivation. (We're learning from them as fast as we can.)

Beef with Red and Green Peppers

2 medium sweet red peppers
2 medium sweet green peppers
1 pound lean tender beef, such as
  fillet of flank steak
2 tablespoons cornstarch
2 tablespoons dark soy sauce
1/4 teaspoon hot red pepper flakes

1 cup corn or vegetable oil
1 cup coarsely chopped scallions
1 teaspoon chopped garlic
1 tablespoon honey
2 tablespoons dry sherry
2 tablespoons fresh or canned
  chicken broth

1. Core and remove the seeds from the peppers. Cut the peppers into thin strips about 1 1/2 inches long.

2. Slice the meat across the grain into thin strips, 1 1/2 to 2 inches long. Place in a bowl and add the cornstarch, soy sauce, red pepper flakes and 2 tablespoons of the oil (the oil prevents the meat from sticking together while cooking). Blend well and let stand 15 minutes.

3. Heat the remaining oil in a wok or skillet large enough to hold the ingredients. When the oil is very hot, add the meat, stirring about 30 seconds until separated. Drain the meat in a sieve over the bowl to catch the drippings and reserve the oil.

4. Wipe out the wok and return 2 tablespoons of the oil to it. Heat the oil and add the peppers, scallions and garlic. Cook over high heat until they are crisp and tender, about 1 minute. Add the honey, sherry and chicken broth. Add the beef and cook quickly, stirring, until just heated through. Serve immediately.

Yield: 4 servings

West Indian Cooking in America

From the hilltop at Blackbeard's Castle, a stone tower named after the brutish pirate who actually plied these waters, the island's major town, Charlotte Amalie, lies stretched out below. It seems tranquil and harmonious. The rooftops are all red, a vestige of the days when corrugated metal was painted with red lead to protect it against the salt air (the paint isn't leaded anymore, of course). And the harbor is the picture of serenity, with mammoth cruise ships and many-masted yachts taking their positions as if some stage director told them where to hit their marks.

Nothing from that hilltop gives you the sense of the frenetic tourism below or of the swirl of influences that shaped all of the U.S. Virgin Islands (St. Croix alone has flown seven flags). But the food on St. Thomas, especially when you find it off the beaten track, hints at it. This is the West Indian outpost of America, a part of a string of islands that have seen the French, the British, the Danes and the Spanish come and go. In the American Virgin Islands, it is the African influence that is particularly strong. During the most virulent days of the slave trade, Africans came straight on through here, many headed elsewhere, but some going no further as they were sold to work the plantations. Later, as freed people, they would work for pay, often as cooks for the rich.

They never lost touch entirely with the food they knew from their homeland, like their beloved okra or their stews. The cooking tradition remains very strong.

"Every West Indian man thinks he knows how to cook," laughed Victor Sydney, when we showed up one day at his restaurant Victor's New Hideout. The restaurant isn't so much hidden away—it's on a hill near the airport, after all—as it is shielded from the tourist's eyes by an unappealing approach that takes you up a road past wrecked cars and a view dominated by a power plant. Once there, though, the restaurant is congenial (the ships in the harbor are in sight), a sea breeze courses through the dining room, aided by ceiling fans. Lilies and hibiscus flowers grace the tables.

And then there's Victor himself, a muscular fellow in a blue T-shirt stretched beyond its maker's intentions, who speaks warmly of his African heritage. Victor came to St. Thomas from Montserrat when he was 17, and he soon got it in his head to open a restaurant, a "hideaway" just down the hill from the present spot. He operated it to great acclaim for 16 years and then moved to the bigger, new place.

Victor was not particularly at ease before our television camera, at first. He was a bit stiff as he showed me the fish dish he was preparing for us, a yellowtail in a sauce rich in peppers and tomatoes, with a serving of fungi on the side. (Fungi is a traditional mixture of cornmeal and okra; as for the fish, since there are more than 500 varieties in these waters, seafood was obviously what we would encounter much of the time.) During the taping, somewhere around the third or fourth take, Victor relaxed, exuding the charm he is known for. Getting into it, he slapped my back with as much vigor as I could handle. I was a fine maker of fungi, he concluded.

If Victor's was a bit off the main road, Ashley's was not, but it was as far from the beaten track in its own way as you're likely to get. It's a ramshackle roadside stand, along the airport highway, the kind of place you don't usually try unless you have some information in advance guiding you to it, which we did. There I ordered goat

Okra's New Life

Crowded onto ships and bereft of anything to call their own, it's said that many Africans on their way into slavery did carry the tiniest luggage with them: okra seeds, hidden in their hair. It was a successful ploy. Their okra made it to the West Indies, and it made it all the way to the American South, too. In the tropical climate of St. Thomas, okra bushes grow as big as trees and you can pick the vegetable right off the bushes as if it were cherries.

On the mainland, just during my lifetime, okra has gone through the same sort of transformation we witnessed with "trashfish." Once widely disdained, except in certain pockets of the country, okra is now a much more widely esteemed treat. The first thing mainland Americans had to overcome was an aversion to the undeniable slipperiness of the vegetable, something that many people associate with sliminess. Initially, that slipperiness was a characteristic they seemed unable to forgive in this vegetable, although they might readily forgive it in an oyster, say, or tapioca pudding. In any event, one cure for the slipperiness is that okra has traditionally been cooked to death so that it would dissolve into an innocuous bit of thickener, for soups mostly. One turn-of-the-century recipe for boiled okra calls for simmering it for half an hour, which, at least, is an improvement over earlier recipes that told you to simmer the poor thing for more than an hour. I like to cook it for somewhere between five and seven minutes, depending on the softness desired. The idea is to keep it tender, not mushy, retaining its sweet taste and brilliant green color.

When you buy okra, use the common sense you would with any vegetable; be sure it seems fresh, not blotchy or flabby or dried out. It can't be stored for long; the best you can do is place it in a paper bag in the bottom section of the refrigerator for a day or two.

water, a simple, savory stew, actually made with mutton. I also felt I couldn't leave this place without tasting bull's foot soup, a fine vegetable concoction thickened with the gelatin from calves' feet. In this adventure into what was for me an unknown world of West Indian cookery, I also had something called a pâté, which was nothing like what I expected. The pâtés here are fried cornmeal turnovers, filled with seafood or meat. Interesting enough as a snack, but a pâté! I felt awfully far from my own roots.

That is, until I wandered into a tiny niche of St. Thomas on the Charlotte Amalie harbor called Frenchtown, a little fishing village, full of restaurants, bars and knowledgeable people shopping for fish fresh off the boat. At one boat was Julien Magras, a 22-year-old fisherman whose lineage can be traced directly to France, selling some of the most startling fish one will find anywhere. He did business on the dock alongside his white 22-foot skiff, with its twin 55-horsepower engines, the fish spread out before him. One, called a red hind, was true to its name, adorned with irregular areas of brilliant red. There was also a multihued triggerfish (called an "ole wife" here; it is inedible until you remove its skin and then it yields sweet white flesh). And there was the bluish doctorfish that I had never seen before, a whole pile of them.

The French who have made their home in St. Thomas came here from the French-settled islands like St. Barthélemy or Martinique. So here I found myself, a Burgundy-born American, on an American island rich in African culture, speaking French to fishermen who made me feel like I was on the shores of Brittany. Too much.

When we drove up the hill to Victor's New Hideout it was because everyone had told us that Victor was the genuine article, a real West Indian cook, offering the best regional food we would find on St. Thomas. We weren't disappointed. Here's what Victor chose to prepare for us, with a little help—that he requested more out of generosity than necessity—from me. The fish and sauce are exactly as he makes it (including the margarine, an ingredient I rarely, if ever, use).

Victor's Steamed Fish

The Sauce

1 quart water

2 tablespoons white wine vinegar

3 onions (about 1 pound), sliced

4 scallions, cut into $^1/_2$-inch lengths (both white and green parts)

1 clove garlic, crushed

1 cup cored, seeded and coarsely chopped sweet red pepper

2 cups chopped, skinless, ripe tomatoes

4 stalks celery, sliced on the diagonal (about 2 cups)

Combine all the sauce ingredients and simmer for 7 minutes. Set aside and keep warm.

The Fish

2 quarts water

salt and freshly ground pepper to taste

$^1/_4$ cup margarine

3 bay leaves

4 sprigs thyme

1 tablespoon white vinegar

juice of $^1/_2$ lemon

1 cup sliced onions

1 stalk celery, sliced thickly

4 $1^1/_4$-pound whole snappers, ole wife or yellowtail, cleaned but with tail and head on

1 cup coarsely chopped fresh coriander for garnish

1. Combine all the ingredients, except the fish, sauce and coriander for garnish, in a large shallow saucepan. Bring to a boil and simmer for 10 minutes.

2. Add the fish to the broth. Simmer for about 7 minutes.

3. Serve over the sauce and sprinkle with the coriander.

Yield: 4 servings

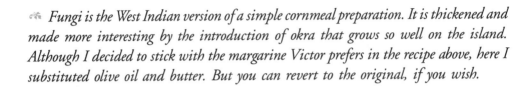

   Fungi is the West Indian version of a simple cornmeal preparation. It is thickened and made more interesting by the introduction of okra that grows so well on the island. Although I decided to stick with the margarine Victor prefers in the recipe above, here I substituted olive oil and butter. But you can revert to the original, if you wish.

Victor's Fungi

I pound cornmeal
3 cups boiling water
2 tablespoons sunflower oil
salt and freshly ground pepper
   to taste

2 tablespoons vinegar
4 cups cooked okra (recipe follows)
2 tablespoons butter
2 tablespoons olive oil

1. Pour the cornmeal into the boiling water with the sunflower oil, salt and pepper and vinegar and cook, stirring, for 5 minutes.

2. Combine the cornmeal and okra, stirring to blend in the soft vegetable, and cook for 5 minutes. Blend in the butter and oil.

The Okra

4 cups okra
6 cups boiling water
2 tablespoons vinegar

2 tablespoons sunflower oil
salt and freshly ground pepper to
   taste

1. Rinse the okra in cold water and drain well. If the stem ends are tough, cut them off and discard. Cut the okra into $^{1}/_{2}$-inch lengths.

2. Combine all the ingredients, bring back to a boil and simmer for 5 to 6 minutes.

Yield: 4 to 6 servings

The next two recipes, goat water stew and bull's foot soup, come from a roadside stand called Ashley's not far from the St. Thomas airport. We had gotten off the plane, and I was starved. I had to try these marvelous-sounding dishes. Actually, the names are more exotic than the actual preparations. Both are simple to make and richly flavored.

Goat Water Stew

4 pounds lean neck and shoulder of lamb, cut into 1¹/₂-inch pieces, including neck bones (goat or mutton meat could be used)
salt and freshly ground pepper to taste
2 cups coarsely chopped onions
1 tablespoon finely chopped garlic
2 tablespoons flour
10 cups water
1¹/₂ cups tomato paste

8 fresh thyme sprigs or 2 teaspoons dried
2 bay leaves
6 whole cloves
4 large carrots, about 1 pound, trimmed, scraped and cut into 2-inch-long pieces
4 white turnips, trimmed and quartered
4 tablespoons coarsely chopped fresh coriander

1. Heat a skillet or cast-iron pot large enough to hold the meat in two layers, add the lamb, and salt and pepper to taste. Cook, stirring until lightly browned, about 5 minutes. Drain the fat.

2. Add the onions and garlic. Cook and stir for about 2 minutes, then add the flour. Blend well. Add the water, tomato paste, thyme, bay leaves, cloves, carrots and turnips. Bring to a boil and simmer for 2 hours or until well done. Skim the foam and the fat from the top. Serve hot in soup plates and sprinkle with the chopped coriander.

Yield: 12 servings

Bull's Foot Soup

4 calves' feet, about 1³/₄ pounds
each
1¹/₂ pounds tripe, cut into 2-inch-
long strips
2 cups coarsely chopped onions
2 tablespoons finely chopped garlic
3 quarts water
1¹/₂ cups tomato paste

2 bay leaves
8 whole cloves
6 large carrots, trimmed, scraped
and cut into 2-inch-long pieces
¹/₂ cup coarsely chopped parsley
salt and freshly ground pepper to
taste

1. A calf's foot when purchased generally includes the hoof and the upper leg bone with flesh and skin attached. Using a sharp boning knife, carve away the meat and the skin from the upper leg bone of each foot. Save all the pieces, including the leg bone. Cut the meat and the skin into pieces about 1¹/₂ inch square.

2. In a large kettle place the pieces, including the bone, and the tripe and add water to cover. Bring to a boil and simmer for 5 minutes. Drain.

3. Return the pieces and the bone to a clean kettle. Add the onions, garlic, the 3 quarts of water, tomato paste, bay leaves, cloves, carrots, parsley, salt and pepper. Bring to a boil and simmer for 4 hours, skimming the foam occasionally. Serve hot.

Yield: 10 to 12 servings

⟶ Curried dishes are great favorites in the West Indies and certainly on St. Thomas, where the best cooks have been preparing food in the West Indian tradition all their lives.

Curried Chicken

1 3½-pound chicken, cut into 10 serving pieces	1 bay leaf
salt and freshly ground pepper to taste	1 cup cubed apple
1 tablespoon olive or corn oil	½ cup diced banana
½ cup chopped onions	1 tablespoon tomato paste
½ cup chopped celery	1½ cups fresh or canned chicken broth
2 teaspoons chopped garlic	½ cup yogurt, drained in cheesecloth or sieve
2 tablespoons curry powder	4 teaspoons chopped fresh coriander

1. Sprinkle the chicken pieces with salt and pepper.

2. Heat the oil in a heavy skillet and add the chicken pieces, skin side down. Cook until golden on one side, about 5 minutes. Brown the other side. Drain the fat.

3. Add the onions, celery, garlic, curry powder. Cook briefly, stirring, until the onions are wilted. Add the bay leaf, apple, banana. Cook for 5 minutes, stirring. Add the tomato paste and chicken broth, stir to blend, cover and simmer for 15 minutes or until chicken is tender.

4. Remove the chicken pieces, place the sauce in the container of a food processor and blend to a coarse texture. Reheat, add the yogurt and blend well. Add the chicken pieces. Bring to a simmer and serve hot, garnished with coriander.

Yield: 4 servings

❧ *The magnificent yacht operated by Club Med—they call it* Club Med I—*often drops anchor in Charlotte Amalie's harbor during the winter. We couldn't resist spending some time aboard her. In the ship's enormous, gleaming kitchen, we discovered that the Club Med chief executive chef, Hans Viertl, has a nice Caribbean touch despite his German background. What follows are two dishes similar to those we prepared aboard ship. The mahimahi—also called dolphin fish although it is unrelated to the dolphin—is readily caught off St. Thomas (one day driving around the island we saw a fisherman selling one that was several feet long from the back of his pickup truck). The preparation here is straightforward and I liked it very much. It was served, at the time, with julienne strips of blanched breadfruit, the exotic apricot fruit and white yams. Those ingredients are not easily purchased on the mainland, and the dish works well enough without them.*

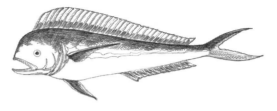

Sautéed Mahimahi

The Sauce

2 tablespoons sunflower oil

3 cups tomatoes, skin and seeds removed, cut into small cubes

3/4 cup leeks, only the white part, cut into julienne strips

salt and freshly ground pepper to taste

1/2 teaspoon seeded chopped hot pepper

1. Heat the oil in a saucepan, add the remaining ingredients and cook for 4 or 5 minutes.

2. Set the sauce aside and keep warm.

The Fish

2 tablespoons sunflower oil

2 pounds skinless boneless mahimahi, in 1/2-pound fillets

2 tablespoons crushed coriander seeds

salt and freshly ground pepper to taste

8 small cherry tomatoes

8 small thin slices of avocado

16 sprigs fresh coriander

1. Heat the oil in a nonstick frying pan large enough to hold all the pieces of fish in one layer.

2. Sprinkle the fish with crushed coriander, salt and pepper. Pat on both sides to be sure the seasonings adhere.

3. Sauté the fish for 2 minutes on each side.

4. To serve, divide the sauce evenly in the center of 4 plates. Place a serving of the fish over the sauce.

5. Garnish each serving with the cherry tomatoes, avocado and coriander sprigs.

Yield: 4 servings

Pineapple and Kiwi Flan

3 cups fresh pineapple juice
2 cups sugar
4 tablespoons water

8 eggs
3/4 cup cubed papaya
3/4 cup coarsely diced kiwi fruit

1. Preheat oven to 350°.

2. Combine the pineapple juice and 1 1/2 cups of the sugar. Bring to a simmer and cook until it reaches 222° on a candy thermometer (or simply simmer for 4 minutes). Remove and let cool.

3. Combine the remaining 1/2 cup sugar with the water and simmer until just caramelized. Do not let syrup burn. It should be light brown. Pour the mixture into each of 6 1 1/2-cup ramekins, swirling the ramekins around to coat the bottom and the sides.

4. In a mixing bowl beat the eggs with a fork. Do not let them become frothy. Strain them into the cooled pineapple syrup. Strain the mixture into the caramel-lined dishes.

5. Set the ramekins in a large pan containing hot water to come halfway up the sides of the ramekins. Place in the oven and bake for 1 hour or until set.

6. Let cool thoroughly before unmolding on individual plates. Garnish with the papaya and diced kiwi.

Yield: 6 servings

Praise the Pig

PELLA, IOWA

On a summer day it can be astonishingly, even painfully, hot at the farm of
Esther and Owen Vermeer, not far from Des Moines. Occasionally, on one of
these brutal days, there is a breeze and you can see it coming from far off—rustling
its way through the Iowa cornfields. But despite the heat on the day we visited, there
was nothing oppressive about the place. The Vermeers, smart and competent people,
are pig farmers who exhibit the cheerfulness of survivors. Through the hard times in
small farming, they managed to make it, managed to pay off the farm and to work
out a marital and business relationship that is remarkable for the affection and
respect that seems to permeate it.

Esther, in cutoff jeans and a pink blouse, was describing the relationship that
developed in the years since 1973 when they bought the farm (140 acres owned
outright, much of the land devoted to crops that feed the hogs).

"Life is a lot different for us now," she said. "Early on we had all these debts.
Sometimes the hogs would get sick and we'd get very discouraged, but we'd get right
back at it. Others dropped out of the business in the bad times, but we didn't; we
waited for the good times. And we picked each other up when we had to."

The Vermeers had children to raise through most of these years, three of them—
born four years apart so that there wouldn't be babies around the farm all the time.
Then in just the past four years, with the children all pretty much able to take care of
themselves, Esther took on more responsibility for the farm. She and Owen decided
that she would be the one primarily responsible for the animals and he would be
mostly responsible for the crops and the handiwork that needed to be done on the
farm, like rebuilding when a tornado ripped apart some of the buildings.

"It's really different for a male farmer to give his wife as much authority as Owen

has given me," Esther said. "But I had to earn it. And a while back we made it legal; we're actually legal partners in this business now."

Esther with her youthful face framed in graying hair may not look like the farmer she is, but Owen fits right in. He's a burly, tall man, wearing bib overalls the day we arrived. Those overalls are a source of some discussion in the family. Esther would rather he didn't dress in any stereotypical way. And at first, he didn't. Then one day he took a role in a local play—as a farmer, of course—and had to wear the overalls. He found them awfully comfortable. And now he wears them around the farm. It's still a source of disagreement, but they've worked it out. He changes when she asks him to and wears them when she doesn't mind.

The couple took us on a brief tour of the farm. The funniest moment happened when we entered a building where a bunch of piglets—adorable, as you might imagine—were jostling with each other to get at their mothers. At first, it looked as though the mothers were being treated cruelly. They were standing between a set of bars so they couldn't lie down or roll over. It turns out this is for the little pigs' safety. The mothers have a habit of sitting on them, in all the confusion and the jostling, sometimes doing considerable harm to the babies.

Esther reached in to grab one of these piglets, held it in her arms and the little pink fellow was obviously happy to be held by her. Now, I'm a farm boy at heart and took the piglet into my arms, too. And it was just what you might see when a stranger picks up any baby, this one began to squeal and squirm (actually squeal is too tame a word for the amount of noise emanating from that little body). I tried soothing it, hugging it; I used the old trick of offering a finger as a pacifier. Didn't work. So we tried another piglet, and it protested, too, louder even than the first. We tried another and by this time it must have been apparent to all of them that they were supposed to give me a hard time because none of them ever let me cuddle up.

There are 1,000 pigs on this farm in various stages of growth and they do grow very quickly. The hogs are ready for market at just six months of age, when they reach a weight of about 240 pounds. Outdoors in the pens some of the older hogs were wallowing in the mud to avoid sunburn and keep cool. Some of them looked like the most contented animals on earth. One pink hog was dozing with its head resting on the butt of a reclining black pig. The pink fellow opened his eyes as we walked by, lost interest, and closed them again.

After we'd seen the farm, Esther and Owen took us into the town, and it was no ordinary place. Pella was settled by the Dutch (Holland, by the way, is famous for its pigs, among other things) and still retains much of its Dutch look. Pella is a Dutch word meaning, we were told, "city of refuge," a reminder that the immigrants were fleeing religious persecution. Everywhere signs are in Dutch and English. A tulip festival turns the town into a mosaic of color every year. A windmill sits at the corner of a park. There are still streets of brick, and the facades of the stores evoke Holland. The place is clean beyond anything you're likely to see elsewhere in these days of tight municipal budgets. And the people are open and friendly, every one of them.

The restaurant we visited was the Strawtown Inn. The name itself is tied to the history of Pella. In 1847, when 800 Dutch immigrants settled in the small town, housing was short. Many of them built sod huts with thatched straw roofs. Most of those thatched-roof houses were concentrated in one section of Pella and that became known as Strawtown. The inn was built in 1855 and served a number of purposes from residential to commercial, but in 1974 it became a restaurant, with Dutch overtones, naturally: the Rembrandt Room, the Delft Room. . . . The menu lists the likes of "borst van eend," a breast of duckling, and "riblap," which is a steak. But it was pork we had been talking about all day, and it was pork we made. Back in the kitchen of the Strawtown Inn, I pitched in to help with a pork chop with dressing—the dressing, in typical Dutch fashion, made ample use of apples and of apple cider.

Lean Times

It is true that pork used to be an extraordinarily fatty and fattening food. It is much less so now. Spokesmen for the pork industry say that from the 1950's to 1983, pigs became 50 percent leaner than they had been. From 1983 to the present, they got to be an average of 31 percent leaner than that. The result is that many pork cuts—the loin that I favor so much among them—are under 180 calories for a 3-ounce portion. That puts the caloric and fat content somewhere between that of a chicken's breast and its thigh.

How did the farmers do it? They started by breeding for more muscular pigs. They also learned to feed the hogs in a more restrained fashion, providing them enough of the right food to keep them healthy but lean— and no more than that. And they learned that 240 pounds was just about the right market weight. In the past, pigs went to market as they got closer to 300 pounds. But after about 240, the hog starts to put on a disproportionate amount of fat rather than muscle.

It's a clear case of an industry figuring out that it had to do something to comply with the consumer's wishes—and then making quite a success of it.

At Pella's Strawtown Inn, they're more likely to make this dish as a stuffed pork chop, cooking it for quite a long time. But, for our benefit, the dish was made with the stuffing—we'll call it a "dressing" in this case—cooked separately, greatly speeding up the process.

Strawtown Pork Chops with Dressing

The Dressing

4 slices white bread, cut into ¹/₂-inch cubes

¹/₂ cup coarsely chopped scallions

1 cup cored, seeded and cut in ¹/₄-inch cubes Granny Smith apples

2 tablespoons celery seeds

¹/₂ cup walnuts, coarsely chopped

2 tablespoons fresh lemon juice

2 cups apple cider

salt and freshly ground pepper to taste

1. Preheat oven to 400°.

2. Combine all the ingredients in a bowl and blend well.

3. Butter a 9-inch baking pan and place the dressing in it, levelling the top with a spatula. Bake for 1 hour.

The Pork Chops

4 center-cut pork chops, ¹/₂ pound each

salt and freshly ground pepper to taste

1 tablespoon coarsely chopped rosemary

1 tablespoon vegetable oil

¹/₄ cup finely chopped onion

¹/₂ cup Madeira

1 cup fresh or canned chicken broth

1 tablespoon tomato paste

1 tablespoon butter

chopped parsley for garnish

1. Sprinkle the chops with salt and pepper and the rosemary.

2. In a nonstick skillet large enough to hold the chops in one layer heat the vegetable oil. Add the chops and cook over medium-high heat for 7 minutes, until lightly browned. Turn and cook another 7 minutes, or until done. Remove the chops and set aside. Keep warm.

3. Pour off the excess fat from the skillet. Add the onion. Cook and stir until wilted. Add the Madeira. Cook and reduce to $1/4$ of its original volume. Add the chicken broth and tomato paste. Cook and reduce by half. Remove the skillet from the heat and swirl in the butter. Check for seasoning.

4. To serve, divide the dressing evenly in the center of each of 4 plates, forming a circle that will be somewhat larger than the chop. Place a chop on top of it. Pour the sauce over and around each chop and dressing. Garnish each plate with 4 Parslied Baby Carrots (page 371), placed evenly around the periphery of the plate. Sprinkle with the chopped parsley or another fresh herb.

Yield: 4 servings

❧ *Since we've been talking about how lean pork can be, I've put my mind to creating several recipes using pork medallions, dense, almost fat-free cuts of meat. Although the cut is the same in each of the next three dishes, they couldn't be more distinct one from the other.*

Grilled Pork Medallions with Herb Marinade

8 boneless pork loin slices, about 3 ounces each, trimmed of excess fat
2 tablespoons olive oil
3 tablespoons fresh lemon juice
$1/4$ cup dry white wine
1 tablespoon dry mustard
2 teaspoons finely chopped garlic

1 teaspoon ground cumin
1 tablespoon chopped fresh rosemary or 2 teaspoons dried
1 tablespoon chopped fresh sage or 2 teaspoons dried
salt and freshly ground pepper to taste
2 tablespoons butter

1. Preheat charcoal or gas grill.

2. Place each pork slice on a flat surface and pound lightly with a mallet or meat pounder.

3. In a shallow dish large enough to hold the pork slices in one layer combine the oil, lemon juice, wine, mustard, garlic, cumin, rosemary, sage and salt and pepper to taste. Blend well.

4. Add the pork slices and turn them in the marinade. Cover with foil and set aside until ready to cook.

5. Place the medallions, reserving the marinade, on the grill and cook 3 or 4 minutes on the first side. Turn and cook 2 or 3 minutes on the second side. Continue cooking, turning them often, for a total of about 8 minutes, or until done. Do not overcook.

6. Meanwhile, heat the marinade for 2 minutes. Add the butter and blend well. Transfer the pork slices to the marinade and cover with foil. Let the meat rest in a warm place for 5 minutes before serving.

Yield: 4 servings

Pork Medallions with Mustard Sauce

8 boneless pork loin slices, about 3 ounces each, trimmed of excess fat

salt and freshly ground pepper to taste

1 tablespoon vegetable or corn oil

$^{1}/_{2}$ cup finely chopped onions

2 teaspoons finely chopped garlic

1 tablespoon red wine vinegar

$^{1}/_{2}$ cup fresh or canned chicken broth

1 tablespoon tomato paste

1 bay leaf

4 sprigs fresh thyme or $^{1}/_{2}$ teaspoon dried

2 teaspoons ground cumin

2 tablespoons Dijon mustard

4 tablespoons chopped parsley

1. Place the pork slices in a shallow dish and sprinkle with salt and pepper.

2. Heat the oil in a nonstick skillet large enough to hold the slices in one layer. When the oil is very hot, add the meat and cook over medium-high heat for 5 minutes or until brown. Turn the slices and cook for about 5 minutes more. Reduce

the heat and continue cooking about 2 minutes longer, turning occasionally. Transfer the meat to a warm serving dish and keep warm.

3. Remove the fat from the skillet, add the onions and garlic and cook, stirring, until lightly browned. Add the vinegar and cook briefly. Add the broth, scraping the bottom of the pan with a wooden spatula to dissolve any brown particles adhering to it. Add the tomato paste, bay leaf, thyme and cumin. Add any juices that have accumulated around the pork. Bring the sauce to a boil, add the mustard and blend well. Simmer for about 5 minutes, then reduce by half over high heat.

4. Spoon the sauce over the meat and sprinkle with the chopped parsley. Serve immediately with Mashed Potatoes and Carrots (page 173).

Yield: 4 servings

Sautéed Pork Medallions with Plums

8 boneless pork loin slices, about 3 ounces each, trimmed of excess fat

salt and freshly ground pepper to taste

1 teaspoon ground cumin

1 teaspoon paprika

2 tablespoons vegetable oil

¹/4 cup finely chopped onion

1 teaspoon finely chopped garlic

¹/4 cup gin

1 teaspoon red wine vinegar

1 cup fresh or canned chicken broth

24 pitted fresh ripe red or purple plums

1 tablespoon tomato paste

2 tablespoons butter

1. Place the pork slices in a shallow dish. Combine salt and pepper, the cumin and paprika and sprinkle the slices on both sides with this mixture.

2. Heat the oil in a skillet large enough to hold the pork slices in one layer. When the oil is quite hot, add the pork and cook over medium-high heat about 5 minutes or until browned.

3. Turn the slices and cook about 5 minutes more. Reduce the heat and continue cooking about 2 minutes more, turning the slices. Transfer the pork to a platter and keep warm.

4. Pour off the fat in the skillet. Add the onion and garlic and cook, stirring, until the onion is wilted and lightly browned. Add the gin, vinegar, chicken broth, plums and tomato paste. Stir to dissolve the brown particles that cling to the bottom of the pan. Add any juices that have accumulated around the meat. Simmer and cook until the sauce is reduced to about 1¼ cups. Add the butter and blend well. Pour the sauce over the medallions and serve hot.

Yield: 4 servings

> *Pork, like turkey, is more adaptable than you might think and I've included here one pretty good example of that. It's a kind of hamburger, you might say, but of course it's nothing like the conventional burger. Instead it's sweet and tangy.*

Pork Burgers Oriental Style

1½ pounds lean ground pork
½ cup chopped scallions
3 tablespoons chopped fresh
   coriander
1 tablespoon grated fresh ginger
2 tablespoons light soy sauce
2 teaspoons finely chopped garlic
½ cup fresh bread crumbs
¼ cup fresh or canned chicken
   broth

salt and freshly ground white
   pepper to taste
¼ teaspoon Tabasco sauce
1 teaspoon vegetable oil
½ cup fresh orange juice
2 tablespoons fresh lemon juice
2 tablespoons butter

1. Place the pork in a bowl and add the scallions, 2 tablespoons of the coriander, the ginger, 1 tablespoon of the soy sauce, the garlic, the bread crumbs, chicken broth, salt and pepper to taste and the Tabasco. Blend well.

2. Divide the mixture into 8 equal portions and form them into hamburger shapes, about 1 inch thick. Heat the vegetable oil in a cast-iron skillet over medium heat. Add the burgers and cook on one side for 7 or 8 minutes. Turn the burgers and cook about 8 minutes more or until done. Transfer to a serving plate and keep warm.

3. In a small saucepan combine the orange and lemon juices and the remaining soy sauce. Reduce by half. Add the butter and the remaining coriander, blend well and pour the sauce over the burgers. Serve with Sautéed Baby Vegetables (page 370).

Yield: 4 servings

  I often use a variety of peppers in a single dish, not just for the flavor differences they bring but also for the color. Here, thanks to the peppers, you'll find a burst of red, green and yellow.

Pork Chops with Peppers

4 center-cut lean pork chops, about
   1¹/₂ pounds in all
salt and freshly ground pepper to
   taste
2 teaspoons vegetable oil
¹/₂ cup finely chopped onions
2 teaspoons minced garlic
1 small sweet red pepper
1 small sweet green pepper
1 small sweet yellow pepper

1 teaspoon ground cumin
2 tablespoons red wine vinegar
¹/₂ cup fresh or canned chicken
   broth
¹/₂ cup Italian crushed tomatoes
1 bay leaf
1 teaspoon rosemary
4 tablespoons chopped Italian
   parsley

1. Sprinkle the chops with salt and pepper to taste.

2. Core and seed the peppers. Cut the flesh into thin strips about 1¹/₂ inches long.

3. Heat the oil in a nonstick skillet large enough to hold the chops in one layer. When very hot, add the chops. Turn them until well browned, about 4 minutes on each side.

4. Pour off the fat in the skillet. Place the onions and garlic in the skillet around the chops and stir well until the onions are wilted. Add all the peppers and the cumin and cook and stir for 1 minute. Add the red wine vinegar, chicken broth, tomatoes, bay leaf and rosemary. Cover and cook over low heat for 20 minutes.

5. Uncover and reduce the liquid, if necessary, to produce a thick sauce. Remove the bay leaf. Just before serving, sprinkle with the chopped parsley.

Yield: 4 servings

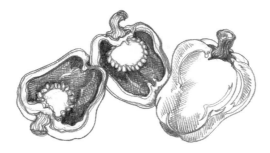

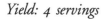 *The traditional use of caper sauce is with mutton or lamb, but over the years I've tried it in lots of different ways, none more successful than this one with pork cutlets.*

Pork Cutlets with Caper Sauce

8 boneless pork loin cutlets, about 3 ounces each, trimmed of excess fat

salt and freshly ground pepper to taste

1 tablespoon vegetable or peanut oil

1/2 cup finely chopped onions

1 teaspoon finely chopped garlic

1/3 cup drained capers

1 tablespoon red wine vinegar

1 tablespoon Dijon mustard

1/2 cup fresh or canned chicken broth

1 tablespoon tomato paste

2 tablespoons butter (optional)

2 tablespoons finely chopped parsley

1. Sprinkle the cutlets with salt and pepper to taste.

2. Heat the oil in a skillet large enough to hold all the cutlets in one layer. When the oil is very hot, add the pork and cook over medium-high heat for about 5 minutes or until browned. Turn the cutlets and cook about 5 minutes more. Reduce the heat and cook about 2 minutes more, turning occasionally.

3. Transfer the cutlets to a warm serving dish. Cover with foil and keep warm.

4. Pour off the fat in the skillet and add the onions, garlic and capers. Stir until the onions are lightly browned. Add the vinegar, Dijon mustard, chicken broth and tomato paste. Stir to dissolve the brown particles that cling to the bottom of the pan. Cook until reduced to about 3/4 cup. Add any juices that may have accumulated around the cutlets and the butter. Blend well. Add the cutlets to the skillet, bring to a simmer and serve immediately. Sprinkle with the chopped parsley.

Yield: 4 servings

The Old Families and
the New Breed

In the raucous, romantic city of New Orleans, tradition is like the Mississippi itself—straining at its boundaries and yet, in large measure, still what it has always been, true to itself and flowing strong. That tradition can be seen ever so clearly in some of the great restaurant families that have made their mark on the city over the decades. For one of the two television shows we did on the city's restaurants, we visited three of those families and their establishments. For the other show, we went off in search of the new breed and found youth and vitality spicing up the old town.

Among the great traditionalists, the descendants of Jean Galatoire, who opened Galatoire's in 1905, are still holding down the fort on Bourbon Street. Nearby, the even older (1840) Antoine's is still in family hands. And away from the Old Quarter, in the Garden District of the city, we visited Commander's Palace, run by the Brennan family, certainly the most adventurous of the preeminent restaurant families. But even the Brennans still have their roots clearly in Creole New Orleans.

Creole, as it refers to cooking, seems to mean many things to many people in these parts. And if you ask five different people, you're likely to get five different answers (counting a blank stare or two). But in New Orleans Creole is generally a reference to the settlers from France and Spain and the food they brought with them. In Creole cooking what you get, for the most part, is a sophisticated, almost traditional French cuisine that is often made piquant by the use of hotter ingredients, such as cayenne pepper, reflecting the Spanish and other influences. And it has been modified by the kinds of herbs and spices that were most available in the area. Cajun, a term frequently uttered in the same breath as Creole, is usually intended to refer to the down-home cooking out in the Louisiana countryside.

The French influence is so strong in the old-line Creole restaurants that, at

Galatoire's, one of the most popular dishes is the French classic trout *meunière*, or with almonds, trout *amandine*. (In a local twist, pompano can replace the trout, and it does spectacularly well here, too.) Galatoire's is so unyielding in the face of changing times that not only does it cling to many of the same dishes it always cooked but it also will not even change some of its own stranger customs. Despite a tremendous clamor to get into the place, for instance, it will not accept reservations. It also does not advertise. One of the family members, Yvonne Galatoire Wynne, explained it to us this way: What if the restaurant advertised and took reservations and then people showed up but could not be seated? Wouldn't it be doing those people a disservice? Well, whatever. . . .

Meantime, the old restaurant sits there amid the strip shows and the jazz joints, its dozen antique ceiling fans turning slowly, doing what it's always done, most notably, selling fresh fish, generally prepared in simple ways. And the people do come. The lines that form outside are legendary. On Friday afternoons, when the city starts to wind down (or up) for the weekend, attorneys send their clerks to hold their places for them. The drinking and the eating can sometimes go on straight through two meals, so reluctant are people to abandon their tables and depart the good cheer.

At Antoine's on St. Louis Street, just off Bourbon, the restaurant's name, in elegant script and framed in a wrought-iron sign, hangs before the entrance. The doors are flanked by lanterns. The menu is still in French. The high ceilings and balloon-style drapes give the main dining room a sense of spacious dignity. And if that dining room is full, there are 14 more, each with its own look, and as you stroll through the rooms, the overall sense is that of walking from one distinct restaurant to another.

Here, the tales are as much a part of the place as the food. Randy Guste, a fifth generation proprietor, eagerly launches into the one about the invention of oysters Rockefeller, served here first in 1899 by Jules Alciatore, proprietor from 1885 to 1930. Jules, it seems, was trying to emulate a traditional snail dish, but with oysters instead. When the sauce kept sliding off the oysters he thickened it with a white *roux* and vegetables. It says in one of the bits of literature offered at a table near the entrance that more than 18 million of these oysters have been sold since. The exact ingredients in the sauce have always been a coy mystery, although it certainly contains scallions, celery and parsley. (And, in any case, other versions abound now; my own effort, which employs spinach, appears later in this chapter.)

In the main kitchen, we participated in the preparation of another of Antoine's

well-known, French-derived specialties, *pommes soufflées,* in which potato slices are deep fried twice. On the first go-round they cook through. When they are plunged briefly into the hot fat the second time they blow up like balloons.

The kitchen is cavernous. The first impression as you walk in is of the 18 or 20 aluminum kettles hanging from the ceiling, most with a capacity of five gallons or more. Just at that entry door sits chef John De Ville—not cooking, of course, in so large an operation—but rather surveying the situation warily as if the weathered wooden stand he sits behind might be the bridge of his ship. "Hey," one of the kitchen helpers shouts to John, "show them your pistol," and everyone in earshot laughs. John, it must be said, does look pretty tough.

At Commander's Palace we ran into a different sort of chef altogether. His name is Jamie Shannon, 29 years old, New Jersey born and bred and a culinary adventurer if ever there was one. Jamie's been at Commander's for only seven years, arriving after stints at the Culinary Institute of America in Hyde Park, New York, and at a Trump hotel in Atlantic City. He rose from saucier to executive chef in five years, inheriting the mantle of many an accomplished chef who came before him. It isn't hard to see why. This tall blond cook is poised, confident and impatient. ("Are we ready, or what?" he inquires at one point during the videotaping, and responds to every challenge with a gung-ho, "No problem, great.") Although the restaurant has a lot of tradition behind it, the place is full of experimentation. Jamie has taken to the new

Creole style of Commander's Palace with tremendous vigor. Sauces are surprisingly light. The salads, such as one with crab meat and avocado, are just right in a restaurant where the leafy, tropical outside and the indoors nearly merge thanks to huge windows and an airy decor. After we looked around the place, Jamie and I cooked soft-shell crabs with Creole sauce.

Our guide for the day was Lally Brennan, a slender young woman in a brilliant red dress, one of the dizzying number of Brennans in the restaurant business in New Orleans. In 1969, the Brennan clan bought Commander's Palace, founded in 1880. But the Brennans had already been running the renowned French Quarter restaurant that bears their name and went on to open others, including Mr. B's Bistro.

Commander's Palace sits in one of the most beautiful residential areas in America. The Garden District, benefitting from a generally warm and humid climate, is a treasury of wide-leafed plants and great live-oak trees, draped in Spanish moss that give their shade to the Greek Revival homes. The area was settled in the early 1800's after Louisiana joined the United States, and people of Anglo-Saxon heritage flocked to New Orleans only to find that the French there were not particularly happy about their arrival. So they moved to the outskirts of town. Instead of moping around as exiles, they created a residential jewel. And people still talk with great vivacity about the history of the place, as they do about everything that has a story attached to it around here.

That avid link to the past has been met by a reaction, a counterpoint that enlivens the restaurant scene here beautifully. I take it to be a sign of great vitality and hope that a city so set in its ways—and good ways they are—is still able to embrace invention and traditions that have not been at home here before.

Take, for example, Kevin Graham, the chef at the Windsor Court, a man of mercurial temperament with an English accent that is not so soft as one often expects among the British. "I don't do Cajun and I don't do Creole," Kevin Graham was saying. "There are enough people doing those things here." What Kevin said he does is "cook." And that's it. And he speaks as emphatically about that stance as he is eloquent in his cooking. His is an international taste that allows him to bring in white asparagus from France or fresh Dover sole. Like many good chefs, he wants the restaurant to express his own preferences. And although he presides over a very big kitchen, it's the kind of place that has a distinct personal touch. He bakes his own bread, even hamburger buns, and makes his own ice cream.

The dining room and the hotel itself are unlike anything we had ever seen before. To give you an idea of the grandness of Windsor Court, in the lobby at teatime, there is, in fact, high tea. The women (and they are mostly women) come for the chamber music, the cucumber sandwiches and the chance to wear their wide-brimmed hats. Upstairs, just off the dining room, there are Joseph Nash lithographs of Windsor Castle rooms and an original Gainsborough depicting the castle itself in the mist. (There's also an original Van Dyke hanging not too far away.)

The walls of the dining room are adorned with paintings of the English countryside. You'd think that all this grand British stuff would force Kevin into typical English cooking and leave him stranded here in New Orleans as a curiosity and not much more. But that isn't the case at all. Instead, he turns out to be the sort of person who worships the basics, Escoffier and all that, and he is a chef who loves to go off on his own. In his kitchen, he and I cooked frogs' legs in Champagne sauce. He also invented a melon and vodka soup on the spot that might get you a bit tipsy, but it was full of flavor. He's a restless man constantly changing the menu, as many as four new menus a week. "I could have it real easy," he told us, "but I don't want that."

The other remarkable new-breed place we visited was Susan Spicer's restaurant, Bayona. It sits in the Old Quarter on Dauphine Street. The name comes from Camino Bayona, as the street was called during Spanish rule. It's a terra-cotta cottage with several relatively small dining areas. One of the most striking is a windowless room surrounded by trompe l'oeil Mediterranean scenes that look out on the countryside, blue-green hills and neat fields. They are so effective they actually make the small space seem large and airy.

Susan, who is tall, slender and modest, has, despite that modesty, attracted a great deal of well-deserved attention as a distinctive cook. She's lived in Holland, worked in Paris, but mostly grew up and learned her trade in New Orleans. She speaks as if she has always had to fight private doubts. "When I went to Paris, I was asking myself, can I hold my own?" she says. "I never felt I was at some very high level. I needed to reassure myself." She says that in Paris she did begin to believe more in her own skills. And, as is powerfully evident now, when she got back to New Orleans she found herself. She works with great poise and charm, producing an eclectic group of dishes that more often than not use the wonderful fresh ingredients that are available here: crawfish, shrimp, fish of various kinds.

My sense of affinity with her is great. She says she cooks "unintimidating" food. Her approach is a lot like mine—well grounded in the basics, but simple, often fast. The duck breast in pepper jelly sauce she cooked while I was there was quite typical. She placed individual portions of Muscovy breast skin side down on the grill and cooked it that way for almost the entire period so as to make the breast very crisp and to render away all the fat. Then, when she turned it on the other side, she exposed it to the heat only briefly. The idea was to keep it pink and moist inside. It was a lovely dish.

Cayenne: A Wake Up Call

Leafing through the classic Picayune's Creole Cook Book, *compiled at the turn of the century and recently revised, you'll find that the ingredients often include the following line: "Salt, Pepper and Cayenne to taste." That gives you an idea of how routinely cayenne is used in the cuisine of New Orleans to give a bit of bite to so many Creole dishes, from potted beef to potato croquette. Two tablespoons of it go into the Creole Seafood Seasoning recipe presented in this chapter.*

Cayenne, bearing the name of a city in French Guiana (where, oddly enough, it is not grown), has the reputation as the hottest of all peppers. Whether or not it is actually the hottest, it is certainly high on the list. It is commercially grown in Louisiana, as well as New Mexico, Africa, India and Mexico. What you find in the store is usually the ground variety (sometimes a blend, using the name "cayenne" in a generic way). It is extremely easy, employing cayenne, to keep turning up the heat of a dish. In fact, it is generally used only for heat and not for the subtle flavoring and other sensations that many similar hot peppers can deliver.

If you've ever wondered why anybody would want to eat hot peppers at all—cayenne or any of the other brutal ones—the psychologist Paul Rozin tries to help with this interpretation: The allure of the cayenne lies partly in our desire to flirt with danger. It certainly seems dangerous—the pain, the gasping, the watering eyes—but it isn't really dangerous at all. We all know that. It is, instead, a stimulating mock confrontation with the enemy. Harold McGee, the scientifically minded food writer, reports that "It is also possible that the brain secretes endorphins, its own opiate substances, in response to a burning tongue, and that these contribute to the pleasurable 'hangover' of a fiery meal."

The following four recipes are all linked. When we cooked the soft-shell crabs Creole with Jamie Shannon, we used his own seasoning mix on the crabs and his own homemade Worcestershire in the Creole sauce. But don't think they have to go together. The seasoning mix is great for any sort of seafood; sprinkle it on steamed, broiled or sautéed fish for that typical Creole tang. The same is true of the sauce, which can be used with anything from fish to chicken or pork. The Worcestershire will, of course, find many uses—from spiking soups to serving as a condiment for beef.

Soft-Shell Crabs Creole with Creole Sauce

vegetable oil for deep frying
4 large soft-shell crabs
8 medium raw shrimp, shelled and deveined
Creole Seafood Seasoning (recipe follows) to taste
1 cup flour

1 large egg, lightly beaten
½ cup milk
3 cups fresh bread crumbs, seasoned with Creole Seafood Seasoning (recipe follows)
Creole Sauce (recipe follows)

1. Preheat oil to 350° in a deep fryer.

2. Meanwhile, clean the crabs (according to the instructions, page 82). Place a raw shrimp in each pocket where the gill has been.

3. Season the crabs with the seafood seasoning and dust them with the flour.

4. In a shallow bowl combine the egg with the milk. Dip each crab into the egg mixture, then into the seasoned bread crumbs. Make sure the crab is well coated. Shake off any excess crumbs.

5. With tongs hold the crab by its body and fry the legs first for about 30 seconds. (This will cause the legs to fold up to the body.) Turn the crab upside down and place carefully in the hot oil. Fry about 3 minutes until golden brown. Remove and drain on absorbent paper; set aside in a warm place. Fry the remaining crabs in the same manner. Serve immediately with the Creole sauce.

Yield: 4 servings

Creole Seafood Seasoning

3 tablespoons chopped fresh
  oregano or 2 tablespoons dried
$^{1}/_{3}$ cup salt
4 tablespoons finely chopped garlic
$^{1}/_{4}$ cup freshly ground pepper
2 tablespoons cayenne

3 tablespoons chopped fresh thyme
  or 2 tablespoons dried
$^{1}/_{3}$ cup paprika
3 tablespoons dried granulated
  onions

Combine all the ingredients thoroughly. Store in a glass jar. Sealed airtight, the seasoning keeps indefinitely.

Note: If you know you don't like all that heat, reduce the cayenne and perhaps the black pepper.

Yield: enough for 4 servings

Creole Sauce

2 tablespoons butter
1 cup julienne strips of onion
1 cup julienne strips of cored
  seeded green pepper
1 cup sliced celery
1 tablespoon finely chopped garlic
1 bay leaf
2 teaspoons paprika
2 cups peeled diced tomatoes or 2
  cups canned crushed tomatoes

4 teaspoons Homemade
  Worcestershire Sauce (recipe
  follows)
4 teaspoons Tabasco sauce or
  Louisiana hot sauce
$1^{1}/_{2}$ tablespoons cornstarch or
  arrowroot
$^{1}/_{2}$ cup water

1. Melt the butter in a large skillet or saucepan. Add the onion, pepper, celery, garlic and bay leaf. Cook and stir until the onion becomes transparent. Add the paprika and tomatoes and stir well. Cook for 3 or 4 minutes.

2. Add the Worcestershire sauce and Tabasco and simmer until the sauce is reduced, about 5 minutes.

3. Combine the cornstarch and the water and stir into the sauce. Bring to a boil, stirring, and simmer for about 2 or 3 minutes. Let cool. The sauce will keep well for 4 or 5 days in the refrigerator. In fact, it is better to make it a day ahead to allow the flavors to meld.

Yield: 2 cups

Homemade Worcestershire Sauce

1 tablespoon olive oil
1/3 cup freshly grated horseradish
2 cups finely chopped onions
1 teaspoon freshly ground pepper
2 jalapeño peppers, finely chopped
1 tablespoon finely chopped garlic
2 cups water
4 cups distilled white vinegar, 4 percent

1 cup molasses
2 cups dark corn syrup
4 anchovy fillets, chopped
12 whole cloves
1 tablespoon salt
1 teaspoon chopped lemon peel

1. In a large saucepan combine the olive oil, horseradish, onions, black pepper, jalapeño peppers and garlic. Cook, stirring, over medium heat until the onions are translucent.

2. Add all the remaining ingredients, bring to a boil and simmer for 1 hour.

3. Strain through a fine strainer or china cap. Store in a Mason jar.

Yield: 3 to 4 cups

At Galatoire's, pompano, a sweet and adaptable fish widely available in New Orleans, is an especially huge seller. And the use of almonds in the butter sauce is both classic French and common among the Creole cooks of New Orleans.

Pompano Amandine

4 skinless boneless pompano fillets, about 6 ounces each
salt and freshly ground pepper to taste
4 tablespoons milk
$^1/_4$ teaspoon Tabasco sauce
$^1/_2$ cup flour for dredging

$^1/_2$ cup peanut or vegetable oil
4 tablespoons butter
$^1/_4$ cup slivered blanched almonds
juice of 1 lemon
4 tablespoons finely chopped parsley

1. Sprinkle the pompano fillets with salt and pepper to taste.

2. Combine the milk, salt and pepper and the Tabasco in a shallow dish.

3. Dip the fillets in the milk and then dredge them in the flour, shaking to remove the excess.

4. Heat the oil in a nonstick skillet large enough to hold the fillets in one layer. Add the fish and cook it over fairly high or moderately high heat about 2 minutes or longer until golden brown on one side. Turn the fish and cook until golden brown on the second side, about 2 minutes longer. Transfer to a serving dish, pour off the oil and wipe out the skillet.

5. Add the butter and the almonds to the skillet and cook until both the butter and the almonds are lightly browned. Add the lemon juice and, shaking the pan, pour the almond butter over the fish. Sprinkle with the chopped parsley and serve immediately.

Yield: 4 servings

When we were talking to Randy Guste, the proprietor of Antoine's and the guardian of the recipe for the restaurant's oysters Rockefeller, we implored him to tell us the ingredients. He smiled; he hinted; but he wouldn't divulge the precise ingredients. Well, never mind. Here's the one I've concocted. When it's done, it looks just about like the one at Antoine's, and I like it a lot. Hope you do, too.

Oysters Rockefeller

24 oysters
1 pound fresh spinach
1/2 cup coarsely chopped celery
1/2 cup coarsely chopped scallions
1/2 cup chopped parsley
1 clove garlic
2 anchovy fillets
4 tablespoons butter

2 tablespoons flour
1/2 cup heavy cream
1/4 teaspoon Tabasco sauce
1/4 cup freshly grated Parmesan or
   romano cheese
2 tablespoons Ricard or Pernod
salt and freshly ground pepper to
   taste

1. Preheat oven to 450°.

2. Open the oysters, leaving them on the half shell and reserving the oyster liquor. Arrange the oysters in a baking pan and chill until ready to use.

3. Pick over the spinach and remove any tough stems and blemished leaves. Rinse well and place in a saucepan. Cover and cook, stirring, until wilted. Drain well and squeeze to remove all excess moisture.

4. In the container of a food processor combine the drained spinach, celery, scallions, parsley, garlic and anchovies. Blend to a fine texture.

5. In a skillet heat 2 tablespoons of the butter. Add the spinach mixture, cook and stir for about 1 minute. Set aside.

6. Heat the remaining 2 tablespoons butter in a saucepan. Add the flour, blend and stir with a wire whisk. Add the oyster liquor, stirring vigorously with the whisk. Stir in the cream, season with Tabasco and cook for about 2 minutes. Add the spinach

mixture, cheese and Ricard, blend well and let cool. Check for seasoning and add salt and pepper to taste.

7. Spoon equal portions of the spinach mixture on top of the oysters and smooth over the tops. Bake for 25 minutes or until piping hot.

Yield: 4 servings

Note: The same mixture works well with hard-shell clams.

❧ *When I first came to the United States, to cook at the 1939 World's Fair in New York, we served frogs' legs in countless number. Some years later, one of New York's great restaurants was named for the frog—La Grenouille. Now this wonderful food has pretty much vanished around the country. But Louisianans seem to still have an affection for frogs' legs. Where they can't be purchased fresh, it remains possible to buy frogs' legs frozen, especially in Asian stores around the country. Here, I offer two options. One is Kevin Graham's elegant dish. The* concassé *in the recipe title merely refers to the abundance of chopped and seeded tomatoes. And the other is my own bistro version—in the expectation that one or the other will entice you into giving frogs' legs a try.*

Windsor Court Frogs' Legs Concassé

1 cup flour for dusting
salt and freshly ground pepper to
    taste
24 small pairs of frogs' legs,
    cleaned (feet removed) and split
3 tablespoons olive oil
1/4 cup finely chopped shallots
1 tablespoon finely chopped garlic

1 bay leaf
4 sprigs fresh thyme or 1 teaspoon
    dried
2 cups peeled, seeded and chopped
    tomatoes
1/2 cup dry vermouth
Tabasco sauce to taste

1. Mix the flour with salt and pepper to taste. Dust the frogs' legs with the seasoned flour.

2. In a heavy large nonstick skillet heat 2 tablespoons of the olive oil. Add half the frogs' legs in one layer. Cook until lightly browned, about 2 minutes. Turn and cook for 2 minutes more. Remove and keep warm. Repeat with remaining frogs' legs and keep warm.

3. Add the remaining 1 tablespoon oil to the skillet. Over medium-high heat cook the shallots and garlic until wilted. Do not burn the garlic. Add the bay leaf, thyme and tomatoes. Cook over high heat for 2 minutes, stirring gently. Add the vermouth and simmer, uncovered, for 5 minutes. Adjust the seasonings with salt and pepper and a dash of Tabasco.

4. Remove the sauce from heat. Spoon one quarter of the sauce into the center of each plate and arrange 6 pairs of frogs' legs around the sauce.

Yield: 4 servings

Frogs' Legs Provençale

24 small pairs or 12 large pairs
    frogs' legs
2 tablespoons olive oil
3 cups peeled, seeded and coarsely
    chopped ripe tomatoes or drained
    canned tomatoes
1/2 teaspoon Tabasco sauce
salt and freshly ground pepper to
    taste

1 bay leaf
1/2 cup milk
1 cup all-purpose flour for dredging
1/2 cup vegetable or corn oil
6 tablespoons butter
1 tablespoon finely chopped garlic
4 tablespoons finely chopped fresh
    parsley

1. Cut off and discard the feet of the frogs' legs and place the legs in a baking dish. To keep the frogs' legs flat as they cook, stick the bottom of one leg through the parallel muscles at the base of the other—in effect crossing their legs at the bottom.

2. Heat the olive oil in a skillet over medium-high heat and add the tomatoes, Tabasco, salt and pepper, and the bay leaf. Cook, stirring often, for about 1 minute. Set aside and keep warm.

3. Pour the milk over the frogs' legs. In a flat dish season the flour with salt and pepper. Drain the frogs' legs and dredge them, one at a time, in the flour. Shake off any excess.

4. Heat the vegetable oil over medium-high heat in one or two large frying pans (nonstick, if possible). Add the frogs' legs and sauté for about 3 or 4 minutes on each side or until golden brown.

5. As the frogs' legs are removed from the pan, transfer them to a warm serving platter to keep them warm. Arrange the legs around the perimeter of the platter.

6. Remove the bay leaf from the tomato mixture and spoon the mixture onto the center of the platter.

7. Melt the butter in a skillet and in it briefly sauté the garlic until golden but not brown. Pour the butter over the frogs' legs and the tomato mixture. Serve immediately with the chopped parsley as garnish.

Yield: 4 to 6 servings

This is the melon soup that Kevin Graham prepared for us so quickly. It's easy, but very elegant.

Chilled Melon Soup with Passion Fruit Sorbet

20 passion fruits
1 cup sugar
2 cups water
2 ripe cantaloupes, peeled, seeded
   and chopped

1 tablespoon honey
1 cup vodka
4 fresh sprigs mint for garnish

1. Cut the passion fruits in half. With a spoon remove the seeds and pulp. Purée the seeds and pulp in the container of a blender or food processor.

2. Combine the sugar and water in a saucepan and bring to a boil. Cook for 2 minutes. Remove from heat and let cool to room temperature. Add the passion fruit purée and mix well.

3. Pour the mixture into an ice cream freezer and freeze following the manufacturer's instructions. Or pour into a wide shallow dish and place in the freezer, stirring every 10 minutes, until the sorbet is smooth and stiff.

4. In a blender combine some of the cantaloupe (reserving 1 cup for garnish), the honey and vodka and blend until smooth. Remove and chill.

5. In each chilled soup plate place a scoop of the sorbet and surround it with some of the melon soup. Garnish with a mint sprig and the remaining cantaloupe.

Yield: 6 to 8 servings

The meunière *style of sautéing fish shows up all over New Orleans. But you rarely see it done with Dover sole. At the Windsor Court, Kevin Graham got us to thinking about this terrific fish. So I thought I'd offer it to you this way.*

Dover Sole Meunière

4 whole Dover sole, cleaned and dark skin removed, about 3/4 pound each

salt and freshly ground pepper to taste

1 cup milk

1/4 teaspoon Tabasco sauce

1 cup flour for dredging

4 tablespoons vegetable or peanut oil

6 tablespoons butter

2 tablespoons fresh lemon juice

4 seeded lemon slices

4 tablespoons chopped parsley

1. Sprinkle the sole with salt and pepper to taste.

2. Combine the milk, salt and pepper and Tabasco in a shallow dish.

3. Dip the fish in the milk, then dredge them in the flour, shaking off any excess.

4. Heat the oil in a nonstick skillet large enough to hold the sole in one layer. Add the fish and cook over fairly high or moderately high heat about 2 minutes or longer until golden brown on one side. Turn the fish and cook until golden brown on the second side, about 2 minutes more. Transfer to a serving dish and pour the oil from the skillet. Wipe the skillet clean.

5. Add the butter to the skillet and cook until it is lightly browned. Add the lemon juice, shaking the pan, and the lemon slices and parsley. Pour the sauce over the sole and serve immediately.

Yield: 4 servings

Here is the recipe for Susan Spicer's grilled duck breasts. It was a treat working with her as she prepared them. The idea is to burn off all the fat, leaving the meat tender and pink. Often people have trouble recognizing it as duck because of the color, texture and absence of fat. Served with pepper jelly, which is ubiquitous in the South, the dish has real personality.

Grilled Duck Breasts with Pepper Jelly Glaze

salt to taste
1 teaspoon freshly ground black
  pepper
4 sprigs chopped fresh thyme or ¹/₂
  teaspoon dried
1 teaspoon chopped fresh rosemary
  or ¹/₂ teaspoon dried
4 boneless Long Island duck
  breasts, 6 ounces each, skin on
  and excess fat trimmed (You can
  buy 2 whole ducks, 4 to 5
  pounds each, and use the legs for

roasting or braising and reserve
the bones to make stock.)
2 tablespoons hot pepper jelly
2 tablespoons finely chopped
  shallots
3 tablespoons sherry wine vinegar
¹/₂ teaspoon minced and seeded
  jalapeño pepper, (optional)
¹/₂ cup Condensed Duck Broth
  (recipe follows) or ¹/₂ cup
  chicken broth
2 tablespoons butter

1. Preheat charcoal or gas grill.

2. Blend together well salt to taste, the pepper, thyme and rosemary and sprinkle on the skin side of the duck breasts. Refrigerate for several hours or let stand for ¹/₂ hour before cooking.

3. Grill the breasts skin side down 8 to 10 minutes over medium heat. Turn and cook 2 or 3 minutes for medium rare. Remove from the heat and let stand on a platter for 5 minutes.

4. Meanwhile, in a small saucepan combine the jelly, shallots, vinegar, jalapeño pepper and duck broth. Cook over medium heat until reduced by half. Add the butter, a little at a time, until the sauce is thickened and glossy.

5. To serve, slice each duck breast into 5 or 6 pieces. Arrange skin side up on a warm plate. Spoon the warm sauce over the slices. Serve with wild rice and the vegetable of your choice.

Yield: 4 servings

Condensed Duck Broth

2 duck carcasses, including the hearts and gizzards (Use livers for other purposes.)
1 cup coarsely chopped carrots
1 cup coarsely chopped onions
$^1/_2$ cup coarsely chopped celery
4 sprigs parsley

1 bay leaf
2 sprigs fresh thyme or $^1/_2$ teaspoon dried
2 whole cloves garlic, unpeeled
8 black peppercorns
5 quarts water

1. Chop the duck carcasses into 2-inch pieces.

2. Brown the pieces of carcasses in a heavy kettle for about 5 minutes. Drain off the fat. Add the carrots, onions, celery and cook, stirring, for about 2 minutes. Add the parsley, bay leaf, thyme, garlic cloves, peppercorns and water. Bring to a boil and simmer, skimming the surface as necessary, for about 4 hours. Strain the broth into a saucepan and discard the solids.

3. In a saucepan reduce the broth over medium-high heat to $1^1/_2$ cups.

Yield: $1^1/_2$ cups

Note: Leftover duck broth can be frozen.

✻ *The simple ways that the young chefs of New Orleans like to employ their seafood put me in mind of the following two dishes, both fast and fresh.*

Sea Scallops with Sweet Peppers and Snow Peas

2 tablespoons butter

2 tablespoons olive oil

1 sweet red pepper, cored, seeded and cut into $^1/_2$-inch cubes

$^1/_4$ pound snow peas, trimmed and washed

$^1/_4$ teaspoon hot red pepper flakes

salt and freshly ground pepper to taste

$1^1/_4$ pounds sea scallops, if too large cut into $^1/_2$-inch cubes

4 tablespoons finely chopped shallots or scallions

3 tablespoons good gin, such as Bombay Sapphire

2 tablespoons fresh lemon juice

4 tablespoons coarsely chopped fresh coriander or fresh basil

1. In large nonstick skillet or wok heat 1 tablespoon of the butter and 1 tablespoon of the olive oil over medium-high heat. Add the red bell pepper and the snow peas. Cook, stirring and tossing, for about 4 minutes. Season with the red pepper flakes and salt and pepper.

2. When the red pepper and snow peas are nearly cooked, add the remaining butter and olive oil. Over high heat add the scallops, shallots, gin, lemon juice, coriander and salt and pepper to taste. Cook and stir for about 2 minutes, until the scallops are heated through. Do not overcook. Serve immediately.

Yield: 4 servings

Steamed Salmon with Yogurt and Coriander Sauce

2 tablespoons Dijon mustard
1/2 cup plain lowfat yogurt, drained
2 tablespoons olive oil
1 tablespoon chopped fresh
   coriander
1/4 cup finely chopped scallions

salt and freshly ground pepper to
   taste
1 tablespoon white wine vinegar
4 sprigs fresh coriander
4 skinless boneless salmon steaks,
   about 6 ounces each

1. Place the mustard, yogurt, olive oil, chopped coriander, scallions, salt and pepper and vinegar in a small saucepan. Blend well with a whisk.

2. Press 1 sprig coriander on each salmon steak. Add salt and pepper to taste. Place the salmon on the rack of a steamer. Cover, bring the water in the bottom of the steamer to a boil and steam for about 4 minutes. Do not overcook. Turn the heat off and let the fish rest in the covered steamer for about 1 minute.

3. Meanwhile, gently heat the sauce until it is warm through. Transfer the fish to a serving plate and serve with the sauce.

Yield: 4 servings

Note: This dish should be served with Boiled Potatoes with Lemon and Parslied Cucumbers (pages 172 and 374 respectively).

Even the Humble Potato . . .

If you want to see a true celebration of food—a paean to America's capacity for producing gorgeous fruits and vegetables and seafood—visit Seattle and the Pike Place market. On a brilliant day (uncharacteristic for the Pacific Northwest) we did just that. The stalls that display the produce do so with an attention to color, symmetry and order that makes each presentation of beefsteak tomatoes, cauliflower and potatoes look like it's posing for a picture. There is gaiety in the air.

At the Pike Place Fish Company in the main building, they're famous for "flying fish." But it's not what you think: A customer orders a fish, any fish, from one of the fellows behind the counter; he calls out to a co-worker who, with the panache of a circus performer, hurls the fish through the air as if it were a football. The receiver of the fish catches it with equal aplomb (despite its slipperiness) and the crowd is delighted—every time.

Before we were stopped in our tracks by this display of agility we were involved in the more serious business of shopping at the market with Caprial Pence, one of the hottest chefs in Seattle. She's a young, ebullient woman who trained, among other places, at the Culinary Institute of America in Hyde Park, New York. That's where she met the man who would become her husband, John Pence. In Seattle, Caprial got a job cooking at Fullers in the Sheraton Hotel and quickly made a national name for herself. John, meanwhile, was doing well in other restaurants.

When the couple decided that the only way they were going to see each other was to open a restaurant together, Fullers evidently couldn't bear the thought of losing her. Instead, she and John were invited to be co-chefs at Fullers and given a free hand in running it, and bringing it, as it turns out, even more acclaim. The partnership, they say, has been good for their marriage, too. They support and inspire each other. They try not to argue, at least not where the staff can see it. During one dispute, they took refuge in the freezer to work things out. "We share responsibilities completely," John said, "money, hiring, everything."

Among the things Caprial and I were buying that day were Russet potatoes, an essential component of some marvelous potato crab cakes with *crème fraîche* that she and John would prepare later in Fullers' kitchen. It's the kind of dish that makes any cook realize how indispensable the potato is to contemporary cooking. Just as if we were to lose rice or pasta, our culinary repertoire would be greatly diminished without the potato.

I got a chance to appreciate potatoes even more when we visited a farmer, Leonard Hanses, who produces them, along with wheat and corn, on the other side of the Cascades from Seattle in what was once just desert. But the Grand Coulee Dam on the Columbia River—completed in 1941 and delivering enough water to the Columbia Basin to irrigate a million acres by 1950—changed everything. It made this part of the country with its long sun-filled days an extraordinarily productive part of America's food chain.

As we walked through the potato fields, Leonard said he preferred this man-made watering system to the natural one. "I like it that way," he said. "I can gauge the

moisture in the soil throughout the week and deliver just the right amount of water." After all that careful measurement, rain can only foul things up, he said.

And the potato, as we learned, is a lot more delicate than it looks. The water is slowly delivered by an irrigation system consisting of piping elevated on braces connected to large tires. As the whole contraption gradually rolls across the field yielding its fine spray, an arm at one end senses the perimeter of the field and adjusts to corners as it responds to a signal from a buried wire outlining the edges of the field. The tubers are plucked from beneath the ground by harvesting machinery that is padded so as to baby the potatoes. Potatoes are alive even after they are removed from the earth (that's why you can place an eye in the ground and a new potato plant will grow from it), and they bruise easily. If they're knocked about too roughly, they respond almost as if they were human, the bruised area darkening, becoming unsightly.

As I stood on this fertile ground with Leonard, we decided to see exactly how many potatoes were crammed together just beneath my feet. There were 12, a dramatic illustration of the soil's fertility. Washington is a major producer of the Russet potato, one of the best for baking and French fries. But potatoes can be prepared so many ways, from simple to elegant. Just think of those potato crab cakes and *crème fraîche,* and take a look at some of the recipes below.

Eye on Potatoes

Potatoes originated in the mountains of South America and only slowly moved to Europe and Asia. Ireland took to them first; Irish Presbyterians settling in New Hampshire brought them back to the New World. The potato's great nutritional value, high in vitamin C and minerals, made it both a boon and a disaster for the Irish, of course, when they came to rely on it so heavily that a crop failure caused the great famine of 1845. We're not that reliant on potatoes these days, but we sure do eat a lot of them.

When purchasing potatoes it is wiser to choose those that haven't begun to turn green. The green areas contain an acid build-up, which is bitter. Don't worry about the eyes. Eyes in the potato will do nothing to harm the tuber as food, unless they have begun to sprout. Sprouts of more than $^1/_4$ inch mean the potato is over the hill for the purposes of good eating. Potatoes with bruises, the darkened areas that result from rough handling, should also be avoided, if possible. The dark spots won't harm you, but their taste will be off. Of course, you can always trim away darkened and green areas.

🌿 *Here are the potato crab cakes that we prepared at Fullers in Seattle. The recipe calls for making your own* crème fraîche—*a cultured cream—but many shops, including supermarkets, sell it these days, too.*

Fullers Potato Crab Cakes with Crème Fraîche

1 large Russet potato, peeled, about
  ¹/₂ pound
2 tablespoons olive oil
1 small red onion, diced
1 sweet red pepper, diced
2 cloves garlic, chopped
1 tablespoon chopped fresh basil
8 to 10 ounces Dungeness or other
  lump crab meat

2 tablespoons Dijon mustard
4 dashes Tabasco sauce
4 dashes Worcestershire sauce
salt and freshly ground pepper to taste
Grilled Scallion Crème Fraîche
  (recipe follows)

1. Place the potato in a saucepan and add water to cover and salt. Bring to a boil and simmer until tender, 20 to 25 minutes. Let the potato cool and grate it, using a medium-blade grater.

2. Heat 1 tablespoon of the oil in a nonstick sauté pan and add the onion, red pepper, garlic and basil. Cook until the onion is wilted. Let cool.

3. In a bowl combine the cooked vegetables with all the remaining ingredients, except the *crème fraîche,* and let stand for 30 minutes. Form the mixture into patties of 2 to 3 ounces each. There should be 8 small crab cakes.

4. Preheat oven to 400°.

5. Heat the remaining 1 tablespoon oil in a nonstick sauté pan large enough to hold the crab cakes in one layer. Sauté briefly to brown on both sides.

6. Transfer the crab cakes to a baking pan and place in the oven for 8 minutes. Serve 2 cakes per person, with a little of the scallion *crème fraîche* spooned over each one or on the side.

Yield: 4 servings

Grilled Scallion Crème Fraîche

¹/₂ cup heavy cream
1 tablespoon sour cream
1 bunch scallions, trimmed

¹/₂ teaspoon olive oil
salt and freshly ground pepper to
 taste

1. Place the heavy cream and sour cream in a bowl and cover with plastic wrap. Let the mixture stand overnight at room temperature. Then refrigerate, covered.

2. Preheat outdoor grill or broiler.

3. Brush the scallions with the olive oil and grill them on the outdoor grill or under the broiler. Chop the scallions coarse and fold them into the *crème fraîche*. Season with salt and pepper.

🖝 *On one television show, I wanted to make a couple of points about potatoes. One was how well they go with lamb and the other was that they can dress up the simplest dish. So I prepared a basic roast leg of lamb, accompanied by* pommes dauphinoises, *the elegant and classic potato and cheese.*

Roast Leg of Lamb with Thyme

1 leg of lamb, 6 to 7 pounds
3 cloves garlic, cut into 12 slivers
1 tablespoon vegetable oil
4 sprigs fresh thyme or 2 teaspoons
 dried

salt and freshly ground pepper to
 taste
1 medium onion, cut in half
 crosswise
³/₄ cup water

1. Preheat oven to 425°.

2. Prepare the lamb by removing most of the outer fat. Remove the hipbone, which runs at a 45° angle from the leg bone. Run a knife along it on all sides to free it. You

will see the ball joint and socket that connect the leg to the hip. Cut through the tendons that join the joint and socket. The bone should now come free.

3. Make 12 small incisions in the meat and insert a sliver of garlic in each.

4. Rub the lamb with the vegetable oil and place it in a roasting pan. Rub with the thyme and sprinkle with salt and pepper. Put an onion half on each side. Place the bone in the pan, too.

5. Roast the lamb on the bottom rack of the oven, basting every 15 to 20 minutes. After 1 hour, remove all the fat from the pan and add the water.

6. Continue roasting for 15 minutes, or until the internal temperature reaches 140° for medium-rare.

7. Remove the lamb from the oven, and place the bone under the roast to serve as a rack. Let stand for 15 minutes as dripping juices enrich the gravy. Carve and serve with the pan gravy, accompanied by Baked Sliced Potatoes with Gruyère Cheese (recipe follows).

Yield: 8 servings

Potatoes have often taken their place among the classic dishes. This is a version of the traditional pommes dauphinoise.

Baked Sliced Potatoes with Gruyère Cheese

3 pounds small Russet potatoes
2 cloves garlic, peeled
1 tablespoon butter
2 cups milk
1 cup heavy cream

salt and freshly ground pepper to
    taste
freshly grated nutmeg to taste
1 cup grated Gruyère or domestic
    Swiss cheese

1. Preheat oven to 400°.

2. Peel the potatoes and cut them into very thin slices less than $1/8$ inch thick. As they are sliced drop them into cold water. There should be 6 or 7 cups. Drain and pat dry.

3. Rub a baking dish (an oval one measuring about 14 by 8 by 2 inches is suitable) with one of the peeled garlic cloves and the butter. Neatly layer the pan with the potatoes.

4. Crush both garlic cloves lightly and put them in a saucepan. Add the milk, cream, salt and pepper and nutmeg and bring to a boil. Strain this mixture over the potatoes, discarding the garlic.

5. Sprinkle the top with the grated cheese. Bake on a baking sheet, to catch any drippings, for about 1 hour, or until the potatoes are tender and the cheese is golden.

Yield: 8 or more servings

Although the potato crab cakes described earlier are extraordinary, they shouldn't diminish the homey satisfaction of plain old potato cakes.

Potato Cakes

4 Russet potatoes, about 1¼ pounds in all
1 egg, beaten lightly
½ cup finely chopped onion or scallions
4 tablespoons flour

2 teaspoons baking powder
¼ teaspoon freshly grated nutmeg
salt and freshly ground pepper to taste
2 tablespoons vegetable oil

1. Peel the potatoes and grate them, using the large openings of a hand-held 4-sided grater.

2. Transfer the grated potatoes to a bowl and add the beaten egg, onion, flour, baking powder, nutmeg and salt and pepper to taste. Blend well.

3. In a large nonstick skillet heat the oil over medium heat and with an ice cream scoop or large spoon drop the potato mixture into the pan to form 8 patties of equal size. Cook until golden on one side, turn and cook on the other side until golden brown. Serve hot.

Yield: 4 servings

Potatoes in a variety of guises are often the easiest and simplest of side dishes to prepare. The recipes that follow, none of them taxing, all make significant contributions to any meal.

Sautéed Potatoes with Garlic

3 pounds Washington or Idaho
   potatoes
salt and freshly ground pepper to
   taste
2 tablespoons olive oil

2 tablespoons butter
2 teaspoons finely chopped garlic
2 tablespoons finely chopped
   parsley

1. Rinse the potatoes and place them in a large saucepan. Add cold water to cover and salt. Bring the water to a boil and simmer for 30 minutes or until tender. Drain immediately.

2. Peel the potatoes. If large cut each in half and cut each half into slices about $^{1}/_{3}$ inch thick.

3. In a large nonstick skillet heat the oil and the butter. Add the potatoes and salt and pepper to taste and cook over high heat, tossing and stirring with care until the potatoes are golden brown. This takes 10 to 15 minutes. Sprinkle with the garlic, and toss well but do not let the garlic burn. Sprinkle with the chopped parsley and serve.

Yield: 6 to 8 servings

Tiny Diced Potatoes

4 Russet potatoes, about $1^{1}/_{4}$
   pounds in all
$^{1}/_{3}$ cup vegetable or corn oil

2 tablespoons butter
salt to taste

1. Peel the potatoes, and cut each into tiny $^{1}/_{4}$-inch or less cubes, dropping them into cold water to prevent discoloration.

2. When ready to cook, drain the cubes in a colander. Run very hot water over them for 10 seconds. Drain well and dry on paper towels or a dishcloth.

3. Heat the oil in a large nonstick skillet over high heat. Add the potatoes and cook, shaking the skillet and stirring the potatoes, for about 6 to 8 minutes until they are lightly browned. Drain well in a colander, and wipe out the skillet. Discard the oil.

4. Heat the butter in the skillet and add the potatoes with salt to taste. Cook, shaking and stirring, for 5 or 6 minutes longer or until the cubes are nicely browned and crisp. Drain and serve hot.

Yield: 4 servings

Baked Mashed Potatoes with Parmesan Cheese

1½ pounds Russet potatoes
salt and freshly ground white
    pepper to taste
1 cup coarsely chopped onions
1 cup milk

2 tablespoons butter
⅛ teaspoon freshly grated nutmeg
2 tablespoons freshly grated
    Parmesan cheese

1. Preheat broiler.

2. Peel the potatoes and rinse them well. Cut the potatoes lengthwise in half. Cut each half into 4 pieces. There should be about 4 cups.

3. Place the potatoes in a saucepan with water to cover. Add salt to taste and the onions and bring to a boil. Simmer for 12 to 15 minutes or until the potatoes are tender. Drain. Put through a food mill or potato ricer into a saucepan.

4. Meanwhile, heat the milk in a saucepan.

5. Add the butter to the milk in the saucepan and stir with a wooden spoon until it is melted. By the spoonful, gradually add the hot milk to the potatoes. Add salt and pepper and the nutmeg and blend well.

6. Spoon the mashed potatoes into an ovenproof serving dish (an oval dish measuring $9^1/_2 \times 6^1/_2 \times 1^1/_2$ inches is suitable). Smooth the top of the potatoes with a spatula and sprinkle with the Parmesan cheese. Place under the broiler until nicely browned.

Yield: 4 servings

Parslied Potatoes

12 small red new potatoes, about
   $1^1/_2$ pounds in all
salt and freshly ground pepper to
   taste

2 tablespoons butter
4 tablespoons finely chopped
   parsley

1. For a decorative touch, with a paring knife remove a thick band of skin around each potato, leaving the rest intact.

2. Wash the potatoes. Place them in a saucepan with water to cover. Add salt to taste. Bring to a boil and simmer for 15 to 20 minutes or until tender. Drain the potatoes, add the butter, parsley and pepper and toss well. Serve hot.

Yield: 4 servings

Boiled Potatoes with Lemon

12 small red new potatoes, about
   $1^1/_2$ pounds in all, peeled if
   desired

salt and freshly ground pepper to
   taste
1 teaspoon fresh lemon juice

Place the potatoes in a saucepan with water to cover. Add salt to taste. Bring to a boil and simmer for 15 to 20 minutes or until tender. Drain. Add the lemon juice and pepper to taste and toss well. Serve.

Yield: 4 servings

I usually use Russet potatoes from Washington or Idaho—especially for baking and frying—but for one of the most elemental of all potato dishes, mashed potatoes, I often choose the ones from Maine or Long Island (although, sorry to say, Long Island is producing fewer and fewer these days). They are naturally moister and easier to mash. In this instance, I've added carrots for their color and sweetness.

Mashed Potatoes and Carrots

1¹/₂ pounds Maine or Long Island potatoes, peeled and cut into ¹/₂-inch slices

¹/₂ pound carrots, peeled and sliced into ¹/₂-inch pieces

salt and freshly ground pepper to taste

1¹/₂ cups milk

3 tablespoons butter

¹/₄ cup chopped parsley

1. Place the potatoes and carrots in a deep saucepan and cover with water. Add salt to taste and bring to a boil. Simmer until tender, about 15 minutes.

2. Meanwhile, warm the milk but do not let it boil.

3. In a food mill (not a food processor, which will produce an unappealing paste), purée the potatoes and carrots as fast as possible so they don't cool. Do this over a saucepan. Add the butter and pepper and beat with a wooden spoon until thoroughly blended.

4. Place the saucepan over low heat and add the milk, stirring constantly with the wooden spoon. After the milk is added, test for texture. Add more milk if a thinner purée is desired. Add the parsley and salt to taste.

Yield: 4 to 6 servings

The Trout Harvest

In a tour of America that had its share of impressive moments, none was more memorable than the time we spent here in the Snake River Canyon. Driving through the canyon on our way to the Clear Springs hatchery, we stopped briefly to witness the single most important reason why this 15-mile stretch of the country produces most of the nation's farmed trout: the Niagara Springs and the others like it bursting from the walls of the canyon. Here, the canyon has sliced through an aquifer, an underground flow of water. The water has been percolating down through lava rock for years, purifying itself as it does. Then, suddenly, it reaches the wall of the canyon and leaps free with tremendous, gushing force, pouring toward the river. It is absolutely clean, and exactly 58 degrees no matter the time of year.

This Niagara and other springs like it provide the wild river with one third of its water. They also make it possible for several trout farmers to prosper. Clear Springs, the largest of the enterprises, funnels off some of the water and runs it through its hatchery, keeping it for 20 minutes or so, then cleaning it before it flows to the Snake as it was intended to do. The water is the perfect temperature for trout, and it is clear, an absolute necessity for these fish. Trout find food with their eyes; that's why trout streams have to be clear to support them.

It's also why, when you look at a newborn trout, as we did at the hatchery, the head is dominated by its eyes. But there were other astonishing things to observe there. The trout eggs (at one point in development you can see the eyes even through the egg) are gelatinous red bubbles. The eggs are kept alive in a vertical clear tube of water that is constantly heaving them up from the bottom and allowing them to settle, in a kind of controlled maelstrom. The reason for all this turmoil is that the eggs are porous and the prenatal fish actually breathe through the shell. The agitation keeps the water oxygenated.

Then, as Dave Erickson, a tall, wavy-haired outdoorsman who is director of technical services at Clear Springs, took us through the steps of farming, we saw how rapidly the hatchlings progressed, ready to go outside into concrete ponds within $2^{1}/_{2}$ months and ready for market in a total of 10 to 14 months. The one hatchhouse we visited contained perhaps three million growing trout.

The hatchery, like all stages of the farming and processing, revealed an intense concern for sanitation. We had to wash our shoes in an iodine bath, for instance, before we could enter the hatchery. The particular concern here is that Clear Springs allows local fishermen to walk through its property down to the river to fish. Wild fish are likely to carry infection with them that might somehow come in contact with the walkways around the hatchhouse and be picked up by the company's workers. Farmed fish would have many fewer natural defenses against infection than the wild ones and that kind of contamination in the hatchery could be catastrophic.

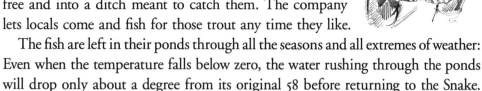

Outside, in the ponds, we saw fish in a wide range of developmental stages, from four-inch lengths at about one ounce up to those that had been there over a year and weighed a pound. And an unusual sight, there beneath the looming black walls of the Snake River Canyon: elderly people fishing in artificial ponds right at the hatchery. It turns out that when the fish are being shipped some of them always leap free and into a ditch meant to catch them. The company lets locals come and fish for those trout any time they like.

The fish are left in their ponds through all the seasons and all extremes of weather: Even when the temperature falls below zero, the water rushing through the ponds will drop only about a degree from its original 58 before returning to the Snake.

The farming of trout, which began decades ago as a means of supplying recreational lakes, is one of the success stories of aquaculture: Transportation and packaging advances in the 1960's meant that fresh trout could be shipped rapidly around the country. What was once a delicacy almost exclusively known to the fisherman is now a treat nearly all of us can have just about any time.

Trout at Home

In buying and handling this very versatile
fish, there are a few things you ought
to keep in mind. The flesh should be
firm and resilient. The skin should be dark,
shiny and slippery, the eyes clear. Trout is a fragile
fish. The Clear Springs people instruct shops
to rinse the fish in a slurry of 50 percent ice
and 50 percent water, stirring gently; then
remove any loose scales from the flesh and keep
the fish refrigerated at 30 to 34 degrees. When you
buy trout in the store be sure that it still
looks fresh and that the shopkeeper has
been making an effort to keep it efficiently
chilled, skin side down on the ice and lightly covered.
The best thing to do once you get it home is to prepare it soon, although it
should last a couple of days well wrapped in the refrigerator, if the shop has
taken good care of it in the first place. When you do cook it, leave the skin
on. The skin helps hold the flesh together as it cooks and adds flavor. The
skin is edible. The bigger bones, if any, are simple to remove. The pin bones
are hardly detectable at all once the fish is cooked.

The great availability and popularity of trout these days was underscored for us when we drove from Buhl to the majestic ski resort of Sun Valley. There, at the Sun Valley Lodge, the chefs are crazy for trout, preparing it a different way each day. Just for the fun of it, I photocopied a list: trout sautéed with Champagne and pine nuts, baked with kiwi and lime in a mustard and sour cream sauce, stuffed with scallops and topped with hollandaise, rolled with crab and shrimp duxelles *in caper sauce. . . . Anyway, it went on and on. The dish we prepared in the Sun Valley Lodge kitchen was a simple sauté with grapefruit, shallots and mint.*

Sun Valley Sautéed Trout with Grapefruit

4 rainbow trout, ³/₄ pound each, butterflied, with bones, heads and tails removed

salt and freshly ground pepper to taste

2 tablespoons olive oil or clarified butter

12 grapefruit sections, membranes removed and quartered, a few pieces reserved for garnish

1 tablespoon finely chopped garlic

2 tablespoons finely chopped shallots

1 tablespoon finely chopped fresh mint

4 sprigs lemon thyme, leaves only, or 1 teaspoon dried thyme

1 tablespoon lemon juice

3 tablespoons lemon-flavored vodka, such as Absolut Citron

2 tablespoons butter

4 sprigs basil or parsley for garnish

1. Sprinkle the trout with salt and pepper. Heat the oil in a nonstick pan large enough to hold all the trout in one layer. Sauté the trout, flesh side down, over high heat for about 1¹/₂ minutes or until lightly browned. Turn and sauté for another 1¹/₂ minutes. Remove, set aside and keep warm.

2. Pour off the excess oil in the pan. Add the grapefruit, garlic, shallots, mint and thyme. Cook briefly just to warm through. Do not brown the garlic. Stir in the lemon juice and vodka.

3. Off the heat, blend in the butter.

4. To serve, place 1 trout on each plate. Spoon a portion of the sauce over it and a little around it. Garnish with an arrangement of Parslied Cucumbers (page 374), basil or parsley sprigs and the reserved pieces of grapefruit.

Yield: 4 servings

⁂ *A variation on the traditional trout* meunière *is this dish with a classy ginger stuffing.*

Trout with Ginger Stuffing

$^{1}/_{4}$ pound shelled and deveined
    shrimp, cut into small pieces
$^{1}/_{4}$ cup heavy cream
1 tablespoon grated fresh ginger
1 tablespoon chopped shallots
dash Tabasco sauce
salt and freshly ground white
    pepper to taste
4 boned brook trout, about $^{1}/_{2}$
    pound each, with the heads and
    tails left on

4 tablespoons milk
4 tablespoons flour for dredging
2 tablespoons vegetable oil
4 tablespoons butter
1 tablespoon fresh lemon juice
4 lemon slices for garnish
2 tablespoons chopped fresh parsley
    for garnish

1. Place the shrimp, cream, ginger, shallots, Tabasco and salt and pepper in the container of a food processor. Purée the mixture until it is smooth and thick. This should take about 30 to 40 seconds.

2. Open up each brook trout. Divide the stuffing into 4 equal portions and spread it evenly over the fillet on the right side of the open trout. Fold the left fillet up and over to enclose the stuffing.

3. Pour the milk into a shallow platter. Mix the flour with salt and pepper on a flat dish. Dip each stuffed trout into the milk, let the excess drip off; then dredge it in the flour mixture, patting to be sure the flour adheres.

4. Heat the oil in a nonstick skillet large enough to hold the trout in one layer without crowding. Add the trout and brown thoroughly on one side. Then with a spatula turn the trout; the cooking should take about 4 minutes on each side, depending on the thickness of the trout. While the fish is browning on the second side, baste it with hot oil from the pan to prevent it from drying out. Transfer to a warm platter, and keep warm.

5. While the pan is still warm, wipe it out with clean paper towels and return it to medium heat. In it melt the butter and cook it, stirring, until it turns hazelnut brown in color. Add the lemon juice. Pour the hot butter over the trout. Garnish with the lemon slices and sprinkle parsley over all. Serve very hot with Sautéed Spinach Leaves (page 369).

Yield: 4 servings

I like to smoke my own fish in a backyard smoker, but smoked trout is quite popular and available these days in shops, as well as many fish stores. Here, I've added gribiche sauce, a kind of highly spiced light mayonnaise.

Smoked Trout with Gribiche Horseradish Sauce

1/2 cup olive oil

1/2 cup vegetable oil

1 tablespoon Dijon mustard

2 tablespoons minced shallots

2 tablespoons minced onion

1 large egg yolk

1 large hard-boiled egg, chopped

salt and freshly ground pepper to taste

3 tablespoons red or white wine vinegar

4 tablespoons freshly grated horseradish

1 tablespoon chopped fresh tarragon

2 tablespoons chopped parsley

4 smoked trout, skinned and filleted

4 lemon wedges for garnish

chervil sprigs and chives for garnish

1. In a bowl combine the olive and vegetable oils.

2. In another bowl combine the mustard, shallots, onion, egg yolk, chopped egg, salt and pepper to taste and vinegar. Blend briskly with a wire whisk. As you do, slowly dribble the combined oils into the bowl to create an emulsion. Add the horseradish, tarragon and parsley and blend well with the whisk.

3. On each serving plate place one trout. Spoon sauce around it. Garnish with a lemon wedge and a sprig of chervil and chives.

Yield: 4 servings

Made in America: Rice

Where does rice come from, anyway? I don't know about you, but I was never very sure. Seems Asian, doesn't it? But I know it's grown in this country, too. Here's a staple that one hardly thinks about at all. This is so even if we use it all the time. Certainly, I admire its capacity to incorporate the flavors of other ingredients and its ability to dress up any dish once a little color—via herbs or vegetables—is added to it. (To that end, I always like to shape each serving of rice by pressing it into a small cup and then unmolding it on the plate.) But as to its origins, it was only recently that I became absolutely clear on it all.

What brought rice home to me, so to speak, was our trip to Texas, one of the biggest of the rice-producing states, most of which are clustered along the Gulf Coast. Not only is rice produced in this country—and has been for 300 years—but so much is grown here that nearly half of it is exported. When we visited one rice processing plant, ARI, not far from Houston, we found ourselves in an industrial setting so large that its scale seemed more suited to steel, perhaps, or, in any event, to something a lot more substantial than those little grains of rice. The size of the export business was demonstrated for us right there, where we saw rice as it was readied for shipment to Saudi Arabia. This one processing plant supplies that nation with 75 percent of its rice.

Another unexpected bit of information: American rice consumption is climbing with great rapidity, ARI's George Prchal told us, doubling from 10 to 20 pounds in just the last decade. But that startling increase masks this fact—four pounds of that 10-pound increase goes to beer. It turns out, George explained, that increasingly beer manufacturers are finding that they prefer rice to other grains in the brewing process.

As we watched the rice move from trucks through the processing procedures, it

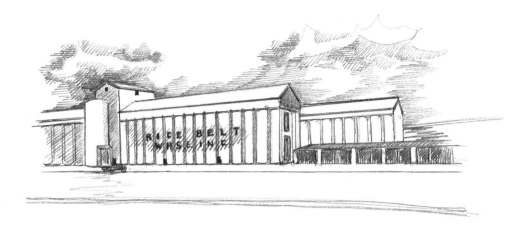

traveled what must have been miles along conveyors and down chutes and into vats. (I asked Butch Hill, another of the company's executives, how many miles he thought a kernel might travel and he scratched his head: "Not sure," he said. "Nobody ever thought about it before.")

All of the rice is hulled, but there the similarity stops. Beneath the hull is the nutritious bran, and brown rice will retain the bran. But that doesn't mean that white rice, bran removed, has lost all its nutritional value. Quite the contrary. In the process called parboiling—one producer uses the term "converted" for this procedure—the kernels are soaked, steamed and dried before they are milled. The rice experts say that this treatment drives the water-soluble nutrients throughout the grain, making it more nutritious. It also makes the rice harder and more compact so that the grains maintain their separateness better. The experts insist that this is not a kind of precooking since the rice actually now requires a bit more time to cook than it would if it hadn't been treated this way. They recommend 20 to 25 minutes for parboiled rice. But I've always disagreed with that advice. I think that a cup of parboiled rice cooked in $1^{1}/_{2}$ cups liquid for 17 minutes will come out perfectly every time, as long as it is simmered slowly and very tightly covered.

As we watched the rice going through its steps, another one of those "taken-for-granted" things came to our attention. The word "enriched" that regularly appears on boxes and bags of rice never meant much to any of us. And, all of a sudden, there we were watching it being enriched. In this process the rice is simply sprayed with iron, niacin and thiamine. Five states—New York, California, Arizona, Pennsylvania and South Carolina—require the enrichment by law. The implication for the cook is that you should not cook rice as if it were pasta, in abundant quantities of water. That will just wash off the nutrients. This is particularly true of ordinary white rice that hasn't been parboiled, since it has lost a lot in the processing, and the enrichment is an attempt to restore some of that.

To see how rice is farmed in America we drove to Lowell Farms in El Campo. Rice is a water-loving grass that must be grown in shallow water and then harvested; the simplest way to bring it in is to drain the field first and call in the big combines. At El Campo, it was harvesttime and Lowell Raun, Jr., and his family—his uncle Norris, niece Lisa, brother Tim and father—were all working the farm, driving combines and trucks to get the rice in quickly. If the place seemed to be frantically busy, though, that impression belied one more of the more dramatic facts about rice in America. Modern farmers like Lowell Raun—with their scientifically leveled fields that allow efficient flooding and drainage, with modern irrigation and mechanical harvesting machinery—have cut the time spent in the field to only seven man-hours per acre. That compares to the 300 man-hours per acre that are still required in parts of Asia.

After all this investigation of rice, we dined on it back in Houston at a delightful restaurant called Café Annie. The restaurant is designed to be the sort of elegant bistro that has been so successful in New York, and, in fact, in Houston it's regarded as a "New Yorkie" restaurant. But its skilled, outgoing chef, Robert Del Grande, came to Houston from California. He was training as a biochemist at the University of California at Riverside. "But I came here," he said, "chasing my girl friend." That girl friend, Mimi, is now his wife. They went into the restaurant business together and appear to have made a great success of it. The dish Robert prepared for us was pan-roasted shrimp on a bed of highly seasoned and creamy rice.

Aromatics

A category of rice that is new to many of us, although it's gaining quickly in popularity, is the aromatics. The two aromatics grown in the United States are Jasmine and Della. Rices in this group are more distinctive in flavor than many others. Usually, people describe the flavor as that of roasted nuts or popcorn. Whatever, the taste is distinctly different and once you try it you may well prefer it to all other kinds of rice. Aromatic rice cooks quickly, just 15 minutes of simmering in a tightly covered pot. When we visited Lowell Raun's farm, we spent most of our time watching him harvest the standard white rice that he grows on 160 acres, but afterward we moved over to a plot of just 40 acres where he grows Jasmine and does it organically.

It was already late in the afternoon, and Lowell and I strode through this beautiful field, chatting. The sounds of nature were all around us. (The frogs start singing when the sun gets low.) And Lowell's particular pride in this field of Jasmine was unmistakable. In fact, while most of his rice goes off to processors to bear the label of their choosing, this rice—the Jasmine—is sold under his own name. On the back of a 2-pound package of Lowell Farms Jasmine it says: "This rice was grown with care by Lowell G. Raun, Jr., 311 Avenue A, El Campo, Texas 77437."

❧ *Risotto—rice made creamy by the gradual addition of liquid—is one of those dishes that seems harder to make than it is. The following, expertly prepared for us by Robert Del Grande at his Houston restaurant, can be cooked surprisingly quickly and makes an impressive appetizer, although it could be a rich main course, too.*

Café Annie's Pan-Roasted Shrimp with Creamy Rice

3 cups fresh or canned chicken broth

2 teaspoons butter

2 cloves garlic, finely chopped

1/4 cup finely chopped onion

1 *chipotle* chile pepper, finely chopped

1/2 cup converted or "parboiled" rice

1/4 cup heavy cream

1 plum tomato, seeded and chopped

2 tablespoons chopped fresh coriander

2 teaspoons lime juice

salt and freshly ground pepper to taste

8 jumbo shrimp, shelled and deveined

1 tablespoon olive oil

4 lime wedges

1. Bring the chicken broth to a boil and hold it at a simmer.

2. In a sauté pan melt the butter over medium heat. Add half of the chopped garlic, 2 tablespoons of the onion along with the chile pepper and sauté until the onion is wilted. Add the rice and sauté for 1 minute.

3. Add 1/2 cup of the hot broth. Boil vigorously until the liquid has nearly evaporated.

4. Add another 1/2 cup of broth and boil until nearly evaporated. Continue this procedure until all of the broth has been used and the rice is tender. If the rice is still too crunchy, add more stock or water.

5. Add the heavy cream, chopped tomato, the remaining onion, the coriander, lime juice and salt. Bring to a boil, then lower the heat and simmer until the rice is creamy and slightly thick.

6. Toss the shrimp with the olive oil and the remaining garlic. Sprinkle with salt and pepper.

7. Heat a heavy skillet large enough to hold the shrimp in one layer until it is very hot. Sear the shrimp on both sides, then lower the heat and cook the shrimp, turning frequently, until the flesh turns opaque, about 3 minutes total cooking time.

8. Serve the shrimp over the rice. Garnish with the lime wedges.

Yield: 4 appetizers or 2 main course servings

Although many rice dishes appear throughout this book, this is a basic preparation—completed in the oven, not on the stove—that I use often and, although it has many applications, it will be required for the Pilaf of Mussels that follows it.

Basic Rice Pilaf

2 tablespoons butter
2 tablespoons finely chopped onion
1¹/₂ cups converted or "parboiled" rice
2¹/₄ cups fresh or canned chicken broth

1 bay leaf
2 stems parsley
salt to taste

1. Preheat oven to 400°.

2. On top of the stove melt the butter in an ovenproof saucepan and add the onion. Cook until wilted. Add the rice and stir well.

3. Add the broth, bay leaf, parsley and salt to taste. Bring to a boil, cover and bake for 17 minutes or until tender. Take out of the oven, remove bay leaf and parsley and toss gently with a fork. Keep warm.

Yield: 3¹/₂ cups

Usually, I prefer to serve my guests by arranging individual plates. But this dish, in which the mussels are baked inside a large dome of rice, is brought to the table as is and served there. Of course, if you like, the portions can be molded into 4 individual servings.

Pilaf of Mussels

3 pounds mussels, well scrubbed
  and with beards removed
2 tablespoons finely chopped
  shallots, plus 1 tablespoon
  chopped shallots
4 tablespoons chopped parsley
6 tablespoons butter
³/₄ cup dry white wine

2 tablespoons all-purpose flour
1 tablespoon minced onion
1¹/₂ cups thinly sliced mushrooms
¹/₂ cup heavy cream or half-and-
  half
salt and freshly ground white
  pepper to taste
Basic Rice Pilaf (preceding recipe)

1. Place the mussels in a kettle, and add the 2 tablespoons finely chopped shallots, half of the parsley, 1 tablespoon of the butter and the wine. Cover and bring to a boil. Simmer for 5 minutes or until the mussels are opened.

2. Strain the cooking liquid and save it. Remove the meat from each mussel. Set aside in a small container, cover and keep warm.

3. Melt 2 tablespoons of the remaining butter in a small saucepan, add the flour and stir with a whisk until blended. Add 1³/₄ cups of the reserved mussel liquid, stirring vigorously with a whisk until well blended. Simmer for 3 minutes, and keep warm.

4. In a skillet heat 2 tablespoons of the remaining butter and cook the onion until wilted. Add the remaining chopped shallots and mushrooms and stir. Cook briefly, add this mixture to the sauce and mix well. Simmer over low heat for 10 minutes. Add the cream and continue cooking for about 5 minutes. Add salt and pepper to taste. Set aside.

5. Preheat oven to 300°.

6. Butter a 1-quart ovenproof bowl. Add 2 cups of the cooked rice. With your fingers or a spoon press the rice against walls of the bowl, leaving a well in the center to contain the mussels.

7. Spoon $^1/_2$ cup of the sauce and 1 tablespoon of the parsley into the mussels and blend. Heat thoroughly, but do not boil, and spoon the mussels into the rice-lined bowl. Cover with the remaining rice and press down to cover the mussels.

8. Cover the bowl with aluminum foil and bake in the oven just to heat through, about 5 minutes. Remove the foil and unmold the rice mold onto a large round warm serving platter.

9. Add the remaining parsley to the sauce, and bring to a boil. Remove from the heat and swirl in the remaining 1 tablespoon butter. Spoon a little sauce around the rice mold and serve the remaining sauce separately.

Yield: 6 servings

Preparing Mussels Pilaf

1. Press most of rice into bowl, creating well in center.

2. Add mussels mixture.

3. Cover with remaining rice, packing it down, and cook.

4. To unmold, place plate over bowl.

5. Invert and lift off the bowl.

I rarely just boil rice and let it go at that. Here's a version that's pretty close to being that simple, except that I've added some lemon juice and Tabasco to brighten it up.

Creole Rice

4 cups water
salt and freshly ground pepper to
  taste
1 cup converted or "parboiled" rice

1 tablespoon butter
$^1/_4$ teaspoon Tabasco sauce
2 tablespoons fresh lemon juice

1. Bring the water with salt to taste to a boil in a saucepan. Add the rice, and stir well. Bring back to a boil and simmer for 15 minutes, stirring occasionally.

2. Drain the rice in a colander. Add the butter, Tabasco, pepper and lemon juice. Blend well.

Yield: 4 servings

Rice, like chicken soup, can be one of those comforting foods that remind you of home and family. Rice pudding is the quintessential example of that. This is my method for preparing it.

Rice Pudding

6 cups milk
1 cup heavy cream
1 vanilla bean or 1 teaspoon pure
  vanilla extract
1 cup converted or "parboiled" rice
$1^1/_4$ cups sugar
$^3/_4$ cup white raisins
2 large eggs

4 tablespoons *crème de* Grand
  Marnier or other orange-flavored
  liqueur
1 tablespoon butter for greasing pan
1 teaspoon ground cinnamon
1 tablespoon grated orange zest
2 tablespoons confectioners' sugar

1. Pour the milk and cream into a heavy-bottomed saucepan and add the vanilla bean. Bring to a boil and add the rice and sugar. Stir often from the bottom to

prevent sticking. Simmer until the rice is tender, about 35 minutes. Remove the vanilla bean.

2. Put the raisins in a small bowl and pour boiling water over them. Let stand until the rice is cooked.

3. Beat the eggs, and add the *crème de* Grand Marnier. Remove the rice from the heat when it is fully cooked and add the eggs to the rice, stirring rapidly.

4. Meanwhile, preheat oven to 400°.

5. Drain the raisins and add them to the cooked rice.

6. Grease an oval baking dish measuring 14 by 8 by 2 inches. Pour in the rice mixture, sprinkle with cinnamon and zest and put the dish inside another flameproof dish or pan.

7. Pour boiling water around the interior dish. Bring the water to a boil on top of the stove and place the double-dish assembly in the oven to bake for 30 minutes or until the custard is set. Remove from the oven and sprinkle with confectioners' sugar. Serve hot or cold.

Yield: 8 to 10 servings

Say Cheese

It was a drizzly, cool morning—7:30 A.M. already quite late in the day on a farm—and David Funk was working his cows. The cows in two lines filed through the shed, moving slowly, their eyes seeming heavy with boredom and their udders heavy with milk. David Funk seemed anything but bored as he moved his machinery from cow to cow, gathering the huge yield a healthy cow can deliver. These Holsteins can give between 50 and 80 pounds (that's the measure the farmers use, not quarts or gallons) of milk a day. The cows here produce milk that is 3.8 percent fat. Some of that will have to be skimmed away to turn it into the standardized 3.5 we buy as whole milk.

David gave us each a taste of the milk, chilled but unpasteurized, just as it had come from the cow. Rich and sweet, it recalled for me those childhood days in rural France when I was a lot closer to the earth than I am now. I got a chance to milk one of the cows by hand—no fun doing it by machine—and was having a splendid time despite the inclement weather.

We'd come to the Funk family farm, not far from Madison, because it was key to understanding the story of the cheese made in this state. It's the cows and the high-quality milk they produce in Wisconsin that has made this state the center of cheesemaking in America. The area has drawn immigrants from all over Europe, notably the Dutch, Italians and, most recently, the French. But the pilgrims who settled here were first, of course, and their cheese—Cheddar (from the area of the same name in England) is one of the state's greatest successes. Although other states produce fine Cheddar as well, Wisconsin turns out more of it, by far, than any other region and its Cheddar is sold all over the country. The area also, thanks to those European immigrants, is now producing a slew of other cheeses, including blue

cheese, Edam and Gouda, mozzarella, Parmesan, Muenster, provolone, ricotta and Swiss.

Although Cheddar started out as an English cheese, it has spawned two purely American varieties: Colby and Monterey Jack, both of which are really variants on Cheddar. Colby, named after a Wisconsin town, is softer and more lacy than Cheddar; and Monterey, after the California city, cured only for three to six weeks, is blander and also softer than Cheddar.

I had watched my mother make cheese on a small scale when I was a child, so I've known for a long time just how milk is converted to cheese, how the cheesemaker separates the curds from the whey and the curds are solidified into this incredible food. But it wasn't until we visited Dave Simon's Cheddar plant in Appleton, Wisconsin, that I saw this process on a large scale, and it took my breath away. Dave sells great quantities of many different Wisconsin cheeses from his store and by mail (Simon's Specialty Cheese, Route 5, Appleton, WI 54915). But the Cheddar—tons of it—he produces himself.

Dave is a big fellow, blond and large boned, who looks as if he ought to be playing guard for the Green Bay Packers instead of making cheese. When we met him, he was dressed in the white uniform he wears while working, which emphasizes the focus on cleanliness that is imperative in cheesemaking (you want only the prescribed bacteria to go to work in the milk; anything else is contamination that could ruin much of the investment), and he wore a floppy white net to contain his hair. It seemed silly on so big a man. Although, I think all of us looked silly enough wearing it through the plant, whatever our size.

The process, as Dave led us through it, starts with tons of milk sluicing into vats. There, the cheesemakers add rennet, an enzyme that coagulates the milk and turns it custardy in about 20 minutes. Next comes the arduous task of draining the whey, the liquid, and leaving behind the curds, the solids. What differentiates one cheese from another, among other things, is the process by which the curds are handled: Are they drained completely of whey or not? Are they innoculated with one culture or another? Is the cheese sprayed with a mold? Any of these factors—and a lot more—go into determining whether the final result is cottage cheese or Cheddar or blue or something else.

We watched as a group of men worked hard and fast to make Cheddar, cutting into chunks the solidifying milk. In long slant-sided vats, the whey drains off. As it does the still-moist curds are compressed into slabs that are repeatedly turned over and slapped down in the vats to encourage more of the liquid to depart and to give the Cheddar its dense texture. Cheddar is not the driest of cheeses but it is quite dry and this vigorous rendering of the whey is central to the process. (Incidentally, whether it is yellow or white depends on whether the natural dye from the annatto seed is added during the process; the dye affects the taste not at all.)

Ultimately, the curds are pressed into shape and cured. Mild Cheddar is cured for only one to three months, sharp from six to nine months. But the curing can go on for perhaps three years. As it does the cheese becomes not only sharper and drier but more granular. We got a chance to taste the Cheddar in each of its states of aging and, when you try it in sequence that way, it's almost as if you're tasting totally different cheeses.

How old can it be? Actually, since cheesemaking preceded refrigeration—as a means of storing milk—by thousands of years, it's hard to spoil it. But refrigeration is recommended these days if you mean to keep cheese in good condition. Tightly sealed and chilled, but not frozen, Cheddar can last for several years. If you've had cheese in the refrigerator for a while and surface mold has formed, just cut it away cleanly. The rest should be fine but it should be eaten within the week, according to guidelines published by the Dairy Farmers of Wisconsin. To remove the chill of refrigerated Cheddar let the cheese stand, covered, for 30 minutes before serving.

The Expert's View

When experts taste cheese for the purpose of making large purchases, they go about it much the way wine tasters might, with great erudition and seriousness. They know how each cheese is supposed to look and taste. Most of us, of course, aren't that skilled. But there are some insights that can be gleaned from the expert's process even for the nonexpert.

First of all, the cheese must be at room temperature to release its odors properly. Does it have any off odor, the expert asks, a fruity smell, for example, that might suggest some alien bacteria at work?

Is its appearance correct? Cheddar should have no holes, for example—again suggesting something unwelcome growing there—but Colby should.

How does it feel? The expert will take a piece of cheese and roll it around in his fingers to check its body, its resistance to pressure. A hard cheese should not be sticky under pressure.

How does it taste? A cheese of medium age might be expected to have a pronounced cheese flavor but not a sense of astringency. (At this point the expert will exhale through his nose, while tasting, in an effort to learn more about the odor of the cheese.) The flavor should be clean. No cheese should leave an acidic aftertaste that lingers.

Although most of us can't and won't go through all of that in buying cheese for the home, it does make sense to purchase cheese from a shop that will let you sample it first. It also makes sense to buy it from a shop that has lots of turnover. This is a more important guideline for the soft and semisoft cheeses than for the harder ones that are less likely to be over the hill. The more familiar you become with a variety of good cheeses, the more self-assured you'll become.

❧ *In Madison, we shopped in the fine farmer's market downtown, accompanied by Odessa Piper, the chef of a restaurant there called L'Etoile. Her place has acquired an intensely dedicated following for, among other things, its inventive and very successful use of local produce. One of her proudest dishes, either as an appetizer or a main course, is a tart with a hickory nut crust filled with Cheddar cheese and arugula.*

L'Etoile's Cheddar Tart with Arugula

$^1/_3$ cup hickory nuts or hazelnuts
1 cup all-purpose flour
salt and freshly ground white
   pepper to taste
11 tablespoons chilled butter, cut
   into small cubes
$^1/_2$ cup water
20 whole pearl onions

1 teaspoon sugar
2 cups small-leaf arugula
$^1/_2$ pound sharp Cheddar cheese,
   shredded
$^1/_2$ cup heavy cream
2 eggs
1 teaspoon fresh thyme leaves

1. Preheat oven to 400°.

2. In the container of a food processor coarsely chop the nuts. Add the flour, salt, 8 tablespoons of the butter and 3 tablespoons of the water. Pulse for 15 seconds or until dough mixture begins to gather into a ball. Wrap the dough in wax paper and refrigerate it for at least 30 minutes before rolling.

3. On a lightly floured board, roll the dough to a thickness of $^1/_4$ inch. Fit it into a 10-inch metal tart pan with a removable bottom and trim away the edges.

4. Place wax paper or foil over the pastry and pour in enough dried beans or raw rice to cover the bottom of the shell. Bake for 30 minutes. Remove the beans or rice and wax paper. Bake for another 5 minutes. Remove from the oven and set aside.

5. In a small skillet place 2 tablespoons of the remaining butter, the onions, remaining water, sugar and salt to taste. Bring to a boil. Simmer until the water has evaporated and the sugar starts to caramelize, about 20 minutes. Set aside.

6. In a small saucepan melt the remaining 1 tablespoon butter. Add the arugula and sprinkle it with salt. Sauté over low heat until wilted. Remove from heat and set aside.

7. To assemble the tart, place the prebaked crust on a baking sheet. Place small handfuls of the cheese at even intervals around and in the center of the tart. Arrange the onions around the cheese. Arrange the arugula in the remaining spaces.

8. In a bowl thoroughly beat the eggs and add salt and pepper and the thyme. Mix well. Pour the mixture gently over the assembled tart. Bake for 25 minutes or until set. Serve lukewarm.

Yield: 4 servings as a main course

One of the great advantages of cheese in cooking is its capacity to melt so beautifully and blend and bind as it does. The choice of cheese, of course, can bring great character to a dish or leave it sadly boring. Blue cheese is one of those with lots of personality; it is a terrific partner for chicken breasts.

Chicken Breasts with Blue Cheese Sauce

4 skinless boneless chicken breast
  halves, about 1^1/$_4$ pounds in all
salt and freshly ground pepper to
  taste
3 tablespoons butter
1 tablespoon flour

^{1}/$_2$ cup fresh or canned chicken
  broth
^{3}/$_4$ cup milk
^{1}/$_4$ pound blue cheese, crumbled
^{1}/$_4$ cup finely chopped onion
^{1}/$_4$ cup dry white wine

1. Sprinkle the breast halves with salt and pepper.

2. Heat 2 tablespoons of the butter over medium-high heat in a heavy skillet large enough to hold the chicken in one layer. Add the chicken and brown lightly on one side. Turn and continue cooking about 5 minutes or until cooked through. Remove the pieces to a platter and keep warm.

3. Meanwhile, heat the remaining 1 tablespoon butter in a saucepan and add the flour, stirring rapidly with a wire whisk. Add the broth and milk, and continue stirring rapidly. Add the cheese and stir until melted.

4. Add the onion to the skillet and cook, stirring, until wilted. Add the wine and stir to dissolve the brown particles that cling to the bottom and sides of the skillet. Stir in the cheese sauce.

5. Place a sieve over a small saucepan and strain the sauce into it, stirring and pushing it down with a plastic spatula to press through as much of it as possible. There should be about 1^1/$_3$ cups sauce.

6. Pour the sauce over the chicken and serve hot.

Yield: 4 servings

Without any doubt one of the best uses of cheese—maybe the way I use it most of all—is in pasta dishes. The pasta offers a canvas just waiting for the cook to come along and give it color. Cheese is one of the finest brighteners. The next several recipes are all for pasta, each quite different in character. This one employs Cheddar to bind together a long-cherished combination of ingredients.

Macaroni Casserole with Fresh Herbs and Cheddar

1½ cups uncooked elbow macaroni
1 tablespoon olive oil
1 cup chopped onions
¼ cup chopped celery
¼ cup chopped sweet green pepper
2 teaspoons finely chopped garlic
1 tablespoon chopped fresh oregano
   or 1 teaspoon dried
2 tablespoons chopped fresh basil
   or chopped Italian parsley
½ cup crushed canned tomatoes

salt and freshly ground pepper to
   taste
2 tablespoons butter
2 tablespoons flour
2 cups milk
2 cups cubed or shredded Cheddar
   cheese
cayenne to taste
¼ teaspoon freshly grated nutmeg
2 tablespoons freshly grated
   Parmesan cheese

1. Preheat oven broiler to high.

2. Bring 2 quarts of lightly salted water to a boil in a kettle. Add the macaroni, stir and simmer until tender. Do not overcook. Drain and rinse under cold water.

3. In a skillet heat the oil and add the onions, celery, green pepper and garlic. Cook, stirring, until wilted. Add the oregano, basil, tomatoes and salt and pepper to taste. Cook and stir for 5 minutes. Add the cooked macaroni and blend well. Set aside and keep warm.

4. Meanwhile, in a saucepan melt the butter and stir in the flour with a wire whisk until well blended. Add the milk, stirring rapidly, and bring to a simmer. Cook, stirring, for about 5 minutes.

5. Remove the sauce from the heat and stir in the Cheddar cheese, salt, pepper and cayenne to taste and the nutmeg. Stir until the cheese melts.

6. Spoon the macaroni mixture into a baking dish measuring 10 by 7 by 2¹/₂ inches. Pour the cheese sauce evenly over the macaroni mixture. Sprinkle the top with the Parmesan cheese and place under the broiler until hot and bubbling and lightly browned.

Yield: 4 servings

Usually, Parmesan cheese is used in relatively small quantities in pasta dishes. Not so here.

Ziti with Creamy Parmesan Sauce

¹/₂ pound ziti
salt and freshly ground white
   pepper to taste
1 cup milk
¹/₂ cup heavy or light cream

pinch cayenne
¹/₄ teaspoon freshly grated nutmeg
¹/₂ cup freshly grated Parmesan
   cheese

1. In a kettle bring 3 quarts of water to a boil and add salt to taste and the ziti. Cook, stirring frequently until tender, about 10 minutes. Drain thoroughly.

2. Return the ziti to the kettle and add the milk, cream, cayenne and pepper to taste and the nutmeg. Bring to a boil and cook about 3 minutes or until the liquid thickens. Add 2 tablespoons of the Parmesan cheese, blend and pour the mixture into a baking dish about 10 by 7 by 2¹/₂ inches.

3. Preheat the broiler to high.

4. Sprinkle the top of the dish evenly with the remaining cheese. Place the dish under the broiler until the top is lightly browned.

Yield: 6 servings

If cheese dominates the preceding pasta dishes, here it merely accents it, while the vegetables move to center stage.

Pasta with Vegetables, Capers and Anchovy Sauce

3/4 pound pasta bows or farfalle

salt and freshly ground pepper to taste

3 tablespoons olive oil

1/2 pound mushrooms, cut into 1/4-inch slices

1 tablespoon finely chopped garlic

1/4 teaspoon hot red pepper flakes

1/2 small zucchini, washed, trimmed and cut into 1/4-inch cubes

1 pound ripe plum tomatoes, cut into 1/2-inch cubes

1/2 cup capers, drained

2 tablespoons anchovy paste

4 tablespoons chopped Italian parsley

4 tablespoons grated Cheddar, Parmesan or pecorino cheese

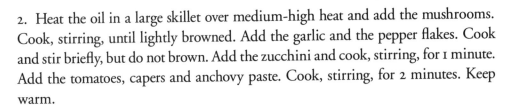

1. Bring 4 quarts of lightly salted water to a boil in a large kettle.

2. Heat the oil in a large skillet over medium-high heat and add the mushrooms. Cook, stirring, until lightly browned. Add the garlic and the pepper flakes. Cook and stir briefly, but do not brown. Add the zucchini and cook, stirring, for 1 minute. Add the tomatoes, capers and anchovy paste. Cook, stirring, for 2 minutes. Keep warm.

3. Meanwhile, drop the pasta into the boiling water. Return to a boil and cook until al dente. Do not overcook. Reserve 1/2 cup of the cooking water. Drain the pasta and return it to the dry kettle. Add the vegetable caper sauce, the reserved cooking liquid, the parsley, salt and pepper to taste and the cheese. Toss and blend well. Serve immediately.

Yield: 4 to 6 servings

🌿 *This is an extremely simple dish, but with blue cheese, which is growing in popularity, and asparagus as main players, it makes quite a statement.*

Fettuccine with Blue Cheese and Asparagus

1¼ pounds fresh asparagus
salt and freshly ground pepper to taste
¾ pound imported fettuccine
2 tablespoons olive oil
2 tablespoons butter
4 ripe plum tomatoes, peeled, seeded and diced

2 teaspoons finely chopped garlic
¼ pound domestic blue cheese, crumbled
4 tablespoons coarsely chopped fresh basil leaves
freshly grated Parmesan cheese

1. Scrape and trim the asparagus. Slice the spears on the diagonal into ½-inch lengths.

2. Bring 2 quarts of lightly salted water to a boil in a kettle. Add the fettuccine. Boil very gently for 9 minutes. Do not overcook. The pasta should be al dente. Reserve ¼ cup of the cooking liquid. Drain the pasta.

3. Heat the olive oil and butter in a kettle and add the asparagus, tomatoes and garlic. Cook over medium heat for 2 minutes, stirring. Add the fettuccine, blue cheese, basil, the reserved water and salt and pepper to taste. Toss well over medium heat. Serve immediately with the Parmesan cheese on the side.

Yield: 4 servings

The Big Catch

Montauk sits at the very tip of Long Island, New York, like a compass needle pointing northeast to New England. It is, in fact, closer as the crow flies to New Bedford, Massachusetts, than it is to Manhattan. And despite the seasonal influx of affluent New Yorkers wan and weary from their long hours in the offices to the west, Montauk is still a fishing village, one with close links in culture and occupation to the great New England fishing regions just across the water. Every summer, Montauk becomes one of the nation's centers for tuna and swordfish.

As we made our way to its old harbor, past the charter boats, we arrived at Great Circle Fisheries, where headless tunas, weighing hundreds of pounds and looking like tapered barrels, lay on their sides awaiting their ultimate fates. The best tuna, Ralph Owen of the Great Circle Fisheries company told us, would go to Japan, where it would be displayed, perhaps, in an auction house before being bid on and then sent off to a *sushi* bar. The Japanese pay more for the fish than Americans do, and it's the middleman's job to get the highest price he can for the fishermen.

The best tuna is not the reddest, as you might imagine. In fact, Ralph told us, with some dismay in his voice, when the fresh tuna industry got going in a big way, the idea was to push it as a "red meat, like beef." But that has backfired. A lot of good tuna is not very red; the color is merely the result of where the fish has been feeding.

Then what is the true test of quality? What do these experts look for? They look for fat content that resembles the marbling in a steak. Each slice of tuna has conspicuous curved lines that resemble tree rings. These are connective tissue in the muscle. Between the curved lines, in high-quality tuna, are faint suggestions of whitish webbing: That's the fat, the true indication of the fish's worthiness. The more fat the better.

To find these big fish, the commercial boats head out from Montauk for 7 to 10 days, or even longer. They follow the fish as far as they feasibly can, all the way north to the Grand Banks off Newfoundland and all the way south to the waters off Cape Hatteras, North Carolina. Unlike many a smaller and more delicate fish, tuna does not seem to suffer in edibility for many days, as long as it is kept well chilled. As we watched, we saw some of the big fellows being carefully packed in crates full of ice to be rushed to Kennedy Airport and thence, of course, to Japan.

Before we left Montauk we wandered over to the charter boat docks again and found a tuna that was certainly staying in this country. A boat called the *Adios* had just come back in with an 80-pound fish that had required more than an hour of hard work, with each of the fishermen on board taking turns, before it could be brought aboard. It was destined to be marinated and grilled.

I got into a good-natured dispute with one of the anglers who described a perfectly good marinade to me but refused to use garlic in it because, he said, "it gives me gas." To make his point, he poked himself in the chest a couple of times with the side of his fist. I don't know. Garlic is just too fine an ingredient to dismiss completely like that. I urged him to give it another try. He said he wouldn't. So be it.

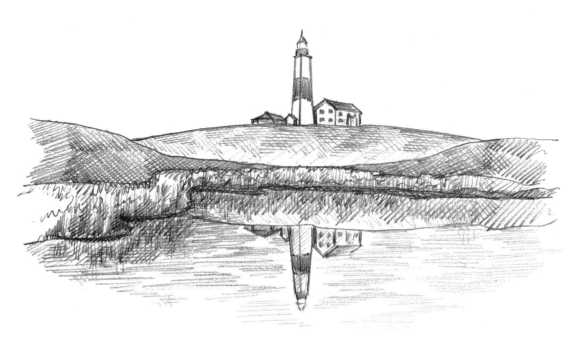

Earlier that day, back at home—I live in East Hampton, not far from Montauk—I had gone lobstering with one of the local watermen. It is still possible, even in these days when population growth has put so much pressure on sea life, to trap plenty of lobster out there past Gardiners Island and toward Block Island Sound. I've gone lobstering often enough in the past in my own power boat and on my own.

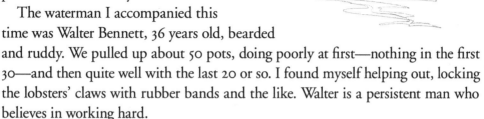

The waterman I accompanied this time was Walter Bennett, 36 years old, bearded and ruddy. We pulled up about 50 pots, doing poorly at first—nothing in the first 30—and then quite well with the last 20 or so. I found myself helping out, locking the lobsters' claws with rubber bands and the like. Walter is a persistent man who believes in working hard.

Walter's family has worked the water, he said, since the "seventeenth or eighteenth century" and he's now actively teaching his own children the ways of the bays and the sea. At one point as he was growing up, Walter recalled, he had the good fortune to be tutored by his parents, grandparents and great-grandparents. "Every day I learned something new," he said. He learned some things that might not seem of immediate importance, but they were. He learned, for instance, how to tell the difference between a male and female horseshoe crab (the male is smaller and has two small hooks to latch onto the female). That's useful because the female's eggs are good bait for eels. And Walter, like so many of the watermen here, doesn't limit himself just to lobster or any one fish. Why should he, when the nearby water is rich in scallops, clams, monkfish and bluefish?

In the evening, the TV crew, as well as those members of my family and friends who happened to be around, dined sumptuously on the bounty of the Atlantic. There was a warm tuna and arugula salad and, of course, the lobster steamed in the naturally salted water hauled in a kettle from Gardiners Bay, just off my backyard.

East End Wisdom

The eastern end of Long Island has no shortage of fish experts. One of the wisest, no doubt, is John Haessler, the proprietor of the Seafood Shop in Wainscott. He opened the shop in 1972, initially just as a sideline (he was teaching fifth grade at the time). Soon the shop became a genuine occupation and now draws people from many miles around, looking for the highest-quality seafood.

John has a lot to say about fish and crustaceans; here are a few of his points:

When you're looking for freshness in a fish, not only should its gills be red and its eyes bright, but it should have no fishy odor, even if it is oily. The notion that oily fish might be allowed a bit more aroma, he says, "is just an excuse."

Fish already cut into steaks should be shiny and, usually, the flesh should be firm and tight with no indication of premature flaking, although there are some exceptions: Codfish will flake naturally when it is cut into steaks.

Lobster should have a hard shell when you buy it; a slightly soft shell is an indication that the lobster will have less meat.

Even if you intend to grill or bake a lobster, parboil it first in a large kettle of water, until the shell just turns red. This will make it easier to split for further cooking and kills the lobster quickly. It also avoids the necessity of stabbing the lobster between the eyes to kill it first, a procedure, he notes, that is sometimes unsettling to home cooks.

A nice thing about marinades is that once you get the knack of it, you can add a little more of this or less of that or substitute similar ingredients that provide interesting nuances. The marinade I use here is a basic one that happens to have a significant contribution from lemon juice to give it a notable tartness.

Broiled Tuna in Lemon Marinade

4 center-cut tuna steaks, about 6 ounces each, 1 inch thick
2 tablespoons olive oil
salt and freshly ground pepper to taste
4 teaspoons mustard seed

1 tablespoon chopped fresh oregano or 1 teaspoon dried
2 bay leaves, broken into pieces
2 tablespoons fresh lemon juice
$^{1}/_{4}$ teaspoon hot red pepper flakes
1 tablespoon chopped garlic

1. Place the tuna on a flat surface and cut away and discard the dark part, if any. In a shallow dish blend the remaining ingredients together well, add the tuna and coat on both sides. Cover with plastic wrap and let stand at room temperature for 15 minutes.

2. Place the steaks in a very hot cast-iron pan. Cook on one side for 3 minutes. Turn the fish and continue cooking for 2 or 3 minutes for rare. If you want it well done, cook 1 minute more on each side. Return the steaks to the dish with the marinade and keep warm. Serve with the vegetable of your choice.

Yield: 4 servings

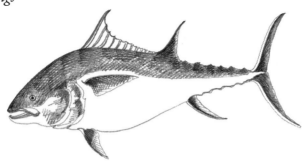

Monkfish, springy and dense, was once among the so-called trash fish because so few people wanted it for anything. But now, of course, it's widely coveted and the price (alas) often reflects that. Its density makes it excellent for a stew as it resists breaking apart during the cooking process.

Monkfish Stew

2 tablespoons olive oil
1 cup finely chopped onions
1 tablespoon finely chopped garlic
1/2 cup finely chopped celery
1 cup finely chopped leeks
1 teaspoon saffron threads or
   turmeric
1/4 teaspoon Tabasco sauce, or to
   taste

salt and freshly ground pepper to
   taste
4 ripe plum tomatoes, coarsely
   chopped
1/4 cup tomato paste
1/2 cup dry white wine
6 cups fresh fish broth or water
2 pounds monkfish fillets
Garlic Croutons (page 286)

1. Heat the olive oil in a large saucepan or kettle, add the onions, garlic, celery, leeks, saffron and Tabasco. Cook until the onions are wilted. Do not brown the garlic. Add salt and pepper to taste. Add the tomatoes and tomato paste and cook for about 5 minutes.

2. Add the wine and fish broth and bring to a simmer. Cook for 10 minutes.

3. Meanwhile, cut the monkfish into 1-inch cubes. Add to the broth, cook and simmer for 5 minutes. Check for seasoning and serve in soup bowls with the croutons.

Yield: 6 to 8 servings

Of all the places I like to take my friends in New York City, none is more convivial than La Cité in Manhattan, where I can always count on the talented young chef Frederic Perrier. When we were looking for a restaurant to tape some creative lobster cookery, I turned to him immediately and, as usual, he didn't let us down. This is his beautiful dish. The sautéed mushroom component uses mushrooms that you may find difficult to come by. Feel free to substitute any fresh mushrooms that are available to you.

Lobster with Ratatouille and Sautéed Mushrooms

The Ratatouille

4 2-pound lobsters
1 medium eggplant, about ¹/₂ pound
2 medium zucchini, about ¹/₂ pound in all
1 large sweet red pepper, halved and seeded
1 large sweet yellow pepper, halved and seeded
1 medium onion

1 large tomato
2 tablespoons olive oil
2 bay leaves
2 sprigs fresh thyme or ¹/₂ teaspoon dried
1 tablespoon chopped garlic
¹/₂ teaspoon saffron threads
salt and freshly ground pepper to taste

The Sautéed Mushrooms

3 tablespoons olive oil
1 tablespoon chopped garlic
2 large shallots, chopped (about 4 tablespoons)
¹/₄ pound *chanterelles*, halved
¹/₄ pound *pleurotes*, halved

¹/₄ pound *shiitake*, halved
4 tablespoons chopped chives
salt and freshly ground pepper to taste

8 whole chives for garnish

1. Plunge the lobsters into a kettle of boiling salted water and poach for 7 minutes. Do this in two batches, if necessary. Remove with tongs and allow the lobster to cool. Remove the meat from the shell and set it aside in a saucepan along with any liquid that has accumulated on the platter. Cover and keep warm. Reserve 1¹/₂ cups of the salted water used to cook the lobsters.

2. Cut the eggplant, zucchini, peppers, onion and tomato separately into cubes of about $^1/_4$ inch.

3. Heat the olive oil in a large sauté pan. Add the onion, then the peppers and then the zucchini. Add the eggplant and tomato. Sauté for 5 minutes, stirring. Deglaze the pan with the $1^1/_2$ cups reserved cooking liquid. Add the bay leaves, thyme, garlic, saffron and salt and pepper to taste. Simmer the ratatouille for about 15 minutes.

4. To prepare the mushrooms: Heat the olive oil over high heat in a large sauté pan. Add the garlic and shallots and cook, stirring rapidly for 30 seconds. Add all the mushrooms and sauté for 5 minutes still over high heat until lightly browned. Add the chopped chives and salt and pepper and remove from the heat.

5. To assemble, heat the lobster in the saucepan with its liquid. Place the mushroom garnish in a circle in the center of each plate. Spoon the *ratatouille* around the mushrooms. Place the lobster pieces on top of the mushrooms and finish with 2 whole chives inserted into the middle pointing up.

Yield: 4 servings

☙ *The lobster in this recipe is steamed, my preferred method most of the time, because I think steaming keeps the meat more tender than other methods of cooking do. I actually place the lobster right in boiling water, but only 2 or 3 inches of it. The trick is to have a kettle wide enough to hold the lobster in one layer and to have a very tightfitting cover so that the steam builds rapidly once the lobster has been dropped into the pot.*

Lobsters with Aïoli Sauce

The Lobsters

salt to taste
8 black peppercorns
1 cup sliced onions
$^1/_2$ cup sliced carrots
1 cup sliced celery
1 bay leaf

4 sprigs fresh thyme or 1 teaspoon dried
$^1/_4$ teaspoon hot red pepper flakes
4 live lobsters, each about $1^1/_2$ to 2 pounds

1. Place about 2 or 3 inches of water in the bottom of a large steamer pot. Add all the remaining ingredients, except the lobsters. Bring to a boil and simmer for 10 minutes.

2. Place the lobsters in the steamer and cover the pot.
Bring the water to a rapid boil over high heat and cook for about 12 minutes. Remove from the heat and let stand for 5 minutes. When the lobsters are easy to handle, remove them and split them, if desired. Crack the claws and remove all the meat. Set aside. Serve with aïoli and Tomato and Arugula Salad (page 225).

Yield: 4 servings

Aïoli Sauce

1 tablespoon finely minced garlic
1 egg yolk
1 tablespoon fresh lemon juice
1 tablespoon Dijon mustard

salt and freshly ground white pepper to taste
1 cup olive oil

Place the garlic in a bowl, add the egg yolk, lemon juice, mustard and salt and pepper. Add the oil very gradually, while beating rapidly with a wire whisk. Continue whisking until all the oil is incorporated and the sauce is smooth and thick.

Yield: about 1 cup

❧ *Typically,* escabèche, *as it is done in Provence, refers to a fish dish that has been sautéed in olive oil first and then covered in a hot marinade. That, as you'll see, is what I've more or less done here.*

Swordfish Escabèche

4 tablespoons olive oil

4 swordfish steaks, about 6 ounces each, 1 inch thick (1¹/₂ pounds in all)

salt and freshly ground black or white pepper to taste

1¹/₂ cups coarsely sliced white onions

1 cup coarsely sliced sweet red peppers

1 cup coarsely sliced sweet green peppers

1 tablespoon chopped garlic

1 cup diced ripe plum tomatoes

4 tablespoons white wine vinegar

¹/₂ cup white wine, such as Riesling

1 bay leaf

4 sprigs fresh thyme or 1 teaspoon dried

2 teaspoons coriander seed

2 whole cloves

2 tablespoons drained capers

¹/₄ teaspoon hot red pepper flakes

4 tablespoons coarsely chopped fresh basil or parsley

1. Heat the olive oil in a nonstick skillet large enough to hold the swordfish steaks in one layer. Add the swordfish with salt and pepper to taste and cook briefly on each side for 1 minute. Remove from the skillet and set aside. Do not discard the oil.

2. Add the onions, peppers and garlic. Cook and stir until wilted. Do not brown. Add the tomatoes, vinegar, wine, bay leaf, thyme, coriander, the whole cloves, capers and pepper flakes, and bring to a boil. Cover and simmer for 5 minutes.

3. Add the swordfish steaks, and distribute the vegetable mixture over the steaks. Cover and cook for 5 minutes. Let cool and refrigerate. Serve cold garnished with the chopped basil.

Yield: 4 servings

❧ *Ginger is so widely available now that it no longer seems exotic. I find myself picking my spots to use it carefully so as not to overdo it. Here it joins thyme and bay leaf in transforming a simple broiled fish into something quite distinctive.*

Broiled Swordfish with Herbs and Ginger

4 swordfish steaks, each about 1 inch thick, total weight about 6 ounces each

salt and freshly ground pepper to taste

4 sprigs fresh thyme

4 slices fresh ginger
1 bay leaf, broken
1 tablespoon vinegar
4 tablespoons olive oil
2 tablespoons butter, melted

1. Preheat oven broiler to high or preheat an outdoor grill.

2. Place the swordfish steaks on a platter and sprinkle both sides with salt and pepper. Place on each steak 1 thyme sprig, 1 slice of ginger and bits of the bay leaf. Sprinkle each steak with the vinegar and olive oil. Cover closely with plastic wrap and let it stand until ready to cook.

3. If broiling, arrange the steaks on a rack and place under the broiler about 6 inches from the source of heat. Broil 5 minutes with the door partially open. Turn the steaks, leaving the door partially open, for about 5 minutes.

4. If grilling, place the steaks on a hot grill and cook for 5 minutes. Turn the fish, and continue cooking for about 5 more minutes. Serve with the melted butter over all.

Yield: 4 servings

꙳ That day we went to Montauk to talk to the fishermen we came back with a magnificent slab of fresh tuna. I served that tuna in a salad as a separate course, followed by the steamed lobster.

Grilled Tuna Steaks with Tomato and Arugula Salad

4 center-cut tuna steaks, about 5
  ounces each
2 tablespoons olive oil
salt and freshly ground pepper to
  taste
4 sprigs fresh thyme or 1 teaspoon
  dried

$^1/_4$ teaspoon hot red pepper flakes
2 teaspoons grated lemon rind
1 tablespoon red wine vinegar
Tomato and Arugula Salad (recipe
  follows)

1. Preheat outdoor grill.

2. Place the tuna on a flat surface and cut away and discard the dark part, if any. Spoon the oil over the fish and sprinkle with salt and pepper, the thyme, pepper flakes, lemon rind and vinegar. Coat well on both sides. Cover with plastic wrap and let stand at room temperature for 15 minutes.

3. Place the steaks on the hot grill, and cook on the first side for 3 minutes. Turn the fish and continue cooking for 2 to 3 minutes for rare. If you want it well done, cook 1 minute more on each side. Return the tuna to the dish with the marinade and keep warm.

4. To serve, place 1 tuna steak on each serving plate, dividing any remaining marinade over the steaks. Divide the salad equally and arrange it over the fish.

Yield: 4 servings

Tomato and Arugula Salad

¹/₄ pound arugula

4 ripe plum tomatoes, cut into
  wedges

1 cup thinly sliced white onions

2 teaspoons finely chopped garlic

¹/₂ cup fresh basil leaves or
  chopped flat-leafed Italian parsley

2 tablespoons red wine vinegar

salt and freshly ground pepper to
  taste

3 tablespoons olive oil

Pick over the arugula and discard any tough stems. In a large salad bowl combine the arugula, tomatoes, onions, garlic, basil, vinegar, salt and pepper and olive oil. Toss well.

Yield: 4 servings

Strawberries and Artichokes

It was the serenest, perhaps the most beautiful day I'd spent in California. There we—the television team and I—were in a strawberry field that did not go on forever. Instead it stopped abruptly, right at the Pacific Ocean. As the sun rose and burnt away the early haze, we could see three distinct bands: the fields, the water glistening, and the baby-blue sky. It was cool, even at high noon in the springtime, and we all had to wear jackets or sweaters or else ignore the goose bumps.

In fact, it is almost always cool here, making it ideal for the growth of strawberries, which flourish in the westerly winds off the Pacific. That cool—almost never freezing—breeze is trapped in the valleys that reach back just off the coast. Strawberry plants maintained at an average temperature of 55° leap into a period of robust sexuality, as Larry Galper explained it to us, that leads to a tremendous production of fruit in this part of the country (75 percent of the total national yield is Californian and the most vigorous part of the state is right here in the rural Watsonville area not far from synthetic, touristy Carmel and bustling Monterey).

Galper, our guide to the nature of strawberries, is a former rodeo rider, science teacher and now full-time farmer, the manager of the Telles Ranch. He is stocky, completely bald and absolutely convinced that a strawberry farm is heaven on earth. The berry he grows is called the Pajaro, a particularly sweet strawberry, and it accounts for about 11 percent of the total we see around the country. Nearly half of the berries that reach us are Chandlers, a bit tarter than the pajaro and, I gather, somewhat easier to grow. Strawberries are grown all up and down the state, with fruit production coming earliest in the year in the south, near San Diego. By April and May the whole state is going full blast, and only in late fall does the production die off. That's why strawberries are available just about all year long at your local grocer.

What struck me at once when I got my first glimpse of California strawberries was that they were all peeking up through long strips of white or clear plastic, the berries and leaves neatly segregated away from the rest of the plant. "These strawberries will never touch the earth," Larry told us. There are two reasons for the plastic. The first is that it keeps the strawberries clean. They can be picked in the dew of early morning when they are coolest and they won't have mud clinging to them, so they'll never need to be washed until they reach your kitchen. (Water, it turns out, speeds the deterioration of the picked strawberry.) The plastic also maintains an even temperature in the earth beneath the berries. The whole procedure—and this is obviously one aspect that attracted Galper so powerfully—has high science written all over it, and there is great respect for the fruit around here.

As proud as the California farmers are of their berries, they are continually trying to improve them, make them more disease-resistant, and more flavorful. There's an active breeding program going on right now at the Telles Ranch, where scientists are striving for all sorts of slight variations. But never mind the subtleties of breeding, the fruit turns out to be astonishing even on the most elementary level. You know those tiny outcroppings, those spots, that cover the whole berry? Those are seeds, each one, and every seed is an individual different from the others. This whole day with Larry made me feel a little like I had fallen into the care of Mister Wizard (I even got to ride a tractor around the farm), and I didn't think I'd see anything again that was as alluring as a field of strawberries.

But artichokes came close. Artichokes—flowers, actually, in the sunflower family, but never permitted to bloom—need precisely the same climate as the strawberry. And like the production of strawberries, we can thank California for carrying nearly

the whole burden for the United States. In fact, the artichoke farming is even more concentrated, with almost all nationally grown artichokes originating in the area of Castroville, a few miles from Watsonville.

For the cook, there's a great deal to learn from a look at the plant. Each one has a primary stem, which produces one main artichoke, then there are secondary and tertiary offshoots, each producing smaller vegetables. The choke—that hairy bit of business, near the vegetable's heart, that we all carve away—is an immature seed. The so-called baby artichoke is not a baby at all, but rather the product of the tertiary stalk. These little artichokes will never mature, which turns out to be a boon for those of us who cook. Little artichokes have no choke and are completely edible. They are so tender that they can be eaten raw. Tony Leonardini, a farmer who was generous with his knowledge and his artichokes, whipped out his little knife right there in the field, sliced a baby artichoke thinly and offered the strips to each of us. Now all we needed was an olive tree, a press to render some oil and. . . .

Both the strawberry and the artichoke are wonderful examples of how eating in America has improved since the days when everything was canned or frozen. Both are chilled as soon as they are picked and then trucked—real fast—to faraway markets where, if they are handled properly, they will still be almost as fresh as if they'd just been picked. Galper says his truckers can get those strawberries to Hunt's Point market in New York in a mere 48 hours or so after they're plucked from their plastic covered beds. To resist deterioration, strawberries and artichokes need to be kept cool, even in the store; lamentably, that's not always the case.

It wasn't until we reached our temporary headquarters—the Highlands Inn, a bit farther south on the northern tip of Big Sur—that I got the chance to do any cooking on this leg of the American journey. There I visited the resort's stunning restaurant, Pacific's Edge, so named because it seems to lean right over the water. Seabirds soar beneath it. Waves smash into rocks and cascade over them, a stone's throw from one's table. I got to meet the restaurant's widely celebrated young chef, Brian Whitmer. He invited me into his kitchen, where inspired by my trekking through the fields—with nothing but strawberries and artichokes on my mind—I persuaded him to join me in cooking with both. We baked a phyllo dough purse, then filled it with sliced strawberries. (This is an adaptation of one of the most popular desserts at the restaurant, one that usually uses raspberries.) And we cooked a salmon dish—Pacific salmon, of course—prominently accompanied by artichoke hearts.

The Best Choice

Strawberries

It's not likely that you'll have the choice of one kind of strawberry over another when you go shopping. But there are, nevertheless, a few things to keep in mind: Strawberries don't ripen after they're picked, so it's up to you to choose the ones that look best right from the start. They should have a rich, red color, with caps that are bright green, not wilted. Refrigerate them as soon as you can, covered loosely in plastic wrap. Like a good wine, you don't want a strawberry to be too cold. So just before serving, allow the berry to come close to room temperature. Don't wash the berries until the last minute. Remember, water tends to break down the flavor and texture. In fact, when you do wash them, do it before you take the cap off so that no water will pour into the center of the berry. As soon as the berry is washed, pat it dry.

Artichokes

Hold each artichoke in your hand and pick the ones that feel heavy for their size. The artichokes should have a consistent green color. In the fall and winter, expect them to be darker or bronze tipped. Stay away from the ones that are spreading or separating, since they're probably a bit too far gone and are likely to be fibrous. To store an artichoke, sprinkle it with water, place it in an airtight plastic bag and refrigerate it. It should stay fresh for a week at the very least.

Strawberries

🌿 *This is the dessert Brian Whitmer, the chef at Pacific's Edge, and I cooked together on my swing through Northern California. It's a simple combination of ingredients resulting in a regal, golden dish. You might want to serve it with a scoop of vanilla ice cream. You'll notice that it includes the use of Grand Marnier, an orange liqueur. I have joined it with strawberries almost habitually over the years because the marriage of the two seems to bring out the best in the berry.*

Strawberries in a Purse

3 sheets phyllo pastry dough (can be purchased in supermarkets)
3 tablespoons butter, melted
6 large strawberries

4 tablespoons sugar
6 tablespoons Grand Marnier
fresh mint leaves for garnish

1. Preheat oven to 375°.

2. Place a sheet of phyllo dough on a flat working surface. Brush well with melted butter. Repeat for second and third sheets of dough. Gently place the second and third sheets over the first sheet.

3. Cut approximately 4 squares, each 6 by 6 inches, in the dough.

4. Slice 4 of the strawberries, rinsed and stemmed, into quarters but keep the quarters together as if the berry were still whole. Place one berry in the center of each dough square. Sprinkle each with 2 teaspoons of the sugar and check to be sure that the edges of the dough are buttered.

5. Bring together the sides to form a pocket or pouch and pinch the sides to seal (see illustration, page 234).

A Phyllo Purse

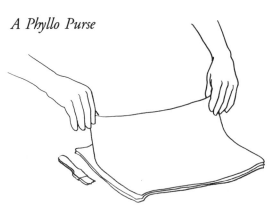

1. Brush sheets of phyllo with butter and stack.

2. Place sliced strawberries on phyllo squares.

3. Pick up two corners and pinch together.

4. Bring up remaining corners.

5. Pinch all sides to seal.

6. Place the pouches in a baking pan and bake for 10 minutes until golden brown. Place 2 pouches on each serving plate. Decorate each plate with the remaining strawberries, diced. Sprinkle with Grand Marnier and the remaining sugar. Garnish with the fresh mint leaves.

Yield: 2 servings

❧ *Strawberry, like pineapple, sorbet is among the cleanest tasting and most refreshing. Here I've taken what is for me an unusual step, by adding jam to the natural fruit. Strawberry sorbet can have a tendency to be a bit too mild and watery, but the jam solves those problems, acting as a binder and flavor booster. Be sure to use the highest quality, purest jam you can find.*

Strawberry Sorbet

3/4 cup sugar
1 cup water
2 pints ripe strawberries

1 cup pure sugar strawberry jam
3 tablespoons fresh lemon juice

1. Mix sugar and water thoroughly in a saucepan. Bring mixture to a boil, stirring. Simmer for 5 minutes and cool under refrigeration.

2. Rinse the strawberries well, drain and pat dry with paper towels. Remove the stems.

3. Place the strawberries and the strawberry jam in the container of a food processor. Purée to a fine texture for about 30 seconds. Add the cooled sugar syrup and the lemon juice. Blend well. Push through a sieve or strainer.

4. Pour the mixture into an ice cream freezer and freeze following the manufacturer's instructions.

Yield: about 5 cups

Note: For an extraordinarily light sorbet, gently beat one egg white with a fork and add to the mixture as it starts to freeze.

This is a variation of a classic dessert, named after a Russian prince, that always employs orange peel and whipping cream. If you like, garnish it with candied violets.

Strawberries Romanoff

2 pints red ripe strawberries
peel of 1 orange
$^1/_2$ cup sugar

$^1/_3$ cup *crème de* Grand Marnier
$^1/_2$ cup heavy cream
mint leaves for garnish

1. Rinse the strawberries well, drain and pat dry with paper towels. Remove the stems.

2. Use a swivel-bladed vegetable peeler to peel the orange. Do not cut into the white pulp. Cut peel into strips.

3. Place the strawberries in a bowl and add $^1/_3$ cup sugar and the *crème de* Grand Marnier, also the orange peel. Blend well gently, cover with plastic wrap and refrigerate.

4. Whip the cream and flavor with the remaining sugar.

5. To prepare for serving: Remove the orange strips from the strawberries, fold in the whipped cream very gently and serve. Decorate with the fresh mint leaves.

Yield: 6 to 8 servings

Like the strawberry farmer trying to refine his berry through breeding, I'm always reworking my cheesecakes. Here, the new touch is the honey in the sauce; and the cake itself is a bit cheesier than you may have experienced before.

Old-Fashioned Strawberry Cheesecake

The Cheesecake

1 tablespoon butter

$^1/_2$ cup graham cracker crumbs

3 packages cream cheese, 8 ounces each, at room temperature

4 large eggs, separated

1 cup sugar

1 teaspoon pure vanilla extract

1 cup heavy cream

The Sauce

2 pints fresh strawberries, washed and hulled

$^1/_4$ cup honey

1 tablespoon fresh lemon juice

4 tablespoons Grand Marnier

1. Preheat oven to 325°.

2. Butter the bottom and the insides of a 9-inch springform pan. Dust the inside with the graham cracker crumbs, reserving 1 tablespoon of the crumbs. Shake off the excess.

3. In the bowl of a KitchenAid or other table-top mixer blend the cream cheese at number 5 setting until smooth, about 40 seconds. Stop the machine and scrape down the sides of the bowl as needed. Add the egg yolks and blend for 15 seconds. Add $^3/_4$ cup of the sugar and the vanilla. Keep beating, add the cream and blend for 5 seconds.

4. In a 2-quart bowl, or a copper bowl, beat the egg whites with a wire whisk or an electric mixer (at medium speed) until soft peaks form. Gradually add the remaining $^1/_4$ cup of sugar and continue beating until stiff but not dry. Using a large rubber spatula, fold the egg whites into the cream cheese mixture.

5. Place the springform pan on a baking sheet and pour the mixture into it. Sprinkle the top with the remaining graham cracker crumbs. Bake for 1 hour. Turn off the oven but do not remove the cake. Leave the door ajar for 15 minutes. Close the door and leave the cake in the oven for an additional 45 minutes. Remove from the oven and place on a rack to cool. Release the spring lock but do not remove the ring. Let cool for at least 2 hours.

6. Make the sauce: Place $^1/_2$ pint of the smallest strawberries in the container of a food processor or blender. Add the honey and the lemon juice. Add the Grand Marnier, and blend well.

7. Just before serving, remove the ring of the springform and place the remaining whole strawberries on top of the cake. Pour the strawberry sauce over the cake.

Yield: 8 servings

Artichokes

❧ *In my restaurant days we used the artichoke to garnish seafood all the time. Frogs' legs and artichokes were a big hit that nobody seems to remember now. But I'd never had artichokes with salmon until I came to Northern California, near Castroville. If you're a cook near Castroville, you figure out how to use artichokes with just about anything. And, luckily, the combination does work quite well.*

Grilled Salmon with Artichoke Sauce

4 whole raw artichoke bottoms with chokes removed before cooking, sliced crosswise into thin slices
2 cups California dry white wine, such as Chardonnay or Sauvignon Blanc
4 tablespoons finely chopped shallots
1 tablespoon freshly grated ginger
$^{1}/_{2}$ cup diced carrots

1 bay leaf
salt and freshly ground pepper to taste
$^{1}/_{2}$ cup peeled seeded tomatoes, cut into small cubes
4 tablespoons butter, softened
4 boneless salmon fillets, about 6 ounces each
2 tablespoons olive oil
$^{1}/_{4}$ cup small dill sprigs for garnish

1. Preheat broiler to high.

2. In a small saucepan add the artichokes, wine, shallots, ginger, carrots, bay leaf and salt and pepper to taste. Bring to a boil and reduce to one third. Add the tomatoes and blend in the butter. Remove the bay leaf and taste for seasoning. Set aside and keep warm.

3. Meanwhile, sprinkle the salmon with salt and pepper. Brush with oil on both sides.

4. If the salmon is to be cooked on the grill, rub the rack lightly with oil. Place the fish on the rack. If the broiler is used, place the fish on a broiling pan about 4 inches from the heat. Cook 3 minutes and turn, for rare. Cook for 2 minutes more. If you prefer medium-done fish, cook a little longer.

5. To serve, place a fillet in the center of each warmed plate. Spoon the sauce and the vegetables over and around the fish. Garnish with the dill.

Yield: 4 servings

If the recipe above, which discards the artichoke leaves, breaks your heart, here's a way to use the whole artichoke in a preparation that can actually serve as a light lunch instead of just as an appetizer.

Stuffed Artichokes

4 large artichokes prepared for stuffing (see instructions on page 241)
$^{1}/_{2}$ pound bulk sausage meat
2 cups finely chopped onions
1 tablespoon finely chopped garlic
$^{1}/_{2}$ teaspoon ground cumin
4 tablespoons fresh chopped coriander or Italian parsley
1 teaspoon chopped fresh thyme or $^{1}/_{2}$ teaspoon dried

1 cup fresh bread crumbs
$^{1}/_{4}$ teaspoon Tabasco sauce, or to taste
salt and freshly ground pepper to taste
1 bay leaf
2 tablespoons olive oil
2 tablespoons red wine vinegar
$1^{1}/_{2}$ cups fresh or canned chicken broth

1. Preheat oven to 375°.

2. In a saucepan or skillet over medium-high heat add the sausage meat and break it up into small pieces while stirring for about 3 minutes. Remove all the fat, add 1 cup of the onions and garlic, and cook briefly. Do not brown the garlic. Add the cumin, and cook, stirring, until the onions are wilted. Remove from heat and let cool.

To Prepare Artichokes for Stuffing

Using a sharp knife to produce a neat flat base, cut off the stems of the artichokes. As the artichokes are cut, rub all surfaces with lemon to prevent discoloration. Slice off the top cone about 1 inch from the tip.

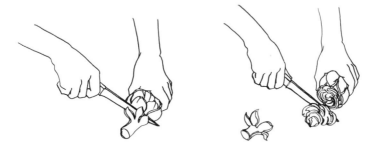

Using a pair of kitchen scissors, cut off the sharp tips of all the leaves about ¹/₂ inch down.

Using a melon ball scoop, hollow out the fuzzy choke in the center, taking care to remove all of it. Turn the artichoke upside down and press down to open up the center to facilitate stuffing. Turn right side up and stuff as desired.

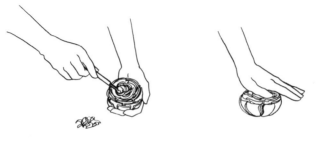

3. Add coriander or parsley, thyme, bread crumbs, Tabasco, and salt and pepper. Blend well.

4. Stuff each artichoke in its hollowed-out cavity and between the leaves, pushing the stuffing down into the bottom.

5. In a flameproof casserole or baking dish large enough to hold the artichokes upright in one layer, scatter the remaining onions on the bottom. Place the artichokes in the dish, bottoms down. Add the bay leaf, broken into small pieces, and dribble the olive oil over the artichokes. Add the vinegar and pour the chicken broth around them. Sprinkle with salt and pepper, bring to a boil on top of the stove and cover tightly with aluminum foil. Place in the oven and bake for 1 hour. Serve lukewarm or cold, with juices spooned around them.

Yield: 4 servings

Artichokes Vinaigrette

4 artichokes, about ³/₄ pound each, prepared for poaching (see instructions on page 243)
salt to taste
1 tablespoon imported mustard, preferably Dijon style

1 teaspoon chopped garlic
2 tablespoons red wine vinegar
freshly ground pepper to taste
³/₄ cup olive oil
2 tablespoons finely chopped fresh herbs, such as parsley or chives

1. Place the prepared artichokes in a large pot and cover with cold water. Add salt. Lay a clean cloth over the artichokes to prevent them from floating. Cover and bring to a boil. Simmer 45 minutes or until tender. Do not overcook. Drain well and let stand until ready to serve.

2. Put the mustard, garlic, vinegar, salt and pepper in a small mixing bowl. Beat vigorously with a wire whisk. Gradually add the oil, beating constantly. Add the herbs.

3. Serve artichokes with sauce on the side.

Yield: 4 servings

To Prepare Artichokes for Poaching

Cut the stems off the bases of the artichokes, leaving the bottoms flat so they can stand upright. Remove any tough outer leaves from the bottoms of the artichoke.

Using kitchen shears, work around the artichoke from top to bottom, trimming about $^1/_2$ inch from the top of each leaf to remove the sharp tips. Lay each artichoke on its side and chop off 1 inch from the top.

Place a thick lemon slice under each artichoke bottom. Tie the lemon to the artichoke with kitchen string. This preserves the artichoke color when cooking.

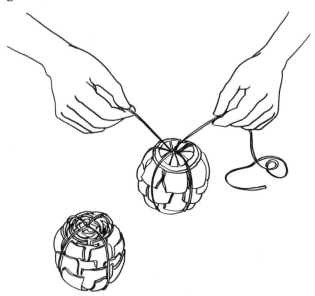

America's Bird

We showed up in the Shenandoah Valley on July 3 to learn a thing or two about the source of American turkeys and we stayed through the Fourth—this was by design, of course. After all, had things just been a little different, it's the turkey that might well have been designated America's official bird. Ben Franklin hoped so and was deeply disappointed when the bald eagle, whose "bad moral character" he deplored, was chosen instead.

Even though the turkey lost out to the eagle, in a strange way, it is fast becoming America's bird now, anyway. The turkey's great and growing popularity (consumption soared from 9.9 pounds per capita in 1979 to 16.2 pounds in 1989) has to do with nutrition and the growing health consciousness of the country. Turkey can be low in fat and calories and now widely available in options consumers didn't have just a few years ago.

No longer are we limited to buying a whole turkey suitable mostly for big gatherings at holiday time; these days turkey parts are common in every supermarket in the country: the breast, the legs and wings, and slices of turkey sold in various ways. (One of the most interesting is the "tenderloin," which is the very tender strip of meat that adheres loosely to the back of the breast. It's just like the more familiar little piece of meat beneath a chicken breast, but the turkey's is larger, of course, and thus more useful.)

Turkey production is now a year-round business on a huge scale. The facilities we visited in Virginia were operated under the auspices of Rocco, Inc., whose Shady Brook Farms label is the umbrella that covers all the independent farmers who supply it. To give you an idea of the volume handled by this, the fourth largest producer in the country, Shady Brook Farms' plant in Dayton, Virginia, processed more than 250 million pounds of turkey in a single recent year.

When we went to visit one of the hatcheries, what we saw was a place obsessed with "biosecurity," which sounds like a C.I.A. term, but actually refers to the steps taken as the consequence of a tremendous dread of any contamination. I had to wear a plastic body suit, plastic booties and a hairnet to pass through the place. We saw the eggs as they were slowly rotated in their incubators, to keep the embryo from adhering to the side of the shell, and saw the hatchlings as they fought their way out of the shell, creating a din in their excitement as they viewed the world for the first time.

Then we watched one of the most peculiar of all the procedures we'd seen in traveling through the country: The birds have to be sexed to separate the toms from the hens. Since birds don't have external, visible sex organs or any obvious defining sexual characteristics at such a young age, their sex is quite a mystery.

Among the only people who seem to have it solved is a contingent of highly trained Asians, who've evidently been raised to work in their trade just as a carpenter might be—or a French chef, for that matter. So the first place that the chicks—they're called poults, actually—are taken is to a group of these experts who quickly determine with exquisitely sensitive, fast-moving hands whether a particular poult is male or female. The turkey growers say that even when an untrained person is shown what to look for that person still won't have the sensitivity to be correct with any regularity. The highly paid sexers—we were told they earn up to $60,000 or $70,000 a year if they're really fast—examine up to a thousand birds an hour.

Another fascinating aspect of the visit was our ride out to one of the Shady Brook ranges, where some 13,000 toms were allowed to roam free in an area of hills, woods and meadows. As we first drove toward one group of 6,000, they looked more like sheep grazing in the distance, all white and clustered together (domestic turkeys are bred to be white so that their skin is not discolored by the pigment of the feathers). We passed them by and reached another group, 7,000 of them. Most were wandering among trees to avoid the midday sun, and it was a very strange sight: a bunch of turkeys strolling in the woods as if it were a park.

They turned out to be an inquisitive group, eager to get closer to us, but scattering when they got nervous. A moment of excitement would be expressed as a wave of gobbling, starting somewhere in the flock, then gathering in volume as every bird joined in so that it sounded like nothing so much as an audience laughing. Individually, they didn't necessarily gobble, but had a range of strange sounds, some seeming to cough, others to hiccup and still others seemed to be barking.

They were a tame bunch, as you might imagine, because they were so accustomed to people. I picked one up and gave it a little kiss (I'm tempted to say peck). It was heavy. These birds, which weigh just over $1/10$th of a pound at birth, are already approaching 30 pounds by the time they are 20 weeks old. (Which leads to another oddity of domestication; the toms are too big to naturally inseminate a hen, and procreation is done exclusively through artificial insemination.)

Only a fraction of Shady Brook's turkeys are allowed the freedom of the range as these were. The company has found no economic advantage (although it's been studied) in identifying for the consumer just which of its turkeys those might be. That's too bad, from my point of view, since free-range birds, I believe, taste better than the others. In any case, I do like turkey, free range or not.

A restaurant we visited in Charlottesville, Va., was the Silver Thatch Inn, a lovely place with one section that was constructed in 1780 by Hessian soldiers taken prisoner during the Revolutionary War. As utterly American as that may be, the chef, Janet Henry, is a talented woman whose influences come from all over the world. She grew up in Kentucky, but traveled widely in the Far East and in many other places, too, notably Mexico. That's why some of the dishes she cooks have a distinctly Japanese touch and others might seem Mexican. What she prepared for us was an ingenious rolled turkey and ham that was stuffed with what she called an ancho chili pudding. It was an extraordinary success: Virginia turkey and corn with a Tex-Mex accent on a beautiful July Fourth.

The Big Giveaway

Ever wondered why turkey is so inexpensive around Thanksgiving? If you thought that it was because the suppliers were glutting the market with cheap birds, you're wrong. What happens is that the markets know that consumers intend to buy turkeys— whole birds primarily—in great number. And every year there is a price war. They want you to come to their store not just to buy the turkey but also all those other things you plan to purchase for the big dinner. As a result they pay full price, or something like it, for the turkey and then take a loss on it—a loss leader, merchants call it—to woo you. The only question is how much of a loss is one store willing to take. Some sell the bird for, say, 29 cents a pound; others just give it away if you buy enough of the other food there on a given day. In other words, turkey at Thanksgiving is a wonderful bargain thanks to that good old competitive spirit.

But it is too bad that the only way you can buy more than one fresh turkey and keep it on hand for later is to freeze it. Some of the turkey industry contends that freezing turkey does it little or no harm. But I think freezing robs it of some moisture; the meat cells rupture during freezing and lose their liquid. That probably matters less, of course, if you intend to grind the turkey or use it in a soup.

My own favorite part of the turkey is the breast, cut into steaks or cutlets or roasted whole. It used to be that the breast without the rest of the bird was regarded as a restaurant commodity and not something for home consumption. Nowadays, of course, turkey breasts are extremely popular everywhere. Most of the recipes here reflect my preference for breast meat. But I also feel that turkey is useful when it is ground as in a meat loaf or lasagne. In many of its uses, it is likely to supply fewer calories than other meats that offer anything near the same level of eating satisfaction.

When Janet Henry prepared this rolled turkey for us, she was ad-libbing, but like all good cooks who try something new, she already knew just what she was doing and what would work. The corn pudding had been on the menu that week anyway, not as a stuffing but as a side dish. Now all she had to do was wrap a tender bit of turkey and a slice of ham around it and give it an appropriate sauce—a tomato relish seemed about right. And indeed it was. The whole invention was simple to prepare and unusual enough to make it the kind of dish we would talk about for some time later.

Silver Thatch Inn Rolled Turkey and Corn

4 fresh turkey tenderloins, about 1 pound in all
8 very thin slices country ham, about ¹/₂ pound in all
Corn and Ancho Chili Pudding (recipe follows)

2 tablespoons olive oil
freshly ground pepper to taste
Tomato Relish (page 253)
blue corn tortilla chips for garnish

1. Preheat oven to 350°.

2. Place each tenderloin between 2 sheets of plastic wrap and pound gently until thin, less than ¹/₄ inch thick. Trim the tendon away and cut the tenderloin in half lengthwise.

3. Trim away any fat on the ham slices and place a slice on each of the tenderloin halves. Spread about 3 tablespoons of the corn and chili pudding evenly over each of the turkey and ham pieces and then roll them neatly, securing the rolls with toothpicks.

4. Heat the oil in a sauté pan large enough to hold all the rolls in one layer. Sprinkle the rolls with pepper and sauté them until they are brown.

5. Transfer the rolls to a baking dish and bake in the oven for 20 minutes. Slice the rolls in half diagonally and remove the toothpicks. Serve with the tomato salsa and garnish with the tortilla chips.

Yield: 4 servings

Corn and Ancho Chili Pudding

5 cups fresh corn kernels
4 tablespoons butter, melted
1 teaspoon baking powder
$1/2$ cup whipping cream
3 dried ancho chilis, ground to a
    powder in a spice grinder or food
    processor

$1/2$ teaspoon freshly ground pepper
$1/4$ teaspoon cayenne
1 teaspoon sugar

1. Preheat oven to 350°.

2. Process all the ingredients in the container of a food processor until well blended; the corn should remain chunky.

3. Pour the mixture into a buttered 8-inch baking dish and bake for 25 minutes. Allow to cool.

Yield: 6 cups

Note: This produces more than is needed for the turkey rolls; save the remainder to use as a side dish another day.

Tomato Relish

4 ripe tomatoes, seeded and diced
$1/4$ cup chopped fresh coriander
1 small red onion, chopped (about
    $1/2$ cup)

$1/4$ teaspoon hot red pepper flakes
freshly ground black pepper to taste

Mix all the ingredients in a bowl. Serve at room temperature.

Yield: about 2 cups

Here's a somewhat simpler recipe capitalizing on the partnership of corn and turkey.

Turkey Steaks with Fresh Corn and Basil

4 turkey breast steaks, about $^1/_3$
  pound each

salt and freshly ground pepper to
  taste

$^1/_4$ cup flour

2 tablespoons olive oil

2 tablespoons finely chopped
  shallots

2 tablespoons red wine vinegar

1 cup peeled and seeded plum
  tomatoes, cut into $^1/_4$-inch cubes

3 ears fresh corn, kernels removed,
  about $1^1/_2$cups

$^1/_3$ cup fresh or canned chicken
  broth

4 tablespoons heavy cream

1 teaspoon Dijon-style mustard

4 tablespoons coarsely chopped
  basil leaves

1. Cover the turkey with plastic wrap and pound it lightly. Sprinkle both sides with salt and pepper and dredege in flour. Remove the excess flour.

2. Heat the oil in a heavy nonstick skillet large enough to hold the steaks in one layer. When it is hot, add the turkey, brown lightly on both sides and cook for about 5 minutes. Transfer to a serving platter, cover with foil and keep warm.

3. Add the shallots to the skillet and cook briefly, stirring. Do not brown. Add the vinegar, cook and stir. Add the tomatoes, corn, chicken broth and any liquid accumulated around the meat. Over high heat, bring to a boil and cook, stirring, for about 2 minutes.

4. Add the cream and mustard. Stir to blend. Add salt and pepper, and cook for 30 seconds. Add the basil and pour the sauce over the turkey. Serve with Sautéed Spinach Leaves (page 369).

Yield: 4 servings

Turkey these days is often used as a beef substitute. Ground, its texture is so similar to that of chopped beef that it turns out to be an extremely useful ingredient in dishes like lasagne, as you'll see if you give this one a try.

Lasagne with Turkey and Tomato Sauce

Tomato Sauce

2¹/₂ pounds ripe plum tomatoes or 4 cups imported crushed tomatoes

1 tablespoon olive oil

2 tablespoons finely chopped garlic

¹/₈ teaspoon hot red pepper flakes

1 teaspoon chopped fresh oregano or 1 teaspoon dried

salt and freshly ground pepper to taste

1. Remove the cores from the tomatoes, cut the tomatoes into 1-inch cubes and put in the container of a food processor. Process until coarsely chopped. There should be about 4 cups.

2. Heat the olive oil in a skillet and add the garlic. Cook briefly, but do not brown. Add the tomatoes, hot pepper flakes, oregano and salt and pepper to taste. Bring to a boil and simmer for 10 minutes.

Yield: about 4 cups

The Lasagne

2 tablespoons olive oil

2 pounds freshly ground turkey meat

1 teaspoon finely chopped garlic

¹/₂ cup dry red wine

3 cups Tomato Sauce (recipe above)

salt and freshly ground pepper to taste

12 lasagne noodles

2 cups ricotta cheese

¹/₄ cup hot water

¹/₂ cup freshly grated Parmesan cheese

2 tablespoons butter, melted

1. Preheat oven to 400°.

2. Heat the olive oil in a nonstick skillet and add the turkey meat. Cook, stirring to break up the meat, until lightly browned. Add the garlic, stir and add the wine. Bring to a boil over high heat and cook until the wine is evaporated. Add the tomato sauce, and salt and pepper. Bring to a boil and simmer for 5 minutes.

3. Meanwhile, bring a large quantity of salted water to a boil. Add the lasagne noodles, one at a time. Cook until tender. Cooking times will vary according to brand. To cool, add 2 cups ice water with a few drops of olive oil mixed in. Drain and spread the noodles, one at a time, on a damp cloth.

4. Lightly grease a 2-quart oblong baking dish. Cover the bottom with a layer of the lasagne noodles.

5. Beat the ricotta with the water to make it spreadable. Spread about $^1/_3$ of the ricotta over the lasagne. Spread a layer of sauce over the ricotta and sprinkle about $^1/_4$ of the Parmesan over it.

6. Continue making layers with the remaining ingredients, but end with a layer of lasagne. Sprinkle with the remaining Parmesan. Drizzle the melted butter over all and bake for 15 minutes or until the lasagne is piping hot and bubbling.

Yield: 4 to 6 servings

A big problem in roasting a whole turkey is in getting all the parts to finish properly, that is, the legs and thighs fully cooked without drying out the breast at the same time. A perfect way to avoid that problem is to do the breast alone. I've described this as breast "with ribs" to indicate that it is similar to the whole turkey, missing only the dark meat sections. Also, I want to distinguish it from the breast steaks and slices that are used in several of the following recipes.

Roast Turkey Breast (with Ribs)

1 fresh turkey breast with ribs, about 4 pounds

1 tablespoon fresh lemon juice

salt and freshly ground pepper to taste

1 tablespoon corn or vegetable oil

2 bay leaves

4 sprigs fresh thyme or 1 teaspoon dried

4 cloves garlic, unpeeled

1 large onion studded with 2 cloves

$1/4$ cup diced carrots

$1/4$ cup diced celery

$1/2$ cup dry white wine

$1^1/2$ cups fresh or canned chicken broth

1. Preheat oven to 450°.

2. Sprinkle the turkey breast inside and out with lemon juice and salt and pepper and spread the oil over the top. Place the breast cavity down in a heavy roasting pan and spread the bay leaves, thyme, garlic, onion with cloves, carrots and celery around it. Place in the oven, cover with foil and bake for 30 minutes.

3. Reduce the heat to 425°. Remove the foil and continue roasting for 15 minutes, basting. Remove the turkey breast from the roasting pan and pour off most of the fat. Return the breast to the pan, skin side up, and pour the wine and broth around it. Continue roasting for 10 minutes, basting occasionally. Remove from the oven and cover with foil. Let stand in warm place for 10 or 15 minutes before carving. Carve and serve with the pan gravy.

Yield: 6 to 8 servings

❧ When we discuss turkey today it is often to praise its incredible adaptability. Here, as a scallopine with prosciutto and cheese, it shows up in a recipe that I don't believe very many people could have imagined just a few years ago.

Turkey Breast Scallopine à la Bolognese

4 slices turkey breast, about $^1/_4$ pound each

salt and freshly ground pepper to taste

flour for dredging

2 tablespoons butter

2 tablespoons olive oil

6 tablespoons Marsala

4 thin slices prosciutto

4 thin slices Fontina or Gruyère cheese

1. Preheat broiler to high.

2. Cover each turkey slice with plastic wrap and pound it lightly with a meat pounder, but do not break the fibers. Sprinkle both sides with salt and pepper and dredge all over in a little flour.

3. Heat the butter and olive oil in a heavy nonstick skillet large enough to hold the turkey in one layer. When it is very hot, add the turkey. Brown quickly over high heat on both sides and transfer to a hot serving platter. Keep warm.

4. Add the Marsala to the skillet and cook, stirring, over high heat until the wine becomes syrupy. Spoon this over the scallopine. Top each slice of turkey with a slice of prosciutto and a slice of cheese and run quickly under the broiler until the cheese melts. Serve immediately.

Yield: 4 servings

If turkey has a drawback in the minds of some people, it is its tendency toward blandness. A full-flavored sauce will take care of that problem very well, as is the case in the following two recipes. The first uses mustard and capers. The second uses mustard seed, tomatoes and an ample helping of herbs.

Sliced Turkey Breast with Mustard Sauce

8 slices turkey breast, about 1¹/₂
   pounds in all
¹/₃ cup flour
salt and freshly ground white
   pepper to taste
2 tablespoons butter
¹/₂ pound mushrooms, thinly sliced

2 tablespoons finely minced shallots
¹/₃ cup dry white wine
¹/₄ cup drained capers
¹/₂ cup heavy cream
1 tablespoon very good Dijon
   mustard

1. Place the sliced turkey on a flat surface and pound lightly with a meat pounder or flat mallet until the slices are about ¹/₄ inch thick.

2. Season the flour with salt and pepper to taste and dredge the slices on all sides. Shake off the excess.

3. Heat 1 tablespoon of the butter in a nonstick skillet and add enough slices to cover the bottom of the skillet without crowding. Cook over medium-high heat until golden brown on one side, about 2 or 3 minutes. Turn. Cook until golden brown on the second side, about 2 minutes. Transfer to a warm serving dish. Add the remaining tablespoon of butter to the skillet and repeat with the second batch of turkey slices. Transfer the slices to a serving dish and cover with foil. Keep warm.

4. To the same skillet add the mushrooms and salt and pepper to taste and shake the skillet. Cook for about 3 minutes. Add the shallots, and cook briefly, stirring. Add the wine and cook, stirring, until it is almost evaporated. Add the capers, cream and mustard. Blend well. Bring to a simmer. Cook, stirring, for about 1 minute. Add the juices that may have accumulated around the sliced turkey. Mix the sauce well and pour it over the turkey. Serve very hot.

Yield: 4 servings

Chunks of turkey breast in a soup give it a lot of character and make for a fine variation on chicken soup. The preparation of this version is made easier by the fact that turkey parts can be purchased in so many different ways these days. Here, as the ingredients specify, all you want is a piece of boneless turkey breast weighing about 1 pound, and I've had no difficulty finding exactly that in the local supermarket.

Vegetable Soup with Turkey and Coriander

2 tablespoons butter

1 tablespoon curry powder (optional)

1 cup chopped onions

4 leeks, about 1 pound, cleaned and cut into $^1/_4$-inch cubes (about 3 cups)

3 carrots, about $^1/_2$ pound, cut into $^1/_4$-inch cubes (about $1^1/_2$ cups)

1 parsnip, about $^1/_4$ pound, cut into $^1/_4$-inch cubes (about 1 cup)

3 potatoes, about 1 pound, cut into $^1/_4$-inch cubes (about 2 cups)

salt and freshly ground pepper to taste

4 cups fresh or canned chicken broth

4 cups water

1 pound skinless boneless turkey breast, cut into $^1/_2$-inch cubes

3 tablespoons chopped fresh coriander

1. Melt the butter in a saucepan. Add the curry powder, onions, leeks, carrots, parsnip and potatoes. Cook, stirring, until the vegetables are wilted, about 5 minutes. Add salt and pepper to taste, the chicken broth and the water. Bring to a boil and simmer for 30 minutes.

2. Add the turkey breast cubes and cook for 10 minutes. Garnish each serving with chopped fresh coriander.

Yield: 8 servings

Salmon Splendor

KETCHIKAN, ALASKA

In the summertime there may be no place in America more exhilaratingly chaotic than Ketchikan, Alaska. In the warm weather, in this small city—with just 13,000 in permanent population—the pulse quickens until the whole place is one adrenaline rush of fishermen, tourists and the industries that serve both. Ketchikan sits on a rough, hilly island. It is not accessible by road, only by ferry, private boat and airplane. The fishing season is so frantic because it is short, May to October, and extraordinarily productive. In less than half a year, Alaska can produce 600 million pounds of spectacular salmon, far outdistancing any other state and, in fact, any competing country.

Ketchikan is one of Alaska's most active fishing centers. College students rush up here from the Lower 48 to join in the harvest. Some of them work on the boats where they usually take home a percentage of the total income, others work in processing plants making $6 to $8 an hour or more. These kids can earn as much as $10,000 in a summer. But the labor is hard, and the unsavory possibility of landing a job on a boat with an excessively tough captain cannot be overlooked (one captain with a crew of five ran through 27 different deckhands in a single summer).

Some of the tourists are here for the salmon, too, but for them the catch, fish and otherwise, can be much more varied than that. Ketchikan is situated in the Tongass National Forest, the largest of all the national forests—500 miles long—and the little city is surrounded by a treasure of northern wilderness, at sea, on land and on ice.

On any given day, the harbor looks like this: Cruise ships drop anchor in the bay right where the fishing boats glide in to pick up their provisions and the crushed ice for their holds. Seaplanes roar up and down, carrying tourists off to see the glaciers. Sports fishermen in charter boats speed out to schools of salmon. Ferries transport people from an airport on an island just off the city's downtown area (there wasn't enough flat land to build one anywhere else). And in the middle of all this activity—in the middle of the cruise ships and ferries, the charter boats, the seaplanes and the commercial fishing fleet—there's bound to be somebody in a kayak, paddling for his life.

The kayak, incidentally, has the right of way.

The city is a blend of factory town and tourist village, with the usual stores selling the usual trinkets. All summer long the processing plants are humming, some canning the salmon, others freezing it, still others smoking it. (As much fresh salmon as can be accommodated by the departing planes is flown out of Ketchikan, too.) Everywhere, you see touches of the different cultures and the different pursuits that have brought such vigorous life to this place. On the main street, there sit two bars next to each other, one called Totem—evoking, of course, the Indian heritage that is still so strong here—the other, suggesting the nautical, called Fo'c's'le. The most colorful part of the city's story may well be Creek Street, so named because it overlooks a rushing stream. At least Creek Street is what people talk about all the time. From the early part of this century into the 1950's it was the red light district. A joke around here is that Ketchikan is where both salmon and men came to spawn.

Anyway, now Creek Street is demure, with respectable shops and apartments and the like.

Somewhere, deep in the National Forest, the fish still have their spawning grounds, untouched and fertile. Even in that stream below Creek Street you can sometimes see the salmon doing what they do: leaping against the current with tremendous energy to return to their birthplace, deposit their eggs and then die. A glance at a map clarifies the big picture. From the Pacific vastness, the sea breaks into bays that are fed by rivers and streams radiating inland like fingers away from the ocean. As the Pacific salmon travel in huge schools toward their final destination, the fishermen try to cut them off before they get into the streams where they will gradually weaken. (The fish in the streams rarely eat and wither and shrivel as they use up their stores of fat.)

The role of the government is to set limits on the number of hours the fishermen can work so that both the fish and the fishermen can flourish. So far the management has been stunningly successful, to judge from the results: bumper harvests in recent years. The regulations are abetted by the many fish hatcheries around Alaska that release salmon into the wild.

Our reason for being here was to witness the fishing and processing firsthand. On the first day we engaged in something like a practice run, heading out to sea to gather Dungeness crabs (another of Alaska's many seafood bonanzas that also include halibut, pollock, cod and shrimp—all of them in staggering quantities). Our guides to the crabbing grounds were the same two charter captains who would navigate the choppy, rocky-bottomed waters to join the salmon fishing boats the next day. Larry Settje, 32 years old with reddish hair and a relatively reserved manner, was the skipper of *Misty Lady*. He'd grown up in Ketchikan and works as a construction contractor when he isn't on his boat. He'd also flown over the area often and knew it by heart. His best friend, Leif Stenford, dark haired and more outgoing, also 32, was our other captain and just as expert in the thrills and perils of the area.

As we raced out of the harbor toward the Dungeness crabs, rain threatened, just

as it did most of the time we were in Ketchikan, an area that gets 13 feet of rain a year. (Repeat: That's 13 feet!) We were heading toward Smugglers Cove, which earned its name when it served as a stopping off place for booze runners during Prohibition. It was our destination now because Leif and Larry had talked to friends who said the crabbing had been good there just a couple of days before. If you know where to look, Leif said, Dungeness crabs aren't that hard to trap. They're indiscriminate gluttons. "They'll eat leftover steak or herring, or Kentucky Fried Chicken—barbecued is best. For some reason, one thing they don't like much is the extra crispy."

The two power boats blasted their way through the chop in the water. In minutes, civilization was left behind and our only companions were the green, mountainous islands, some of them capped with snow; we were in the purest wilderness. The clouds hovered over the mountaintops, seeming to rise from them, as if the mountains were on fire. Eagles wheeled overhead. It wasn't a trip for amateur boatmen. These dark waters required expert guides, like the ones we were fortunate enough to have. When we arrived at Smugglers Cove, the early information proved correct. We pulled up traps that turned out to be inhabited, sure enough, by the big and meaty Dungeness. Gloves were necessary during this job: The impressive crabs, possessed of impressive claws, like to reach for the fingers of their captors, as they did for mine.

The next day we raced out into the waters again for one of the most breathtaking experiences we were to have all summer long in our journeys through America. As we started out, it was 52 degrees, and the weatherman had described the waters as calm. The salmon fishermen we planned to meet were working behind an island that could be reached either by a short course through some open Pacific waters or by a route that would take an hour longer but was far more tranquil, through sheltered seas. It was evident early on that the weatherman's information was not correct. The water was decidedly rough.

That chop was still no threat, but it was a clue. It could mean that the open sea might have swells as high as 10 feet, Larry told us. He explained that it wasn't their height that was the problem so much as the way the underwater terrain forced the swells to build and roll rapidly, one chasing after the other, so that a boat couldn't recover before it was hit again. He remembered the day he was out there in not 10- but 15-foot swells, and all he could see through his window was a green wall washing over the boat. The craft somehow defied nature and logic and stayed afloat. But he won't—can't—forget it.

Now Larry reconnoitered a bit. In addition to the immediate chop in the water, he saw whitecaps in the distance. "When there are whitecaps out there," he said, "it's really smoking on the other side." We took the longer route, of course.

As we approached the fishing boats—58-footers deploying nets called purse seines—we knew the fishermen there had located big schools of salmon. An occasional salmon could actually be seen jumping, acrobatic evidence of many more below. This was the beginning of July and the pinks were running in full force in the waters off this part of Alaska. Pinks are small salmon used predominantly in canning, and the fishermen need to bring in a great many to make much money on them. (More profitable are the "money fish": the king salmon, which can grow to a monstrous 120 pounds and is highly coveted, as well as the coho and sockeye.)

The seining boat we joined was the *Nikki Lee,* with its weary captain, 36-year-old Don Newman. He'd been out in this same spot just off the barren island since 2 A.M.; and he would fish there more or less constantly from 6 A.M. till 9 P.M. When we boarded the ship he was temporarily idle, waiting his turn to drop net again. The nature of seining forces the boats to take turns when there are several in an area. The big seine net is dropped very rapidly into the water from the back of the boat. Then the net is held taut at the other end against the current by a small, powerful (200-horsepower) skiff. The effect is to create a wall that prevents a school of salmon from passing. When there are more than a couple of boats in 'the same waters, one boat may find itself cutting off the flow of fish so completely that a nearby crew will catch almost nothing.

In purse seining the outstretched net is pulled back in through an agonizingly slow dance between the mother boat and the skiff. The little skiff's engine bellows as it labors to haul the net toward the boat while the boat moves toward it, forming a circle. (A deckhand with a long tool that looks something like a bathroom plunger strikes the water to create sufficient commotion to keep the fish down and in place as the net encircles them; this job was entrusted to me for a while.) As the circle is tightened, the net is hauled up and toward the boat, forming a sack, or purse. This purse, as we watched, captured thousands of salmon in a single effort. Unloaded, the fish filled the deck wall to wall until the crew nudged them into a hold full of seawater chilled to 31 degrees to keep them fresh.

The deckhands aboard the *Nikki Lee* were typical of the young people we saw working all over Ketchikan. Four of the five men were already college graduates. Dean Vincent, 23 years old, teaches third grade in Ketchikan when the summer is over. Tim Cunningham, also 23, was going back to graduate school to study the fishery business. They were all bright and well spoken, motivated and in love with the work.

On land, where we visited the Phillips Cold Storage Company, salmon were being cleaned and flash-frozen by a corps of congenial, fast-working youngsters.

They were chatting and laughing, with music blaring. Some of them worked on the "slime line"—it's really called that—cleaning fish, while others pushed trays of the cleaned salmon into zero-degree walk-in freezers.

The next step is to take the hard-frozen fish and glaze them with ice. The glazing is part of a broad effort to maintain the Alaskan salmon at the highest possible level of quality. The glaze, a thin film of ice encasing the whole fish, acts as a coat of armor preventing dehydration and freezer burn. It's accomplished by dropping the fish into a stream of water that instantly freezes when it makes contact with the deep-chilled bodies. (As they float along in this glazing stream, it's the strangest sight: headless salmon still swimming, it seems, upstream.)

The freezing business is big here, just as canning and smoking are, because the short season means that only a certain amount of the large harvest will get out fresh. Then the rest of the salmon must be prepared for sale during the remainder of the year, one way or the other.

But those aren't the only ways to preserve Alaska salmon for the wintertime. To learn more about the smoking of salmon and some of the more exotic salmon preparations, we visited the pleasant Norwegian-style home of Fran Hamilton, on a hillside overlooking the harbor. Mrs. Hamilton is a smartly dressed modern woman blessed with a rich heritage. She is a Tlingit Indian of the clan Bear Under the Eagle. The Tlingits are the second largest native group in Alaska (Eskimos are the first), and they were fishing here thousands of years before Europeans made landfall.

The day we arrived Mrs. Hamilton, her 92-year-old mother, Emma Williams, and her daughter Patsy Mitchell were all there to show us to the backyard where their smoker held chunks of salmon. Mrs. Hamilton also brought out containers of dried salmon, along with salmon that was both dried and salted and salmon preserved in a variety of other ways.

It was delightful to be able to sit there at the picnic table, talking to the eldest of the family, Emma Williams, who took pains to tell me just how she prepared her charbroiled salmon. She would marinate it first, she said, in layers of seaweed, brown sugar, soy sauce, fresh lemon, garlic, onion powder and a bit of white wine. Then grill it.

It would be hard to get me to appreciate salmon any more than I already do. Witness the fact that this book presents salmon recipes in many of its chapters in addition to this one, but I must say that for days after leaving Alaska I was still craving more of it.

Clear Thinking

There's a good deal of confusion these
days about salmon. A salmon steak
bought in the fish store might be fresh from
the wild, fresh from the farm, frozen and
thawed or still frozen. The virtue of each of
these states is widely debated. Restaurant chefs
often prefer farmed salmon because its quality
tends to be consistent and it is available year round.
But critics of fish-farming point to the chemicals
used in the production of the fish (among other
things they are fed artificial dye to make their
flesh pink because their diet doesn't create the color
as it would in the wild). Also, there is the potential
for water pollution in ill-managed farms.

Some people say the wild salmon will taste better
than the farmed and it is much valued because of that, while others can
discern no difference. And what about frozen salmon? Freezing the fish
may tend to diminish its quality, as freezing does with many other foods.
But if freshness is paramount—and it is—modern freezing methods are
more apt to deliver a fresher-tasting fish than a fishmonger who has kept his
"fresh" salmon around too long.

So the best advice to the consumer is not to put too much stock in any one
assertion about the quality of salmon. If it is in good condition, fresh or
thawed salmon will have no fishy odor and it will be firm. If it is frozen, be
sure that it is frozen solid.

❧ Steaming is among the purest ways of preparing salmon, leaving the fish tasting entirely of itself. That sense of naturalness is only enhanced by an herb-enriched, light dressing.

Steamed Salmon Fillets with Green Vinaigrette

$^1/_3$ cup chopped fresh herbs, such as chervil, parsley or coriander

$^1/_3$ cup coarsely chopped scallions, including greens

4 tablespoons coarsely chopped chives

1 tablespoon chopped fresh tarragon

1 teaspoon minced garlic

6 tablespoons olive oil

2 tablespoons wine vinegar

1 tablespoon Dijon mustard

salt and freshly ground pepper to taste

1 hard-cooked egg, quartered

4 skinless boneless salmon fillets, about 6 ounces each

24 large basil leaves

1. Combine the herb of your choice with the scallions, chives, tarragon, garlic, oil, vinegar, mustard and salt and pepper to taste in the container of a food processor or blender. Blend until the herbs are finely chopped. Do not overblend. The ingredients should retain some texture.

2. Add the quartered egg and blend it in coarsely.

3. Pour water into the bottom of a steamer. Season the fillets with salt and pepper and place them on a steamer rack. Lay 4 basil leaves over each, cover the steamer and bring the water to a boil. Steam for 3 or 4 minutes. Do not overcook. This dish should be served cold or at room temperature.

4. Transfer the fish fillets to a serving plate and spoon some of the vinaigrette over them. Garnish with remaining fresh basil leaves and pass the remaining sauce separately.

Yield: 4 servings

**This recipe shows how adaptable salmon is. Here it is completely transformed, presented in a dish that is rich and elegant. Note that the ingredients should be cold.**

Salmon Yogurt Mousse with Champagne Sauce

1 pound very cold skinless boneless
    salmon fillets, cut into 1-inch
    cubes, the bones reserved for
    making the sauce
salt and freshly ground white
    pepper to taste
1/8 teaspoon freshly grated nutmeg
dash of Tabasco to taste

1 egg
3/4 cup plain yogurt, drained and
    cold
3/4 cup cold half-and-half
1 teaspoon soft butter
2 1/2 cups Champagne Sauce (recipe
    follows)

1. Preheat oven to 400°.

2. Place the cubed salmon in the container of a food processor. Season with salt and pepper, nutmeg and Tabasco. Add the egg and blend for 10 seconds. Continue blending while adding the yogurt mixed together with the half-and-half. Blend for about 30 seconds or until the mixture has a fine texture.

3. Butter the insides of four 1 1/2-cup soufflé dishes. Chill them in the refrigerator. Spoon equal portions of the mixture into the soufflé dishes. Smooth over the top and cover loosely with aluminum foil.

4. Place the dishes in a high-sided heatproof metal pan and pour hot water into the pan to come halfway up the sides of the dishes. Place the pan on top of the stove and bring the water to a boil. Transfer the pan to the bottom rack of the oven and bake for 20 minutes.

5. Test for doneness by inserting an instant thermometer into the mousse. If the thermometer registers 140° or if the end comes out clean, the mousse is done. Unmold the soufflés onto a warm plate and serve with the sauce.

Yield: 4 servings

Champagne Sauce

reserved bones from the salmon
  fillets
2 cups Champagne
$^1/_3$ cup water
1 clove garlic, peeled
1 bay leaf
2 sprigs parsley
4 tablespoons sliced shallots

salt to taste
6 peppercorns
4 tablespoons butter
2 tablespoons flour
$^1/_4$ teaspoon cayenne
1 cup heavy cream
2 teaspoons fresh lemon juice

1. Place the fish bones in a small saucepan. Add the Champagne, water, garlic, bay leaf, parsley, shallots, salt and peppercorns. Bring to a boil and simmer for 20 minutes, until the liquid is reduced to $1^1/_2$ cups. Strain.

2. Melt 2 tablespoons of the butter in a saucepan and, using a wire whisk, stir in the flour. Add all the stock from the saucepan, stirring vigorously, until the mixture is thickened and smooth. Add the cayenne. Simmer over low heat, stirring occasionally, for 15 minutes.

3. Stir in the cream. Bring the sauce to a simmer and add the remaining butter and the lemon juice. Stir briefly and serve with the mousse.

Yield: $2^1/_2$ cups

✿ *Alaska isn't far from Russia, so it isn't surprising that my mind turned to a Russian dish when I was thinking about Alaskan salmon. There was once a tavern owner in the Russian town of Torjok, between Moscow and St. Petersburg, named Pojarski. His specialty was ground meat dishes and a number of them carry his name to this day. But these patties are made of salmon, and they are meant to emulate his approach.*

Salmon Cakes Pojarski

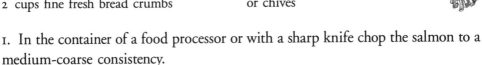

1 1/2 pounds very cold skinless
    boneless fresh salmon fillets
salt and freshly ground white
    pepper to taste
1/4 teaspoon freshly grated nutmeg
1/4 teaspoon cayenne, or to taste
2 cups fine fresh bread crumbs

3/4 cup drained plain yogurt
3/4 cup cold heavy cream
2 tablespoons vegetable oil
6 tablespoons butter
2 tablespoons fresh lemon juice
4 tablespoons chopped fresh chervil
    or chives

1. In the container of a food processor or with a sharp knife chop the salmon to a medium-coarse consistency.

2. Place the salmon in a cold bowl, season with salt and pepper, nutmeg and cayenne and blend well with a wooden spatula. Add 3/4 cup of the bread crumbs and blend.

3. Combine the yogurt and the cream with a wire whisk. Pour the cream mixture into the bowl, a little at a time, beating vigorously, until all of it is absorbed.

4. Divide the mixture into 12 equal portions and shape into patties about 3/4 inch thick. Smooth the tops over with the spatula. Dredge the patties lightly in the remaining 1 1/4 cups bread crumbs.

5. Heat the oil in a nonstick frying pan over medium heat. When the oil is hot, add 6 of the patties and cook on the first side for about 3 minutes or until golden brown. Turn gently and cook 3 or 4 minutes longer. Transfer to a warm platter. Repeat with the remaining 6 patties.

6. Wipe out the pan with a paper towel, add the butter and cook over medium heat, shaking the pan until the butter turns hazelnut brown. Add the lemon juice, blend well and pour the hot butter mixture over the patties. Garnish with the chervil and serve immediately. Suggested side dish: Fresh Green Peas with Pearl Onions (page 369).

Yield: 6 servings

❧ *The* en papillote *method of cooking fish is really a way of steaming the fish in the oven. Enclosed in foil or paper, the fish and any accompanying vegetables fuse beautifully. The dish presented here is a modified version of one we enjoyed at the Westmark Cape Fox in Ketchikan. It employs not only the salmon of the region but also its spectacular Dungeness crab.*

Cape Fox Salmon en Papillote

heavy-duty aluminum foil or
   parchment paper
^{1}/$_2$ cup julienne strips of carrot
^{1}/$_2$ cup julienne strips of celery
^{1}/$_2$ cup julienne strips of onion
^{1}/$_2$ cup dry white wine
4 tablespoons butter

6 ounces Dungeness or other lump
   crab meat, drained
4 salmon fillets, 1^1/$_2$ pounds in all
salt and freshly ground white
   pepper to taste
^{1}/$_4$ cup chopped parsley

1. Preheat oven to 450°.

2. Spread a large sheet of heavy-duty aluminum foil or parchment paper on a flat surface. Invert a 12-inch round cake pan or plate on the foil and trace around the pan with a sharp knife to make a 12-inch circle. Repeat 3 more times.

3. In a saucepan combine the vegetables and the wine. Bring to a boil and reduce the wine by half. Remove from the heat. Swirl in 2 tablespoons of the butter, add the crab meat and stir.

4. In a frying pan melt the remaining 2 tablespoons butter. Place the foil or paper rounds on a flat surface and brush them with the melted butter. On each round slightly below the center, place a salmon fillet. Top with some of the crab meat mixture. Sprinkle with salt and pepper.

5. Fold the foil or paper to enclose the contents completely, while leaving some room for expansion. Crimp the edges as tightly as possible to seal. Arrange the packages on a baking sheet and bake for 10 minutes. To serve, fold the casing back and sprinkle the salmon and vegetables with the parsley.

Yield: 4 servings

Beyond San Juan

PONCE, PUERTO RICO

Puerto Rico is really many places. It is a tropical American island replenished by the continuous stream of its people going to the mainland and coming home. It is, at least in the minds of many mainlanders, little more than the city of San Juan, dominated by tourism. But then there's the rest of Puerto Rico, a region startling in its diversity. The island is only 110 miles long and 35 miles wide, so it is easy enough to drive away from the tourists and directly into the central mountains, whose sounds and sights tell you that you have somehow arrived in the heart of the Third World, and then, from there, to drive to a place like Ponce, a Spanish city resonating with European elegance.

To get a feel for the people, the life and the food beyond San Juan, we hit the road, taking the superhighway from San Juan toward Ponce, but getting off it before Ponce, deep in the mountains in a place called Guavate, an area on the outskirts of the city of Cayey.

Here, just past a bend in the tortuous road, we drove into an astonishing stretch of a half-mile or so in which a haze of charcoal smoke and roasting pig wafted over the road like drifting fog. The street was lined with *lechoneras,* rustic open restaurants, each with a whole pig roasting in front. Some had chickens and sausage hanging over the coals, too. We chose an establishment called Lechonera La Reliquia. The restaurant was painted deep green and plastered with beer signs and Marlboro men. The mountain breeze was constant (a good thing, too, otherwise the smoke would not have moved at all) and it was cooler up here than down below in San Juan. Thanks to radios, traditional Spanish music filled the air almost as thickly as the smoke did. Cars and trucks, many of their drivers oblivious to the need for mufflers, roared through the little town.

The proprietor of Lechonera La Reliquia, César Rodríguez, was kind enough to

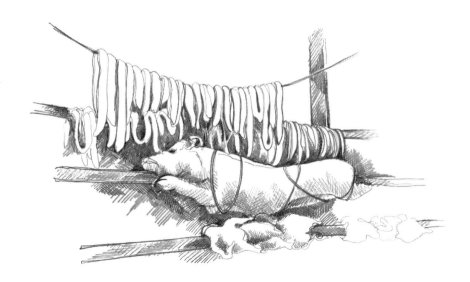

take us behind the scenes. While one pig was on display out front, two others were slow-cooking in a garage structure attached to the restaurant. They were turning slowly on a spit over charcoal cement-block bins covered with corrugated metal. Each of the pigs had been hand-rubbed with *adobo,* the ubiquitous Puerto Rican seasoning combination that usually includes crushed pepper, oregano, garlic, salt and maybe lime juice. The shortcut employed by many local cooks is to buy a dried *adobo* mix and just use that (but I've put together what I believe to be a rather authentic version to go with the roast pork below). After the pig is slow-cooked for several hours in a bin, it is moved outside to continue cooking in public.

This slow-cooking method is ancient, and it makes sense: The fat is all rendered (the pig starts at 140 pounds and ends up at about 90) but as the fat departs the pig it bastes the meat, keeping it moist. After such long cooking, the skin of the pig is crisp and the smoky flavor from real wood charcoal is soft but clear. When the pork is served, Mr. Rodríguez doesn't fool around: He cuts enormous hunks of it with his machete and piles it on plates. It's quite a feast, and one that serves the people in the area as a symbol of home, the way pastrami has always meant home to many New Yorkers.

Proof of that was a chat we had with Humberto Bermúdez, a 23-year-old artillery repairman. He had just gotten back from the Iraqi front during the Persian Gulf War and he was still wearing his desert fatigues. Not two hours after landing in San Juan he was standing at this *lechonera* in Guavate, dining on roast pork with his fiancée, Rosa García. "I rushed right here," he said, "because after all that time in the desert I needed a little civilization." Humberto told us that all his life he had been taking the back roads of Puerto Rico to find the best food. But now it seemed better than ever. "I appreciate it so much now," he said. "What little I had has become my kingdom."

After perhaps too much pork, chicken and beer, we departed Humberto's kingdom for a place as unlike it as you could imagine. We headed down out of the mountains onto the dry, hot southwest coast to the Lajas Valley. There, only 35 inches of rain falls each year compared with the 175 inches in the north and the 250 high in the mountainous rain forest. As it turns out, that 35 inches is the perfect quantity of rain to nourish some of the biggest, sweetest pineapples on earth.

At a place called Finca Carmen we saw and tasted a kind of pineapple called Big Head, so named because it can grow to 20 or 25 pounds (although it usually is sold at around 8). This pineapple is one of the wonders of Puerto Rico and people come from all over the island to admire the Big Heads and take a couple of the monsters back with them.

But the dry heat in the valley, after so much driving, was exhausting and we were a sunburnt tired bunch as we made our way back east into yet another world, the lovely Spanish city of Ponce. There, we were restored by the beauty of the place and the balmy evening.

For dinner, we could find no restaurant of any special allure right there in the center of town—as pretty as it was with its plaza and cathedral—but we were fortunate enough to be guided just a short distance away to the Los Caobos area. There we visited a restaurant called Lydia's, where many of us had a fine seafood *asopao* and others enjoyed seafood in garlic sauce; both are dishes that I've presented, with a few touches of my own, in recipes below.

Coriander

Before this trip, I never really appreciated how much coriander is the signal flavor of so many Puerto Rican dishes. It surprised me because coriander, also called cilantro or Chinese parsley, is not particularly widely used in Spain these days (although it must have been once, since cilantro is the Spanish name for the herb). It is little known in France or England and only recently has it become widely available in the United States. I don't know whom to thank for that sudden familiarity, the Asians who use it all the time, perhaps, or the Mexicans who also employ it with near abandon. In any event, we're all the richer for encountering it here, those of us, that is, who find the flavor pleasing. Coriander is one of those herbs that seem to repel some people. It has a musky, soapy flavor that often dominates a dish. The name stems from the Greek koris, which means bug, supposedly because some of the ancients thought it smelled like bedbugs. Anyway, these days some people can't live without it, and I can understand that. As for me, lately I've been using it almost as often as its sweeter cousin, parsley.

One thing to remember is that when a recipe calls for fresh coriander, you can't substitute coriander seeds; the flavor isn't the same. The herb, which looks like broad-leafed parsley, is often sold with its roots intact, which makes it easy to store: Just place it in the refrigerator in a tall glass of water and lightly cover with plastic wrap.

When we visited a restaurant called *Puerta a la Bahía* in Salinas, about two-thirds of the way from San Juan on the way to Ponce, we certainly knew we had left San Juan far behind. Salinas is a quiet, exquisite fishing village. It sits on a sheltered bay where the fishermen regularly come in with octopus or huge spiny lobsters. Salinas, we were told, is known for its mojita, *the simple sauce offered below. The trick is, of course, to serve it with a lobster cooked to perfection. The broiling-baking method here is meant to ensure that the lobster does not dry out under the broiler (as it usually does when broiling is used alone).*

Lobster with Mojita Sauce

Mojita *Sauce*

2 sweet red peppers, about ³/₄ pound

¹/₃ cup olive oil

6 cups onions, sliced into ¹/₄-inch rings

16 ounces crushed tomatoes

10 black peppercorns

3 bay leaves

salt to taste

1 tablespoon garlic, crushed

1. Preheat broiler or charcoal grill. Place the peppers under the broiler or on the grill and cook them on all sides until the skin is well charred. When cool enough to handle split the peppers in half, core them and discard the charred skin. Cut the peppers lengthwise into ¹/₄-inch strips.

2. Place the olive oil in a large saucepan, then add all the remaining ingredients. Simmer for 3 or 4 minutes and set aside. Remove the bay leaves. Keep warm.

The Lobster

4 live lobsters, 1¹/₂ pounds each

1. Preheat broiler.

2. Kill each lobster by inserting the tip of a large chef's knife between the eyes. Turn the lobster on its back and run the knife through the body toward the tail to cut in half. Pull away and discard the tough sac at the head of the lobster.

3. Place the lobsters, shell side down, 4 inches from the broiler's flame for 4 minutes. In a 425° oven finish the lobster by baking for 5 minutes.

4. To serve, place some of the sauce on each plate and 1 lobster over it. Spoon sauce over the lobsters.

Yield: 4 servings

❧ *I call this a fish stew "à la Puerto Rico" because it is my version of an* asopao, *combining as it does some of what I learned on my journey across the island with some of my own French notions of how to prepare the dish.*

Fish Stew à la Puerto Rico

2 tablespoons olive oil
¹/₂ cup finely chopped onions
¹/₂ cup finely chopped leeks, white part only
¹/₂ cup finely chopped celery
1 tablespoon finely chopped garlic
1 teaspoon fennel seeds
¹/₂ teaspoon saffron stems
2 cups ¹/₂-inch cubed fresh tomatoes or 2 cups canned peeled tomatoes
1 cup dry white wine
¹/₂ teaspoon Tabasco sauce

3 cups Fish Broth (recipe follows)
1 bay leaf
2 sprigs fresh thyme or ¹/₂ teaspoon dried
salt and freshly ground pepper to taste
1¹/₄ pounds skinless boneless fish fillets, such as monkfish, tile or red snapper, cut into 1-inch cubes
1 pound mussels, well cleaned
2 teaspoons Ricard or anise-flavored liquor
¹/₄ cup chopped parsley

1. Heat the oil in a saucepan. Add the onions, leeks, celery, garlic, fennel seeds and saffron. Cook, stirring, until wilted. Do not brown. Add the tomatoes, wine, Tabasco, fish broth, bay leaf, thyme and salt and pepper to taste. Stir and cook over medium heat for 15 minutes.

2. Add the fish to the pan with the mussels. Cook over medium heat for about 5 minutes or until the mussels have opened. Stir in the Ricard and add the parsley. Serve piping hot with Garlic Croutons (recipe on page 286).

Yield: 4 to 6 servings

Fish Broth

3 pounds fresh fish bones, including the head, but with the gills removed
6 cups water
1 cup sliced leeks, green part only
1 cup coarsely chopped onions

4 sprigs parsley
1 bay leaf
3 sprigs fresh thyme or 1 teaspoon dried
6 whole peppercorns

1. Chop the fish bones.

2. Combine all the ingredients in a kettle or saucepan. Bring the mixture to a boil and simmer for 20 minutes. Strain and discard the solids. Leftover broth can be frozen.

Yield: 6 cups

Garlic Croutons

1 loaf French bread
2 cloves garlic, peeled

2 tablespoons olive oil

1. Preheat broiler to high.

2. Rub the crust of the bread all over with the garlic cloves. Cut the bread into ¹/₂-inch-thick slices and sprinkle one side with the olive oil.

3. Place the bread slices on a baking sheet under the broiler until they are golden. Turn and broil on the other side until brown.

Yield: 4 to 6 servings

➣ *Certainly the most indelible day of our visit to the island was the day on the road lined with* lechoneras, *the roast pig restaurants, each with a whole pig cooking out front. I don't expect many readers to try that. But you can experience something similar by spit-cooking a pork butt, slowly so that it self-bastes just as those huge pigs do, and employing the traditional* adobo, *a combination of seasonings that Puerto Ricans apply to most grilled meats and fish.*

Barbecued Shoulder of Pork

1 square pork butt, about 7 pounds, with skin if possible
3 tablespoons all-purpose *Adobo*

Seasoning (recipe follows)
4 tablespoons fresh lime juice

1. Preheat oven to 350° or prepare barbecue spit.

2. In a small mixing bowl combine the *adobo* seasoning and the lime juice. Blend well.

3. Place the meat in a flat dish and make a few gashes around it. Rub the seasoning into the gashes, cover with plastic wrap and set overnight in a cool place or refrigerate.

4. Place in the oven for roasting or on the barbecue spit. If roasted, place a pan underneath to catch the fat. Roast for $3^{1}/_{2}$ hours, basting often, until done. Internal temperature should be 170°. Slice and serve.

Yield: 8 to 10 servings

Note: If gravy is desired, remove all the fat from the drippings pan, add $1^{1}/_{2}$ cups fresh or canned chicken broth to the pan. Bring to a boil while scraping the bottom of the pan. Strain.

Yield: about 1 cup gravy

Adobo Seasoning

1 cup salt
6 tablespoons chopped fresh
   oregano or 3 tablespoons dried

3 tablespoons freshly ground pepper
2 teaspoons turmeric
2 tablespoons finely chopped garlic

Crush all the ingredients to a fine texture in a mortar or use a spice grinder. Keep refrigerated until needed.

Yield: $1^{1}/_{3}$ cups

✎ *Avocado is plentiful on Puerto Rico and brings a beautiful touch of the tropics to any dish.*

Shrimp with Avocado and Sweet Red Pepper

1¹/₂ pounds large shrimp, shelled
   and deveined
4 tablespoons fresh lime juice
2 tablespoons freshly chopped
   oregano or 2 teaspoons dried
¹/₄ teaspoon hot red pepper flakes
salt and freshly ground pepper to
   taste

2 small ripe avocados
2 tablespoons butter
2 tablespoons olive oil
1 sweet red pepper, cored, seeded
   and cut into ¹/₄-inch-wide strips
1 tablespoon finely chopped garlic
4 tablespoons chopped fresh
   coriander or basil

1. In a mixing bowl combine the shrimp, 3 tablespoons of the lime juice, oregano, pepper flakes, and salt and pepper to taste. Blend well, cover with plastic wrap and let stand for 30 minutes or longer.

2. Peel the avocados and remove the pits. Cut the flesh into ¹/₂-inch-thick slices. Place in a small bowl, add the remaining tablespoon of lime juice and mix gently so the flesh does not discolor.

3. Melt the butter and olive oil in a large nonstick skillet or frying pan over high heat. Add the red pepper, cook and stir for 30 seconds. Add the shrimp and the marinade. Cook, stirring, for about 2 minutes. Add the avocado and garlic. Cook and stir for 1 minute. Do not overcook. Add the coriander. Blend well. Serve immediately.

Yield: 4 servings

✎ *The inspiration for this dish and the next was a visit to Lajas, where they grow the huge, sweet pineapple called Big Head. As it happens, on the same day we visited a passion fruit farm that had once been a vineyard but failed because the area had a tendency to flood. The same structures that once supported vines now supported passion fruit, creating an eery canopy of fruit that I was able to walk beneath in dense, cool shade.*

Fresh Pineapple with Passion Fruit

1 large ripe pineapple	1/2 cup LaGrande Passion Liqueur
1/4 cup sugar	4 ripe passion fruits
2 tablespoons fresh lime juice	4 to 8 sprigs fresh mint

1. Trim off top and bottom of the pineapple with a knife. Slice down the sides to remove the skin and any brown fibrous eyes.

2. Cut 8 even slices across and with a small round cookie cutter cut out the fibrous hard center of each slice.

3. In a flat dish place the pineapple slices and sprinkle with the sugar and the lime juice. Pour the passion fruit liqueur over the fruit. Cover with plastic wrap and refrigerate until serving.

4. For serving, place 1 or 2 slices of pineapple in the center of each plate. Spoon the marinade over it.

5. Cut the passion fruits in half and with a spoon remove the fruit and place over the pineapple slices. Decorate with mint sprigs.

Yield: 4 to 8 servings

Pineapple Sorbet

1 4- to 5-pound ripe pineapple
½ cup sugar

5 tablespoons fresh lemon juice
1 large egg white, slightly beaten

1. Trim off the top and bottom of the pineapple with a sharp knife. Slice down the sides to remove the skin and any green flesh. Dig out any brown fibrous eyes. Quarter the pineapple and remove any woody flesh.

2. Slice each pineapple quarter and put in the container of a food processor. Add the sugar and lemon juice. Blend to a fine purée.

3. Place the purée in an ice cream freezer and freeze following the manufacturer's instructions. When the purée begins to freeze, add the egg whites and resume freezing.

Yield: 10 servings

❧ *Outside Ponce, at a restaurant called Lydia's, several of our crew had seafood or chicken in a superb garlic sauce that seemed to me to be rather close to the one I present here, especially if you choose the coriander over the basil option.*

Chicken Strips with Garlic Butter

4 skinless boneless chicken breast halves

salt and freshly ground pepper to taste

1 tablespoon chopped fresh oregano or 2 teaspoons dried

2 tablespoons flour

2 tablespoons butter

2 tablespoons olive oil

4 ripe plum tomatoes, skinned, seeded and cut into dice

1 tablespoon chopped garlic

4 tablespoons chopped fresh coriander or basil

2 tablespoons fresh lime juice

1. Using a sharp knife, cut the breasts in half crosswise, then lengthwise into strips $^1/_2$ inch wide.

2. Blend well salt and pepper to taste, oregano and the flour in a flat dish. Add the chicken pieces in one layer. Stir to season keeping each strip separate.

3. Heat the butter and oil over high heat in a skillet large enough to hold the chicken in one layer. Add the chicken pieces, cook and stir until lightly browned, for about 3 minutes. Add the tomatoes and garlic and cook, stirring, for 3 minutes more. Add the coriander and lime juice, continue cooking and blend well. Serve immediately.

Yield: 4 servings

The Lentil Land

As we traveled across the nation, meeting so many of the people who produce its food, a realization began to dawn: This far-flung country is even more varied than one could ever imagine. Some regions are so distinct that they have evolved into completely specialized niches where climate, soil, history and people combine in some unique way. And it may be that the food produced in one of these utterly idiosyncratic niches will come from that spot—and almost nowhere else in the nation. Lentils, a legume barely known to many Americans, are a spectacular example. Almost every lentil in the country comes from a single 200-mile-long area in Eastern Washington and Western Idaho called the Palouse (derived from the French word for green lawn). Here in the summer the green lentil flourishes in plots that stretch endlessly into the distance.

The hills here are nothing like what we'd seen anywhere else. Formed eons ago by windblown volcanic ash, they are smooth and rhythmic like sand drifts in the desert. In the summer they are cloaked in velvety greens and browns. These are the colors of the lentils—and the closely related vegetable called the dry pea—that are green as they grow, then brown as they dry before being harvested. Making the patchwork more dramatic are plots of stark black soil, idled by agreement with the government. The soil is so black because the ash has made it extremely rich.

The warm summer air is dry but there is much more rainfall throughout the year here than there is not too far to the West, where the mountains cut off the westward flow of moisture from the Pacific nearly entirely. We had a splendid view of the Palouse from two separate viewing points. One was from Steptoe Butte, 3,612 feet high, a mountain that was too tall to be covered over by the prehistoric ash that created the hills below. The other spot was a farm owned by Lee Druffel and his family that looks down into a valley where the Snake and Clearwater rivers meet. Far

below the farm are the towns of Lewiston and Clarkston, so named because Lewis and Clark camped along the rivers during their exploration. From the Druffel farm, you can see Oregon 70 miles away, easily, through the clear Western air.

It turns out that although this little area is ideal for lentils, they might never have been grown here were it not for the Seventh Day Adventists who settled the Palouse early in the century. They were vegetarians who needed the legumes for their great nutritional value in the form of all the minerals and protein they supply. It wasn't until after World War II that anybody started serious commercial production. And that, in some measure, required the influx of immigrants into the country from cultures that knew all about lentils, people of the Mediterranean and from India, for instance. Even so—and this may be changing as the dietary virtues of this high-fiber vegetable become better known—most of the lentils produced in the United States are exported.

I, of course, with my European background, have never been a stranger to lentils. I've used them in soups and salads and other dishes for as long as I can remember. But I think they are still one of America's biggest secrets, so versatile and easy to cook and yet so little used.

Around these parts of Washington and Idaho lentils are much better known and more widely eaten. Joanne Druffel, Lee's wife, even made some lentil cookies for us, using them as you might use oats. Theirs is one of those magnificent American families that manages to work a big productive farm mostly just using the family's own resources. Lee's father, Gerald, was there helping out the day we visited. We met two of Lee's three sons, Nathan, 11, and Allen, 7. But we never did see Justin, 14, because he was off elsewhere on the farm driving a Mack truck. Later, we visited Gerald and Carol Druffel's Victorian home, built in 1896 on land that Carol's family homesteaded in 1876.

We got to try lentils at a wittily designed and intelligently operated restaurant called Café Spudnik in the sparkling university town of Moscow, home of the University of Idaho. The restaurant is owned and run by 30-year-old Denver Burtenshaw who has studied and traveled widely in Europe and Asia. The predominant colors of his restaurant are black and white, and the whimsical Denver likes to dress in black, too. He uses lentils in a variety of ways, in an Indonesian salad, for instance, and in a soup made rich with sour cream. The day we were there he employed simply cooked green and red lentils as a backdrop for another of Idaho's prizes, trout.

Convenience Food

Lentils are about as carefree a vegetable as nature ever invented. Once they dry out in the fields, are harvested and packaged for the consumer, the real work and worry are over. It's hard to make them rot or spoil. Kept in a cool, dry place, they can outlast any of us. There's no trick to preparing them. You have to wash them and pick out any loose debris, then boil them in liquid—water or stock. The usual ratio is two cups of liquid for every cup of lentils. The common green and brown lentils take 20 minutes or so after the liquid is brought to a simmer (test to see if they are tender) but the Red Chief variety is even faster, about 10 minutes.

Like other similar legumes, they are easy to sprout at home, and the sprouts can be used in salads or as a garnish. The technique is to place 1 cup of lentils in a jar or bowl. Cover with lukewarm water and let stand overnight. Next day, drain the lentils thoroughly. Line a baking sheet with several thicknesses of paper towels or cheesecloth. Spread the soaked lentils over the toweling. Completely cover them with a double layer of paper towels. Moisten the towels evenly until thoroughly dampened. Set aside overnight. Repeat the dampening procedure the next day, too. By the third day, the lentils will have sprouted with tails of about ¹/₂ inch. Use them right then or store them refrigerated in a sealed container or plastic bag for up to a week.

🌿 *The dish Denver Burtenshaw prepared for us at Café Spudnik made the point that lentils, which may seem drab, can actually dress up a dish with considerable color and flavor, particularly if the lentils used are of different colors, as is the case here.*

Café Spudnik's Pan-Fried Trout and Lentils

2 cups dried green lentils, washed and picked over

salt and freshly ground pepper to taste

2 sprigs fresh thyme or 1 teaspoon dried

2 bay leaves

2 whole cloves garlic

5 tablespoons butter

7 tablespoons extra virgin olive oil

1 cup Red Chief lentils, washed and picked over

2 teaspoons freshly ground pepper

4 boned brook trout, 1/2 pound each, cleaned, with heads and tails left on

1 teaspoon turmeric

1/2 teaspoon hot red pepper flakes

1 cup flour

1/4 pound diced pancetta or bacon, blanched in water to remove the salt, then finely diced

1/2 medium sweet onion, such as Walla Walla, chopped finely

2 tablespoons finely slivered garlic

1/2 lemon

chopped fresh herbs of choice or whole edible flowers for garnish

1. Place the green lentils in a saucepan with 4 cups water, salt, 1 sprig of the thyme, 1 bay leaf, 1 clove garlic and bring to a boil. Simmer for 20 minutes or until tender. Add 2 tablespoons of the butter, 2 tablespoons of the olive oil and salt and pepper and blend well.

2. Place the Red Chief lentils in a saucepan with 2 cups cold water and add salt, the remaining thyme, garlic clove and bay leaf and set aside.

3. Wash the trout and pat it dry. On a large plate combine salt, the 2 teaspoons pepper, the turmeric, pepper flakes and flour and mix well. Roll the trout in the mixture to coat evenly.

4. Meanwhile, bring the Red Chief lentils to a boil and simmer for about 10 minutes or until tender. Add 1 tablespoon of the butter, 2 tablespoons of olive oil and salt and pepper to taste and set aside.

5. Heat a heavy skillet and add the pancetta and onion. Stir until the pancetta is almost brown and the onion is soft. Add the remaining 2 tablespoons butter, the remaining 3 tablespoons of olive oil and sliced garlic. Cook until the garlic is soft but not burned. Remove the mixture from the skillet and stuff equal amounts of it in each trout.

6. Return the skillet to the heat and place the stuffed trout in the pan. Cook for 3 minutes on each side, until the trout is golden brown and cooked through. Sprinkle each trout with lemon juice.

7. To serve, place 1 trout in the center of a plate. Place alternating spoonfuls of the red and green lentils around the trout. Garnish with the fresh herbs or edible flowers.

Yield: 4 servings

❧ *Just as Denver did in his recipe above, I like to use lentils to accompany other dishes. He used stuffed trout, in quite a delicate preparation in which the lentils were prepared very simply and placed alongside. The next three recipes offer distinctly different lentil salad accompaniments to three very different meats: tongue, skirt steak and lamb.*

Beef Tongue with Mustard Sauce and Lentil Salad

1 cooked beef tongue, available in plastic wrap in supermarkets	2 tablespoons white vinegar
¼ cup prepared imported mustard	salt to taste
1½ teaspoons dry mustard	2 tablespoons finely chopped fresh dill
1 teaspoon sugar	Lentil Salad (recipe follows)
⅓ cup peanut, vegetable or corn oil	

1. The size of cooked beef tongues varies greatly. If you have too much to serve your guests, simply save leftovers for another use, such as in sandwiches. You may wish to

reheat the tongue briefly as indicated on the package, in the plastic bag, about 20 minutes without boiling.

2. Cut away and discard the gristly, throaty and unsightly part of the tongue. Peel and slice as much of the tongue as desired and arrange it on a platter.

3. Put the prepared mustard in a mixing bowl and add the dry mustard and sugar. Stir with a whisk to blend. Gradually add the oil, stirring. Add vinegar and salt. Stir in the dill. On each plate serve the tongue with lentil salad and the mustard sauce on the side.

Lentil Salad

$^1/_2$ pound dried green lentils, washed in a colander and picked over

3 cups water

1 bay leaf

1 clove garlic, peeled

1 small onion, studded with 1 clove

salt and freshly ground pepper to taste

3 sprigs fresh parsley

2 sprigs fresh thyme or $^1/_2$ teaspoon dried

4 tablespoons finely chopped onions

1 tablespoon finely chopped fresh parsley

1 teaspoon finely minced garlic

$^1/_2$ cup peeled, seeded and diced tomatoes

1 tablespoon red wine vinegar

3 tablespoons olive oil

1. Put the prepared lentils in a saucepan. Add the water, bay leaf, garlic, onion and salt and pepper. Tie the parsley sprigs together with the thyme sprigs, if using, in a bundle and add to the liquid. Bring the lentils to a boil and cook, partially covered, until tender, about 20 to 30 minutes. Do not overcook. The lentils must be tender but not mushy. Remove from the heat, remove the onion, garlic, bay leaf and parsley bundle and discard them. Drain the lentils well.

2. Transfer the lentils to a large bowl. Add the chopped onions, chopped parsley, garlic, tomatoes, vinegar, olive oil and salt and pepper to taste and toss gently to blend well.

Yield: 4 to 8 servings

Hanger or Skirt Steak with Warm Lentil Salad

8 cups water

1 pound dried lentils, washed in a colander and picked over

1 cup finely diced carrots

1 bay leaf

3 sprigs fresh thyme or 1 teaspoon dried

salt and freshly ground pepper to taste

1 tablespoon Dijon mustard

3/4 cup olive oil

1/4 cup red wine vinegar

1 cup finely chopped onions

4 tablespoons finely chopped chives or parsley

4 skirt steaks, about 1/2 pound each, trimmed of excess fat

1 tablespoon ground cumin

1 tablespoon vegetable oil

2 tablespoons butter

2 teaspoons finely chopped garlic

2 tablespoons finely chopped parsley

1. Place the water in a large saucepan. Add the lentils to the pan with the carrots, bay leaf, thyme and salt to taste. Cover and simmer for 20 to 25 minutes. Do not overcook. Drain and remove the bay leaf and thyme sprigs.

2. In a large bowl combine the mustard, olive oil, vinegar, chopped onions, chives and salt and pepper to taste. Blend well with a wire whisk. Add the lentils and blend well.

3. Sprinkle the steaks on both sides with salt and pepper and cumin and brush with the vegetable oil.

4. In a cast-iron skillet large enough to hold 2 steaks at a time brown the steaks over high heat for 3 minutes for medium-rare. Turn and continue cooking until thoroughly browned, about 3 minutes more. Remove to a warm platter. Repeat the procedure for the 2 remaining steaks.

5. Pour off the fat from the skillet and reduce the heat. Add the butter, garlic and parsley and cook briefly. Add any juices from the platter of steak and blend well. Pour the sauce over the steaks and serve immediately with the lentil salad.

Yield: 4 servings

Note: Any leftover lentil salad may be served cold or reheated.

Medallions of Lamb with Shallot Sauce and Lentils

2 skinless boneless loin of lamb, about 1½ pounds in all

salt and freshly ground pepper to taste

1 tablespoon olive oil

4 cloves garlic, peeled

1 tablespoon chopped fresh rosemary or 2 teaspoons dried

2 tablespoons finely chopped shallots

¼ cup dry white wine

¼ cup fresh or canned chicken broth

1 tablespoon butter

Lentils with Balsamic Vinegar (recipe follows)

2 tablespoons coarsely chopped parsley

1. Cut the lamb into 12 equal pieces. Sprinkle with salt and pepper.

2. Heat the olive oil in a nonstick skillet large enough to hold the lamb pieces in one layer. Add the lamb, the garlic cloves and the rosemary. Brown the lamb over relatively high heat quickly on all sides and cook, turning, about 4 minutes for rare. Remove the lamb pieces to a warm platter and keep warm.

3. Add the shallots to the pan and cook briefly, stirring, until wilted. Add the wine and chicken broth. Cook and reduce to about ⅓ cup. Swirl in the butter and any juices that have accumulated around the lamb. Blend well, taste for seasoning and remove the garlic cloves if desired. Keep warm.

4. To serve, divide the lentils with balsamic vinegar equally among 4 warm plates. Place 3 pieces of lamb over the lentils and spread some of the shallot sauce over the lamb. Garnish with the chopped parsley and serve immediately.

Yield: 4 servings

Lentils with Balsamic Vinegar

2 cups dried green lentils, washed in a colander and picked over

4 cups water

salt and freshly ground pepper to taste

1 medium onion, studded with 2 cloves

1 bay leaf

2 sprigs fresh thyme or $1/2$ teaspoon dried

1 tablespoon butter

1 teaspoon finely chopped garlic

$1/2$ cup finely chopped onions

$1/2$ cup finely diced carrots

1 tablespoon balsamic vinegar

1. Put the lentils in a saucepan and add the water and salt to taste. Bring the water to a boil and add the onion, bay leaf and thyme. Cover and let simmer for 20 minutes until tender. Drain, reserving $1/2$ cup of the cooking liquid, and remove the bay leaf.

2. Meanwhile, heat the butter in a saucepan and add the garlic, chopped onions and carrots. Cook, stirring, until the onions are wilted. Do not brown. Add the balsamic vinegar and the reserved cooking liquid. Add pepper to taste. Cover and simmer for 5 minutes.

3. Add the drained lentils to the carrot mixture and bring to a boil. Simmer for 2 minutes.

Yield: 4 servings

≈ Even people who are basically unfamiliar with lentils probably know them from lentil soup. Lentils are spectacular in providing body, color and nutrition to a very simple preparation.

Lentil Soup

2 tablespoons butter
1/4 pound smoked ham, cut into small cubes
1/2 cup coarsely chopped onions
2 teaspoons chopped garlic
1/2 pound dried green lentils, washed in a colander and picked over
5 cups fresh or canned chicken broth

2 cups water
1 bay leaf
2 sprigs fresh thyme or 1/2 teaspoon dried
1 tablespoon red wine vinegar
salt and freshly ground pepper to taste
4 tablespoons coarsely chopped chervil

1. Heat 1 tablespoon of the butter in a kettle or deep saucepan. Add the ham, onions and garlic. Cook briefly until the onions are wilted. Add the lentils and 4 cups of the chicken broth, the water, bay leaf and thyme. Bring to a boil. Simmer for 25 to 30 minutes. Remove 1/2 cup of the soup with some lentils and set aside. Discard the bay leaf and thyme sprig. Remove the pan from the heat.

2. With a wire whisk mash the lentils to make a coarse purée. Return the soup pot to the stove and bring to a boil. Add the remaining 1 cup chicken broth and the reserved 1/2 cup soup. Add the remaining 1 tablespoon butter and the vinegar. Check for seasoning and serve, sprinkled with chervil.

Yield: 4 to 6 servings

In the Groves

We were in central Florida, having dinner with Quentin Roe, one of the state's citrus commissioners and a packer and grower of fruit. Before we were very far into the meal, Quentin decided to put on a show. He called for an orange and a citrus knife. He was going to demonstrate, he said, "how Floridians really eat an orange." So he cut off the cap of the orange, peeled most of the skin, leaving the rind intact, cut a hole into the top of the fruit in the shape of an inverted pyramid and then shoved as much of his face into it as would fit. Quentin rotated the orange, squeezing as he went.

When it was over he stopped slurping and looked up at us in triumph. At one time or another, that night or the next day, as we explored an orange grove, just about everybody in our group would give it a try. The amazing thing is that the system works remarkably well in extracting what seems to be all of the juice, with surprisingly little mess. (See the illustration on page 313.)

Quentin is tall, young—32 years old—and candid. He can dive into an orange or right into a discussion of some of the problems the orange industry in his state has been trying to overcome. For one thing, Florida Valencias, the most commonly sold of the Florida oranges, are rather ugly. They are often green and marred by wind and bugs and other assailants. They look as if they've been batted around a bit. They're thin skinned so that they don't peel as well as the thicker-skinned orange beauties grown in the arid West (although Floridians assert that their oranges are juicier and more flavorful).

"It's the tropical climate," Quentin said. "It's as if we were growing in Cuba or Honduras," meaning more insects, more storms, more heat. The reason some of the oranges never get entirely orange is that the nights aren't as cool here as in the more arid regions where the nip in the air stops the chlorophyll from developing in the skin.

Hot and humid as this place may be, the next day dawned as a blessing, relatively cool and dry (despite dire forecasts of rain just 12 hours earlier), as we headed off to see some of Quentin's oranges close up. It was late in the season—June—when even the late-blooming Valencias had just about ended their production period. But many of the trees were still bright with fruit, the mature oranges, as well as next year's little fellows, still hard and deep green. Most of the state's oranges are shipped November through May; a Florida orange that's still around in, say, August, has been kept in storage. The state's total production is 70 percent of all the oranges grown in America. The fact that Florida's oranges just about disappear in the summertime leaves the field clear for the California crop for a while.

Not surprisingly, while Floridians have been trying to get out the word that their fruit is better-looking on the inside than on the outside, this superficial ugliness is a trait they'd love to eliminate completely if they could. Researchers have, in fact, been developing a new orange to grow in the state's heat and humidity, a fruit called the Amber Sweet. It grows in a tree that shelters it better from wind, has a thicker skin to peel easier and has excellent color in December and January. But the research, according to Quentin, wasn't far enough along, when we were there, to start a move toward marketing.

Our journey into the heart of Florida was instructive because this is a state, after all, known more for its beaches and theme parks than anything else. Yet here in central Florida, as soon as you put a little distance between yourself and Disney World in Orlando, the production of food is the main business in the vast, lush flatlands baking in the sunshine. Not just oranges and other citrus fruit, but tomatoes, corn, lettuce, strawberries—and all sorts of other things that grow here to feed the state and much of the country.

It's a fact that wasn't lost on Mark Rodriguez, proprietor of a restaurant called Jordan's Grove, in Maitland, just outside of Orlando. "There are all these wonderful vegetables available to us," he said, "and then there's the fish, from the east coast and from the west coast, Atlantic and Gulf."

On the day we were at Jordan's Grove, Mark prepared grouper fillets with a relish of chopped fruit. The grouper was a 40-pounder hauled into the kitchen and cut into fillets on the spot by Clair Epting, Mark's executive chef. Grouper is a fine fish for cooking, with springy, dense flesh that's a little like monkfish but not as extreme in those characteristics as monkfish can be. Other fish available to central Florida's cooks include the triggerfish that's so popular in the Caribbean, sea trout, wahoo, dolphin (the fish, not the porpoise, often called mahimahi), and flounder caught, among other places, off Port Canaveral in the shadow of the space shuttle launchings.

The cooking you can find at this restaurant and elsewhere in Florida benefits from many benign influences, with New Orleans not far away and the Caribbean practically in the neighborhood. If that weren't enough, at Jordan's Grove there's also just a touch of the Amish of Lancaster, Pa.—Clair Epting hails from there and although he got most of his cooking experience elsewhere, he remembers that while he was working in a kitchen in Dallas the chef Jacques Pepin, an old and good friend of mine, was in town, offering a brief course. Clair took it and says he was particularly impressed by a method Jacques showed him for preparing strawberry jam simply by leaving strawberries in a screen-covered jar in the sunshine and taking them in at night. "It was a lot like the sort of thing my grandparents would do," he said as his mind drifted back to his Amish background. Somehow, that simple demonstration seemed to validate Clair's Amish heritage for him. It reminded him of his affection for straightforward cooking, employing the freshest conceivable ingredients with a deep respect for their own naturalness. But, of course, these days that's the way a lot of America thinks and cooks. Things are looking up.

Food of the Gods

*Although Quentin Roe, the citrus man, has no trouble
reaching a high level of enthusiasm about just about
any citrus fruit, it is a particular tangerine
that causes his eyes to go almost misty
with admiration. The tangerine is the
Royal Lee and it is barely available anywhere.
Like a flower that just blooms for a moment, the
Royal Lee tangerine has what Quentin describes "as a very narrow
window—it reaches full color from about December 1 to December 15." To
hear Quentin's description, it sounds as though anybody growing it is doing
it more as a hobby than as a job. "There's no promotion around it and
hardly anybody knows about it," he says. To make things even more
mysterious, this tangerine looks just about like any other.*

*But the flavor of it . . . "it's the food of the gods," Quentin says. "It's just
what I imagine the Greek gods would eat for dessert, so sweet and pure,
absolutely the ideal fruit."*

*Now, of course, when we were there, late spring, no Royal Lees were
around to be tasted and it was easy to suspect that this incredible fruit
might be more myth than fact. But Quentin assured us that it was real. He
urged us to write to him in the fall to find out how to get our hands on the
fruit of the gods. And we mean to:*

*Wm. G. Roe & Sons, Inc.,
P.O. Box 900,
Winter Haven, FL 33880.*

🐝 *Here is the true Floridian method for enjoying an orange, according to Quentin Roe:*

Remove the cap, peel half of the orange (leaving rind), and cut out the pyramidal hole. Cup the bottom of the orange in your hands. As you rotate and squeeze, drink the juice from the hole.

🐝 *With this clever idea, the Jordan's Grove restaurant brings sparkle to a simply prepared grouper fillet by accenting it with an uncooked fruit relish, a kind of compote. The relish is served alongside the fish rather than on top so that it doesn't stain the fish red with its raspberry juice. When discussing it with Mark Rodriguez in the restaurant kitchen he suggested several variations. One of them added jalapeño pepper to the relish to give it some heat, and that's the way I'm offering it here.*

Sautéed Grouper with Orange-Jalapeño Relish

1 tablespoon chopped fresh tarragon

2 cups orange sections, membranes removed, cut into triangles

2 cups grapefruit sections, membranes removed, cut into triangles

1 cup raspberries

1 teaspoon finely chopped jalapeño pepper

4 skinless grouper fillets or other firm white-fleshed fish, $^1/_2$ inch thick, about 6 ounces each

salt and freshly ground pepper to taste

$^1/_2$ cup flour for dredging

1 tablespoon vegetable oil

4 sprigs fresh tarragon for garnish

1. Combine the tarragon, orange and grapefruit sections, raspberries and jalapeño in a bowl. Mix together and allow to stand for at least 15 minutes.

2. Sprinkle each fillet with salt and pepper to taste and dredge in the flour. Shake off any excess flour.

3. Heat the oil in a nonstick pan large enough to hold all the fillets in one layer. Place the fish in the pan and cook for 3 minutes on the first side or until lightly browned. Turn and cook 3 minutes longer. Do not overcook.

4. Serve each fillet with relish as an accompaniment on the plate. Place a sprig of tarragon on top of each fillet.

Yield: 4 servings

This orange pie is Clair Epting's twist on Key Lime pie. He has also used grapefruit with great success. And he has given it a nice touch by turning to pistachio nuts for the crust. Shelling the nuts can be a pain, but some stores sell them already shelled. Alternatives that work well are peanuts and hazelnuts.

Orange Pie with Pistachio Crust

2 cups unsalted shelled pistachio
  nuts, finely ground
$^3/_4$ cup brown sugar
$^1/_2$ cup flour
2 tablespoons butter, softened

2 cups fresh orange juice
3 cups sweetened condensed milk
  (Eagle brand)
4 large egg yolks
2 tablespoons orange zest

1. Preheat oven to 400°.

2. To make the crust, combine the ground nuts, sugar, flour and butter in a bowl and blend. Place the mixture in a deep 9-inch pie plate and, with the fingers, neatly press the crust into shape.

3. Bake the crust for 5 minutes. Remove from the oven and allow to cool.

4. Pour the orange juice into a saucepan, bring to a boil and reduce to $^1/_3$ cup. Allow to cool to room temperature.

5. Meanwhile, prepare the filling. In a bowl combine the condensed milk and yolks and blend thoroughly with a whisk. Add the reduced juice and the orange zest. Pour the filling into the prebaked shell.

6. Bake the pie for 5 minutes. Remove the pie and refrigerate it overnight or for at least 12 hours so that the filling sets enough for easy slicing.

Yield: 4 to 6 servings

Orange butter sauce is a version of the old favorite beurre blanc, *but the acid this time, instead of vinegar, is orange juice, and the change is sweet and subtle. I've used an orange butter sauce twice in this chapter for two very different dishes. The first sauce, however, is much richer than the second and has a stronger orange flavor. It's got the strength for a grilled shrimp dish—but you pay the price in calories.*

Grilled Shrimp Brochettes with Orange Butter Sauce

24 jumbo shrimp, about 1¹/₂ pounds, shelled and deveined
1 sweet red pepper, cored, seeded and cut into bite-sized squares
1 yellow pepper, cored, seeded and cut into bite-sized squares
1 cup fresh orange juice
¹/₄ cup finely chopped shallots

4 tablespoons butter
salt and freshly ground white pepper to taste
2 ripe plum tomatoes, peeled, seeded and cut into small dice
2 tablespoons olive oil
2 tablespoons chopped fresh coriander

1. Preheat charcoal grill.

2. Place 6 shrimps on each skewer, alternating each with a piece of the red and yellow peppers. Set the skewers aside.

3. In a saucepan combine the orange juice and shallots and reduce by half on top of the stove. Add the butter and salt and pepper to taste. Blend well with a wire whisk. Add the tomatoes. Set aside and keep warm.

4. Brush the brochettes with the olive oil and place over the hot grill. Cook for 2 minutes on each side. Do not overcook. Arrange each brochette on a serving plate, pour some of the sauce over it and sprinkle with the chopped coriander.

Yield: 4 servings

Broiled Fish Fillets with Orange Butter Sauce

$^1/_4$ cup fresh orange juice
1 tablespoon butter
3 tablespoons olive oil
salt and freshly ground pepper to
   taste
$^1/_2$ cup diced peeled seeded plum
   tomatoes

4 skinless boneless white fish fillets,
   such as red snapper, blackfish,
   sea bass or lemon sole, about $1^1/_2$
   pounds in all
$^1/_4$ cup chopped fresh chives

1. Preheat broiler to high.

2. In a saucepan reduce the orange juice by half over high heat. Add the butter, 2 tablespoons of the olive oil, salt and pepper to taste. Blend well with a wire whisk. Add the tomatoes and set aside.

3. Brush the fish on both sides with the remaining 1 tablespoon olive oil. Sprinkle with salt and pepper and arrange the fish in an unheated broiler pan. Broil the fish about 2 to 3 inches from the heat source for 3 to 4 minutes or until the fillets are just cooked through. Transfer the fillets to a platter, pour the orange sauce over them and garnish with the chopped chives.

Yield: 4 servings

* *A fruitier, softer vinaigrette is rendered by the use of orange instead of, say, lemon. It is meant to harmonize with the orange peel and orange sections in the salad and it strikes me as a very successful combination.*

Warm Salmon Salad with Orange Vinaigrette

2 tablespoons fresh orange juice
1 tablespoon Dijon mustard
1/3 cup olive oil
2 tablespoons red wine vinegar
Tabasco sauce to taste
salt and freshly ground white
  pepper to taste
2 tablespoons julienne strips of
  orange peel
2 tablespoons finely chopped
  shallots

1 head radicchio
1 head bibb lettuce
1/2 pound arugula
2 orange sections, trimmed,
  membranes removed
1 1/2 pounds skinless boneless
  salmon fillets, cut into 4 equal
  pieces
1 tablespoon vegetable oil

1. To make the vinaigrette, combine the orange juice and mustard in a small bowl. Beat briskly until the mixture begins to thicken. Gradually add the oil, vinegar and Tabasco, and continue to beat. Add salt and pepper to taste, the orange peel and the shallots and mix well.

2. To make the salad, tear the radicchio, bibb lettuce and arugula into pieces and in a large bowl combine them with the orange sections. Pour 2/3 of the dressing over the salad and toss well. Divide the salad among 4 serving plates.

3. Cut each fillet into thirds lengthwise. Then cut each strip on the diagonal into 2-inch-long pieces. Heat the vegetable oil in a nonstick skillet and cook the salmon over medium-high heat on both sides for a total of about 2 minutes or until done. Do not overcook.

4. Place the salmon over the greens, and drizzle the remaining vinaigrette over the fish. Serve immediately.

Yield: 4 servings

❦ *The sectioning of grapefruit, as described in the following recipe, is a neat trick. I've watched too many people botch a job that really isn't all that difficult. What you're looking for is a well-shaped section without the bitter membrane.*

Broiled Chicken Breasts with Grapefruit

2 large ripe grapefruits
2 tablespoons olive oil
2 teaspoons grated fresh ginger
2 teaspoons dry hot mustard
2 tablespoons chopped fresh coriander

salt and freshly ground pepper to taste
4 skinless boneless chicken halves, about 1¼ pounds in all
4 tablespoons chopped scallions

1. Using a knife, remove the skin of the grapefruit. Starting at the top and cutting in a circular fashion, remove the grapefruit skin; do not let any membrane remain on the surface of the fruit. Use a knife to pluck out each section by slicing down along each side of the membrane that radiates out from the center of the fruit. When the sections are removed, squeeze the remains of the grapefruits by placing them in a piece of cheesecloth or a strainer. There should be about ³/₄ cup juice. Place the sections in a baking dish and put aside.

2. Using a wire whisk, blend together the grapefruit juice, olive oil, ginger, mustard, coriander, salt and pepper. Pour the grapefruit juice mixture into a shallow baking dish and add the chicken. Cover with plastic wrap and let marinate for ¹/₂ hour.

3. Meanwhile, preheat broiler to high. Remove the chicken from the marinade and broil it in the broiling pan 3 to 4 inches from the source of heat for about 4 minutes on the first side.

4. While the chicken is broiling, add the marinade to the baking dish with the grapefruit sections. Place the dish on the bottom of the oven.

5. Turn the chicken over and broil it for 3 to 4 minutes more until done. Combine the chicken and the grapefruit sauce and serve.

Yield: 4 servings

This is similar to a soufflé I often prepare but the difference is the use of crème de Grand Marnier, *which helps make the soufflé smoother.*

Creamy Grand Marnier Soufflés

1 tablespoon butter
$^1/_3$ cup plus 3 tablespoons sugar
6 eggs, separated
1 tablespoon finely grated orange rind
$^1/_4$ cup fresh orange juice with the pulp

2 tablespoons *crème de* Grand Marnier
1 tablespoon confectioners' sugar
Orange Sauce (recipe follows)

1. Preheat oven to 450°.

2. Rub the bottom and sides of four 1 $^1/_4$-cup individual soufflé dishes with the butter. Sprinkle the insides of the 4 dishes with 1 tablespoon of the sugar.

3. Place the egg yolks in a bowl and add the $^1/_3$ cup sugar, the orange rind, orange juice and *crème de* Grand Marnier. Beat with a wire whisk until blended.

4. In a clean copper bowl or the bowl of an electreic mixer, beat the egg whites until stiff. Shortly before the whites are stiff, beat in the remaining 2 tablespoons sugar.

5. Fold $^1/_3$ of the egg whites into the egg yolk mixture. Beat the remaining egg whites briefly again. Fold the remaining whites into the yolks rapidly and thoroughly. Spoon the mixture into the soufflé dishes. Run your thumb around the periphery of the inside of each dish to create a hollow in the mixture that will allow for expansion when baked.

6. Place the dishes on a baking sheet and put them in the oven. Bake 10 to 12 minutes. Sprinkle the confectioners' sugar through a sieve over each soufflé. Cut a hole in the center of each soufflé and spoon a small amount of the sauce into each hole, saving the rest to serve on the side.

Yield: 4 servings

Orange Sauce

1 cup apricot preserves or jam
1/2 cup water
1/2 cup orange sections, cut into
 pieces

1 teaspoon grated orange rind
2 tablespoons *crème de* Grand
 Marnier

Place the preserves and water in a saucepan and cook over medium heat, stirring, until blended and smooth, about 5 minutes. Add the orange sections and orange rind. Remove from the heat and stir in the Grand Marnier. Serve.

Yield: 1 3/4 cups

The Food and Wine
of Napa Valley

It had been nearly 10 years since I'd last seen my old friend Maurice Nayrolles, a tall, formal man, with a surprisingly quick smile. I knew he had left New York for somewhere else, but we'd lost touch entirely. When we met again it was at the Meadowood, a resort he runs now, in the nation's finest wine region, the Napa Valley of California. In some ways, he was my perfect introduction to this startlingly fertile area. As we sat and talked, we were two erstwhile Frenchmen in a region that is absolutely American and at the same time as international as any place can be.

With mist clinging to the tops of the evergreens just outside the picture windows of the dining room, Maurice told me how congenial he found Napa to be. "When I came here for the first time," he said, "it reminded me of the three countries I knew best in Europe." There were the oak trees of southern Portugal, the fig trees and the olives of Italy and France—and, of course, the vineyards are everywhere in Napa. It is the wine-growing that most defines the character of the people and the life here, he said. "There's a *joie de vivre* and a love of food. People are close to the land; that's part of it, but wherever you find great wine you find great food." The rich red Cabernets, the stout but smooth white Sauvignon Blancs and the clean Chardonnays are not precisely the same as the wines I knew in Burgundy and Bordeaux, but they bring their own, American contribution with them. And it is splendid, to be sure. The Muscovy duck in a Cabernet sauce that the accomplished chef Henri Delcros prepared for us at Meadowood was ample testimony to that.

It's been more than 150 years since the first wine was produced in the Napa Valley, but the tremendous surge in its popularity, along with its refinement to the point where it is among the world's best, is really only a phenomenon of the post-World War II era. If, 30 years ago, you were looking for a place to dine decently here, you likely would have been out of luck. Now, predictably, the food has joined hands with the wine, to the immense good fortune of anyone traveling through the Napa Valley. Wine seminars and cooking classes have sprung up in several places; most notable among them, perhaps, are the cooking classes run by another friend from back East, Madeleine Kamman, who lives here now and teaches at the venerable Beringer winery. I was invited to cook for a private gathering at Beringer's one night, and the quail with grapes you see in this section was my contribution to a sumptuous evening in which a young chef named Jerry Comfort supervised the cooking of everything else. It was very Californian: fresh, kind of woodsy and sophisticated at the same time. I remember best the hickory-roasted venison and morels and also the crisps of phyllo with blue cheese and arugula.

The valley offers cafés and bistros as well as restaurants of considerable elegance. In the height of tourist season, according to one estimate, more than 10,000 meals are served in the valley on any given Saturday. (That statistic can serve as a caution, too: If you can, it's far better to avoid those summer Saturdays and the bumper-to-bumper traffic in favor of a more leisurely fall or spring weekend.) A great many of Napa's meals will be at least good; some will be wonderful. And many will display the culinary signature of the valley: absolute freshness. "It's all here," Maurice Nayrolles said as we continued to chat. "Everything I need is grown or produced in the valley, the fruits and vegetables, the livestock."

For me that point couldn't have been made more powerfully than it was at Tra Vigne, an Italian restaurant—Cal-Ital is what some people are calling it—that draws deeply on some of the best Italian cooking traditions and at the same time takes Napa for everything it's worth. Michael Chiarello is the young chef at Tra Vigne who found himself looking, as he puts it, for a "point of difference," a way of differentiating himself from all the other young chefs in the valley. So—with the business sense of his father who was a banker and the cooking sense of his mother who thrived on turning out from scratch the kinds of food she knew from the old days in Calabria—Michael decided to take the local meats, fish and dairy products and prepare them himself from Step One, with no middleman. The results of this hard work would be sold in the restaurant, once a winery building, and also in a store on the property.

To make his own prosciutto, he buys 300 fresh hams a year from neighboring Sonoma and other nearby areas. Each ham, he told us, must be a right hind leg, because pigs tend to lean on it more than on the left and the muscle is firmer. He, and those who work for him, will rub the hams with salt until their hands are raw.

Later in the process the meat will be rinsed and trimmed, then hung in a curing room above the store. It takes six to eight months to produce a leg of prosciutto at Tra Vigne. Michael likes to demystify the whole effort: "It's really just a Smithfield ham," he says, "but without the smoking at the end." And when he talks about the price some prosciutto brings, he laughs: "dried pig! it's just dried pig!"

In wooden barrels near the curing room, he makes his own vinegars from over-the-hill local wine. The smoked salmon is cured on the premises. And some sausage and cheese, including a lovely, creamy mascarpone, are also turned out right here. This kind of hands-on activity can be a disaster of course, when the end product is inferior, but in every case I could find no fault with anything Michael had courageously attempted. In his airy, popular restaurant, he serves the likes of grilled rabbit, wild mushrooms and roasted polenta. The dish we made together in his kitchen was a delicate smoked-salmon pasta—*orecchiette* is what we used as the pasta but other shapes would work as well—in a sauce of fish stock and wine.

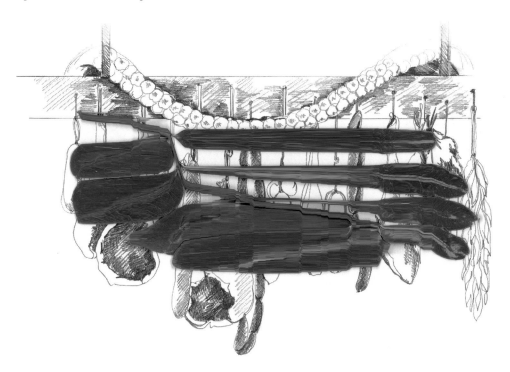

The most often talked about aspect of wine's partnership with food is the drinking of the one while eating the other. And most of the time you'll read about the search for pairings of the two that allow for mutual enhancement. (When you hit the right marriage, you know it: The two will go together, as the food writer William Rice once put it, "like peanut butter and jelly.") But the aspect of the partnership that has always interested me most is more direct: cooking with wine.

Here the marriage is so much more intimate: The wine actually becomes part of the food, impregnating it with flavor, or saucing it or, in some instances (in marinades), even tenderizing it. The most serious mistake home cooks—or anybody else—can make is to choose a bad wine for cooking. I'm not saying that you must use the best bottle in the house, that would be silly; so much nuance is lost in the heat. But keep in mind that wine used in cooking will often be reduced to its essence, as the moisture is removed, and that essence better be at least good enough.

These days, as heavy sauces with cream and flour are shunned for lighter ones, wine seems to be playing a greater role than ever. One of the easiest saucing methods used by chefs all the time for sautéed poultry or beef or fish entails deglazing a pan with a cup of white or red wine.

TO DEGLAZE: After you've cooked the meat, take it out of the pan and pour off most of the fat. Add to the pan 2 tablespoons of chopped shallots and cook briefly. Pour in the wine, stirring over high heat for a minute or two, to reduce the liquid and also to dissolve the solid particles clinging to the pan (stick-free pans, designed so those necessary solids won't cling to them, are obviously a bad choice for this procedure). Then, off the heat, swirl in a tablespoon of butter (this must be done off the heat because butter cooked too vigorously will make the sauce greasy). Pour the sauce over the meat and sprinkle with chopped fresh herbs. Just a little deglazed sauce will do the trick.

In the Napa Valley people are obsessed with wine and grapes the way Wall Streeters are obsessed with money. So while it may seem like gilding the lily when I added the grapes to the wine sauce at the end of the preparation of this neat little quail appetizer, I felt I'd paid homage, as best I could, to the local fixations. Actually, grapes used this way have a strong role in traditional cooking and are not excessive, but just right.

Braised Stuffed Quail

1/4 pound lean bulk sausage
livers and gizzards from quail,
  coarsely chopped
1/2 cup chopped onions
6 tablespoons chopped shallots
2 teaspoons chopped garlic
1/2 cup raisins
1/2 cup chopped apple, cut into 1/4-
  inch cubes
1/4 teaspoon ground cumin
1/8 teaspoon ground cinnamon
1/4 cup instant couscous
1/8 teaspoon hot red pepper flakes
1 3/4 cups fresh or canned chicken
  broth, simmering

salt and freshly ground pepper to
  taste
4 tablespoons gin
4 tablespoons chopped fresh
  coriander
8 quails, boned except for the
  wings, thighs and leg portions
  (reserve liver and gizzard for
  stuffing)
4 tablespoons butter
4 fresh thyme sprigs or 1 teaspoon
  dried
1/2 cup California Chardonnay
1 teaspoon tomato paste
40 seedless white grapes

1. To make the stuffing, heat a medium saucepan. Add the sausage meat, livers and gizzards and cook for about 3 minutes, stirring to break the sausage meat into small pieces.

2. Add the onions, 3 tablespoons of the shallots and the garlic. Cook, stirring until the onions are wilted. Add the raisins, chopped apple, cumin, cinnamon, couscous, pepper flakes, 1 cup of the hot broth and salt and pepper to taste.

3. Bring to a boil, stirring. Cover tightly. Remove from the heat and let stand for 5 minutes. Add the gin and coriander. Blend well with a fork and divide the mixture into 8 portions. Set aside and let cool.

4. Salt and pepper the cavity of each quail. Using hands, place the stuffing in each quail. Crisscross the legs and tuck the tips of wings backward and under so that they are held in place. Gently reshape the quail into its original form.

5. Sprinkle the quails with salt and pepper.

6. Add 2 tablespoons of the butter to a saucepan large enough to hold the quails in one layer. Melt the butter over high heat. Place the quails in the pan, breast side down, and brown them over medium-high heat on each side for a total of 6 or 7 minutes or until lightly browned.

7. Pour off the fat. Add the remaining 3 tablespoons shallots, thyme, the wine, remaining ³/4 cup chicken broth and tomato paste. Blend well. Add grapes. Cover and cook over medium heat for 6 or 7 minutes more.

8. Remove the quails to a serving plate, keep warm. Swirl the remaining 2 tablespoons of butter into the sauce. (If thyme sprigs were used, remove them.) Divide the sauce and grapes evenly over each quail and serve.

Yield: 4 servings

One of the Napa cooks who made me feel most comfortable in his kitchen was Henri Delcros, a highly skilled chef who'd run a one-star Michelin restaurant in France and now was doing excellent work here. The duck he prepared for us, a locally raised Muscovy, was done in the two-stage process that allows the breast to remain rare while the tougher legs are cooked longer. The breast, cooked this way and then sliced before serving, looks a lot like beef. If you've never tried it before, be brave; it is not gamey but rather tender and subtly flavorful, given a boost by the rich Cabernet.

Meadowood Muscovy Duck

2 Muscovy ducks (female), about 4 pounds each
2 tablespoons vegetable oil
salt and freshly ground pepper to taste
1/2 cup chopped onion
1/2 cup carrots in small cubes
2 tablespoons finely chopped shallots
2 teaspoons finely chopped garlic
4 sprigs fresh thyme or 1 teaspoon dried

1 bay leaf
4 cups California Cabernet
1 tablespoon tomato paste
4 ounces pancetta or salt pork, cut into small cubes
16 pearl onions, peeled
1/2 pound whole chanterelles or other mushroom
2 tablespoons butter

1. Preheat oven to 400°.

2. Remove the legs and thighs from each duck; they will be cooked separately from the breast.

3. Heat 1 tablespoon of the vegetable oil in an ovenproof saucepan large enough to hold the 4 legs. Sprinkle the legs with salt and pepper, add them, skin side down, and cook over medium-high heat until brown. Turn and brown the other side. Remove the fat.

4. Add the chopped onion, carrots, shallots, garlic, thyme and bay leaf. Cook and stir until the vegetables are wilted. Add the wine and tomato paste, and bring to a boil. Cover and place in the oven for about 45 minutes or until done.

5. In a small saucepan add the pancetta or salt pork, and cook until some of the fat is rendered. Add the pearl onions and cook covered for 2 or 3 minutes. Add the mushrooms and cover again. Cook for 5 minutes or until the onions are tender.

6. Heat the remaining 1 tablespoon oil in a small ovenproof saucepan. Sprinkle salt and pepper on the duck breasts and brown lightly in the pan, about 5 minutes. Turn the breasts and place in oven for 7 to 8 minutes. The breasts should be rare. Remove the fat and set the breasts aside. Keep warm.

7. When done, remove the duck legs from the pan and set aside. Bring the pan liquid to a boil on top of the stove, and reduce by half. Add the reduced sauce to the saucepan with the pancetta, onions and mushrooms. Bring to a boil and simmer for 2 minutes. Remove the sauce from the heat, and swirl in the 2 tablespoons of butter.

8. To serve, slice the breast on the diagonal into about 6 slices for each breast half (the meat will look something like rare beef); separate the legs from the thighs. Divide the breast meat and dark meat on warmed plates into 4 to 6 portions. Serve the sauce only over the dark meat.

Yield: 4 servings

My friend Maurice Nayrolles told me how pleased he was to see some of the very things in Napa that were so familiar to him from his time in Europe. Here's a Cornish hen sauté that, if I'd been presenting it in some other context, I would have described as Provençale, referring to its French origins. But it is rendered here exactly as they might do it in Napa now, with local olives, the freshest vegetables possible, and a fine Napa Valley wine.

Sautéed Cornish Hens with Olives

2 tablespoons olive oil

2 Cornish hens, 1¹/₂ pounds each, cut into 8 pieces (4 breasts with the wing and 4 legs)

salt and freshly ground pepper to taste

1 cup chopped onions

2 leeks, cut into small cubes (about 1¹/₂ cups)

1 tablespoon finely chopped garlic

2 cups cubed into ¹/₂-inch pieces peeled plum tomatoes

24 green olives stuffed with pimientos

4 sprigs fresh thyme or 1 teaspoon dried

¹/₂ cup dry white wine, such as California Chardonnay

1 cup fresh or canned chicken broth

1 bay leaf

1 teaspoon saffron threads or turmeric

Tabasco sauce to taste

4 tablespoons chopped fresh basil

1. Heat the olive oil in a heavy skillet large enough to hold the pieces of Cornish hens in one layer. Sprinkle the pieces with salt and pepper to taste. When the oil starts to become hot, add the hen pieces, skin side down. Cook over medium-high heat until lightly browned, about 5 minutes. Turn and cook 5 minutes more.

2. Add the onions, leeks and garlic, and cook, stirring, until wilted, about 2 minutes. Add the tomatoes, green olives, thyme, wine, chicken broth, bay leaf, saffron, Tabasco, salt and pepper to taste. Stir and scrape the bottom of the skillet to dissolve any brown particles on it. Cover tightly and simmer for 10 minutes.

3. Remove the thyme sprigs, if used, and the bay leaf. If there is too much liquid, reduce the sauce a bit. Sprinkle with the chopped basil and serve.

Yield: 4 servings

Of all the uses wine can be put to, one of the most important is in what we French call fumet de poisson, *fish stock. Here, in the exquisite pasta dish Michael Chiarello and I cooked at his Tra Vigne in St. Helena, the* fumet *was combined with cream and transformed into a pasta sauce that would be adorned with Pacific salmon smoked right at the restaurant. Here's that recipe, slightly adapted; if you can't find the smoked salmon trimmings, prepare the* fumet *with a pound of fresh fish bones instead, preferably including the head (gills removed).*

Michael's Orecchiette and Smoked Salmon

2 tablespoons butter
1 yellow onion, diced
1 fennel bulb, diced
1/2 pound smoked salmon trimmings (the inexpensive leftovers from the local deli)
2 cups dry white wine, such as Chardonnay
1/3 cup good vodka, such as Absolut
1 bay leaf

4 sprigs fresh dill
10 black peppercorns
1 pound *orecchiette* pasta or other shaped pasta of your choice
1 1/2 cups heavy cream
1/2 pound smoked salmon, cut into 1/2-inch strips
1/2 cup chopped dill
salt and freshly ground pepper to taste
1 ounce salmon caviar (optional)

1. Melt the butter in a heavy saucepan and add the onion and fennel; cook briefly over medium heat until the vegetables are wilted. Add the salmon trimmings, white wine, vodka, bay leaf, dill sprigs and peppercorns. Simmer, uncovered, over low heat for 20 minutes, skimming any foam from the top. Drain through a very fine strainer. Set aside. There should be about 1 cup fish stock.

2. Bring a pot of salted water to a boil and add the pasta. Cook following the instructions on the package.

3. While the pasta is cooking, start the sauce. Bring the salmon stock to a full boil and reduce by half. Whisk in the cream and simmer until reduced by one third. Set aside.

4. When the pasta is done, drain it. Bring the sauce back to a simmer and add the smoked salmon strips, chopped dill and salt and pepper to taste. Toss the pasta with the sauce. Garnish with a bit of the caviar on each plate, if desired. Serve at once.

Yield: 6 servings

For this steak dish, I've used a variation of the deglazing technique described earlier in this chapter (see page 326). Here the strength of the wine is moderated by the addition of stock and the whole preparation made more complex with tomato paste and peppercorns. But it is still, at heart, a sauce using wine as the deglazing agent.

Steak with Green Peppercorns

4 boneless strip sirloin steaks with excess fat removed, about 6 ounces each
salt and freshly ground pepper to taste
1 tablespoon corn or vegetable oil
4 tablespoons finely chopped shallots
1/2 cup dry red wine, such as Pinot Noir or Cabernet

1/4 cup fresh or canned beef broth
1 teaspoon tomato paste
4 tablespoons dried green peppercorns
3 tablespoons butter
4 tablespoons finely chopped parsley

1. Sprinkle the steaks with salt and pepper to taste.

2. Heat the oil in a cast-iron skillet or other heavy skillet large enough to hold the steaks in one layer over high heat. Add the steaks and brown them on the first side for 3 minutes for medium rare.

3. Turn and continue cooking until they are thoroughly browned, about 3 minutes more. Remove to a plate and keep warm.

4. Pour off the fat and reduce the heat to medium high. Add the shallots and cook briefly until wilted. Do not brown. Add the wine over high heat and reduce to one quarter. Add the broth, stirring to dissolve the brown particles that cling to the bottom of the skillet. Add the tomato paste, peppercorns and any juices that may have accumulated around the steaks.

5. Reduce the sauce by slightly more than half and stir in the butter. Check for seasoning, place the sauce over the steaks and garnish with the parsley.

Yield: 4 servings

When you hear that old rule about white wine with fish and red wine with meat, it is of course something many of us don't pay much attention to anymore. These days you see red wine frequently used with monkfish, eel, pike and in fish stews. In every case, it is meant to join fish that have naturally assertive flavors. To my mind, it goes especially well with salmon, as the following dish will demonstrate. (And, certainly, drink a good red wine with it.)

Baked Salmon Fillets with Feta Cheese and Coriander

4 tablespoons olive oil
$^{1}/_{2}$ cup chopped onions
1 tablespoon finely chopped garlic
$^{1}/_{2}$ cup dry red wine, such as a Cabernet or Pinot Noir
4 tablespoons capers
1 tablespoon fresh chopped rosemary or 1 teaspoon dried
1 teaspoon chopped fresh oregano or $^{1}/_{2}$ teaspoon dried
$^{1}/_{8}$ teaspoon hot red pepper flakes

$^{1}/_{2}$ cup crushed canned tomatoes
12 pitted black olives
salt and freshly ground pepper to taste
4 skinless boneless salmon fillets, about 6 ounces each
$^{1}/_{3}$ pound crumbled feta cheese
2 tablespoons anise-flavored liquor, such as Ricard
4 tablespoons chopped fresh coriander

1. Heat 2 tablespoons of the olive oil in a saucepan. Add the onions and garlic, and cook briefly while stirring. Add the wine, capers, rosemary, oregano, pepper flakes, crushed tomatoes, black olives, salt and pepper to taste. Bring to a boil and simmer 5 minutes.

2. Preheat oven to 475°.

3. Pour 1 tablespoon of the remaining olive oil into a baking dish large enough to hold the fish in one layer. Arrange the fish, skin side down, and sprinkle with salt and pepper. Pour the tomato sauce around the fish fillets, brush the top of the fillets with the remaining olive oil and sprinkle with the crumbled feta cheese.

4. Bake for 5 minutes and sprinkle with the Ricard. Transfer the dish to the broiler and broil for 5 minutes. Do not overcook the fish. Sprinkle with the chopped coriander and serve immediately.

Yield: 4 servings

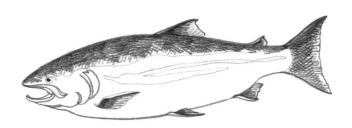

broth that is meant to be eaten along with the food it cooked. Here is one of my favorites.

...Be sure the zucchini aren't overcooked, they should be crunchy.

Rolled Fillets of Sole à la Nage

4 large skinless boneless lemon sole
   fillets, about 6 ounces each

2 small zucchini, $^1/_2$ pound

1 pound mussels

4 thin slices ginger

2 sprigs fresh thyme or 1 teaspoon
   dried

1 bay leaf

2 cups dry white wine, such as
   California Chardonnay

12 baby carrots, all about the same
   size, trimmed and scraped

salt and freshly ground pepper to
   taste

8 tablespoons butter

2 tablespoons finely chopped
   shallots

8 sprigs fresh coriander, coarsely
   chopped

1. Place the fillets on a flat surface. There is a thin line running lengthwise down the center of each fillet. Run a sharp knife down the center of it to divide the fillets. This will produce 8 fillets. Keep refrigerated. Trim off the ends of the zucchini and slice into thin rounds.

2. Scrub the mussels thoroughly and drain. Place the mussels in a saucepan, add the ginger, thyme, bay leaf and the wine. Cover tightly, bring to a boil and cook for 30 seconds or until the mussels are opened. Let cool, remove the meat from the shell, set aside and strain the liquid with a fine strainer. Save the liquid.

3. Place the carrots in a saucepan and cover with water. Salt to taste. Bring to a boil and simmer for 7 minutes or until tender. Drain. Keep warm.

4. Roll the fish fillets up like small jelly rolls. Insert a toothpick to hold them together. Use 1 tablespoon butter to grease the bottom of a skillet just large enough

to hold the rolls in one layer. Arrange the rolls so they are upright in the skillet. Sprinkle the shallots over them and add salt and pepper to taste.

5. Pour the reserved mussel broth over the fish. Cover the skillet tightly and bring to a boil. Simmer for about 3 minutes. Do not overcook. Strain the cooking liquid and keep the rolled fillets warm.

6. Transfer the cooking liquid to a saucepan and place over medium heat. Reduce to two thirds. Add the remaining butter, bit by bit, to the saucepan, beating rapidly with a wire whisk. Add the zucchini and simmer for 10 seconds, stirring with a fork. Keep very hot.

7. To serve, place 2 fillets standing up in a deep dish or soup plate. Arrange 3 carrots and a few mussels around the fillets. Pour over all the broth with the zucchini. Garnish with coriander sprigs. Serve hot.

Yield: 4 servings

Note: This dish should be served with a fork and a soup spoon since the liquid is half the fun.

Spa Cuisine

've been familiar with spa food for a long time now. My good friend Seppi Renggli produced some elegant cooking under that rubric in his days at The Four Seasons in Manhattan. And before him, I remember the incredible inventiveness of Michel Guérard who created spectacular, dietetic dishes for his spa, Eugénie-les-Bains, in France. He called it *cuisine minceur* and replaced the flavorful fats in his dishes with bursts of herbs and spices. I've been watching the trend for more than 40 years, actually, and not so long ago came out with my own version of lighter cooking in a book called *Pierre Franey's Low-Calorie Gourmet.* (In fact, I've been lowering the fat content of my cooking so routinely now, that most of the recipes I publish in one place or another are much lighter than they would have been, say 15 years ago.)

My low-calorie efforts generally lean heavily on vegetables and chicken and seafood. I stay away from cream or flour-based sauces and instead usually employ a reduction of stock or wine, or vinegar or just water (see deglazing discussion on page 326). Soups and sauces can be thickened and made smooth with puréed vegetables, mushrooms being especially good for this task. I like to burn away the animal fat in many dishes through searing meat and then discarding the rendered fat. I also have found that a great deal less cooking oil can be used than I once thought was the case with no loss of flavor, although a nonstick pan is often required.

All that said, I had not visited one of the nation's growing number of spas until the day we drove up the winding driveway to the Canyon Ranch in the Berkshire Mountains of Massachusetts (it bears the same name as its parent spa in Tucson, Arizona). The first thing we saw was the massive columned mansion, built for a businessman named Giraud Foster in 1897 and intended to look like the Petite Trianon at Versailles. The mansion had fallen into disuse by the time it was picked up by the Canyon Ranch people in the mid-1980's. And I do mean picked up. They refurbished the main house to create the dining room and a big modern kitchen. Then they built a sprawling complex of buildings to house the guest rooms and the recreation facilities.

It's the recreation possibilities that wow guests most when they come here, I think. The place has every manner of body shaping machine, an immense indoor pool for swimming laps, as well as an outdoor one, and gyms and classes and, it just goes on in an almost overwhelming array of options.

But food and nutrition are central to the whole affair. And what they're trying to do at Canyon Ranch seems to be part of a recent trend among the diet designers at weight-loss spas, those establishments we used to call the fat farms. Now, they are downplaying the idea that you would come to such a place simply to lose weight (you might even, they say, be among the few who need to gain a few pounds in the right places). What you come for is to unwind and get yourself in the right frame of mind to eat better and exercise more as your life goes on. It is not—as we were told by the spa's vivacious young nutritionist, Margaret Zukas—a program of deprivation. But, if you're a smoker, you'll have to hide out in the mountains, or somewhere, to break out that pack of cigarettes. And if you're a drinker, there's no wine or any other alcohol served with meals. The absence of alcohol makes sense in such highly weight-conscious situations, of course, since it sneaks in calories very quickly.

The core of the diet is a formula: 60 percent carbohydrates, 20 percent fat and 20 percent protein. This is in the spirit of the latest national guidelines for cutting fat intake generally. It's a bit more energetic than some, which call for 30 percent fat, and less rigorous than others, which urge a total of 10 percent—a nearly unobtainable goal for a great many people. The daily caloric intake that many people shoot for at Canyon Ranch—and they're advised not to go any lower—is 1,000 calories for women and 1,200 for men. But the menu allows guests to eat as much as they like. Except that as they eat, they know exactly what they're doing. The dishes on the menu, as well as those announced by the waiter, are accompanied by written or spoken calorie and fat counts.

The entry for the chicken marsala I had during my first meal there, a dinner, read like this: "Broiled chicken breast finished with marsala, wine, shallots and fresh mushrooms . . . 270 . . . 4." The 270 referred to the calories and the 4 to the grams of fat. In addition to the half chicken breast—which was moist, lightly but pleasantly seasoned and cut into two pieces to make it look more substantial, I suppose—I had garlic soup, a large green salad with something called "jet fuel" dressing and bits of tuna on top, bread, and a tiny slice of Boston cream pie, washed down by a cinnamon-apple drink. The total came to 700 calories, a hefty dinner for the spa, but a good deal lighter than I am likely to consume at a restaurant anywhere else. I joked with my companions, "I feel full now," I said, "but in two hours who knows. . . ." The truth is my hunger was satisfied completely for the whole evening, and I found myself looking forward to seeing what else this spa had to offer the next day.

In the kitchen I worked with Barry Correia to prepare a very beautiful dish (visual appeal is mandatory in low-calorie cooking since you don't want the food to look like it's a punishment), a vegetable strudel with a sauce of puréed red pepper.

But Keep the Butter

At the Canyon Ranch, I was pleased to see that the menu listed not just margarine but also butter (50 calories to the serving and 6 grams of fat, with the margarine also 50 and 6). For a long time, margarine had many folks bamboozled, I think. Margarine was being eaten as if it were dietetic. People would slather it on bread in a fit of righteousness. Well, of course, ordinary margarine is just as fattening as butter. In more recent research, margarine has shown itself to be a little riskier on the cholesterol front, too, than anyone had thought before (although, evidently, still preferable to butter for those on rigid diets).

Over the years, incredibly, more and more people were giving up the absolutely magnificent taste of butter, a central flavor in many dishes, and substituting this greasy, phony stuff of dubious health benefit. So much harm done to so much food!

My low-calorie approach to butter has been to avoid it altogether as a spread (you just use too much that way) but include it wherever its flavor is necessary for the success of a dish. Even then I use it judiciously, often a third or less of the volume that I would have employed in the past. Sometimes, I mix butter and olive oil, a very effective combination in terms of taste, and the olive oil is better for your cholesterol count than the butter. One trick is to add a bit of butter at the very end of the preparation of a dish so that the flavor isn't lost. An example: Add as little as 1 tablespoon of butter to a sauce, at the end, swirled in off the heat. Thus, if the sauce is for 4 servings, a mere 25 calories is being added to a dish, and that is an inconsequential amount, even if you're shooting for, say, 1,500 calories a day. But the difference in flavor is incalculable.

Although I prepared that excellent strudel with Barry Correia, the chef at the Lenox, Massachusetts, Canyon Ranch, it is actually the creation of Bernd Schmitt, the German- and Swiss-trained chef of the parent spa in Tucson. In his recipe, you'll notice that Bernd goes to great lengths to avoid the use of salt, employing Mrs. Dash, a combination of dried seasonings instead. To cut calories to the absolute minimum, he employs a thin coating of vegetable spray. Bernd has an excellent sense of colors, and he garnishes the dish lavishly, with among other things, yellow teardrop tomatoes, which are about the size of cherry tomatoes. For many of the dishes prepared at the spa, the cooks use vegetable stock. This is simply the reserved liquid from cooking vegetables at other times.

Canyon Ranch's Vegetable Strudel

5 cups vegetable stock or water

1 cup broccoli florettes

1 cup asparagus spears (split lengthwise if they are thick), cut on the diagonal into 1-inch lengths

1 cup julienne strips of carrot

1/2 cup chopped red onion

1/2 cup sliced *shiitake* mushrooms

2 cups shredded savoy cabbage

1 cup cored seeded julienne strips of sweet red pepper

4 sheets phyllo pastry dough, unseparated

2 tablespoons Mrs. Dash

vegetable spray, such as Pam

Red Pepper Coulis (recipe follows)

1/2 cup julienne strips of beets for garnish

1/2 cup yellow teardrop tomatoes for garnish

chervil sprigs for garnish

1. Preheat oven to 350°.

2. Fill a pot large enough to hold your collander or strainer with ice cubes and water.

3. In a stock pot bring the vegetable stock to a boil. Blanch all the vegetables but the cabbage and the red pepper in the boiling stock for 2 minutes or until al dente. Remove, drain and plunge into the ice water to stop the cooking and keep the vegetables crisp. Remove vegetables from the water and place on a clean towel. Pat dry completely.

4. Place the phyllo pastry on a dry tabletop or cutting board and spread the cabbage down it in a lengthwise mound that will form the base for what will be a rolled

strudel. Leave about an inch of dough uncovered at both ends of the cabbage mound.

5. Place all the remaining vegetables including the red pepper over the cabbage. Season with Mrs. Dash.

6. Gently roll up the strudel (it will roll over 2 times), and leave a strip of 1 inch at the end. Spray the strip with the vegetable spray and fold it over to seal. Spray the ends of the strudel and fold them in to seal.

7. Use the vegetable spray to grease a baking sheet, and place the strudel on it. Bake for 25 minutes.

8. To serve, cut the strudel on the diagonal into 8 pieces, 2 for each serving. Spread the red pepper coulis evenly over each plate and place 2 pieces of the strudel on top of it. Arrange the beet strips and teardrop tomatoes around it. Garnish with the chervil sprigs on top.

Yield: 4 servings

Red Pepper Coulis

4 sweet red peppers, cored, seeded and diced
¹/₂ cup chopped shallots
¹/₂ tablespoon chopped garlic
¹/₂ tablespoon chopped fresh thyme
¹/₂ tablespoon chopped fresh tarragon

1 cup vegetable stock (liquid reserved from cooking vegetables at other times; if you don't have any, use water)
¹/₂ tablespoon chopped mint

1. Place all the ingredients, except the mint, in a saucepan with the vegetable stock and bring to a boil. Remove from the heat.

2. Place the mixture in the container of a blender or food processor and blend until smooth. Just before serving, add the mint and blend briefly.

No one ever got fat eating mussels. They are a marvelous food if you're watching calories. And, with nothing else adding fat to this dish, I've allowed it to luxuriate in ¹/₄ cup olive oil, which spread among 4 servings is much less than it seems.

Mussel Salad with Angel Hair Pasta

¹/₄ pound fine angel hair pasta
salt and freshly ground pepper to
    taste
4 pounds mussels
1 bay leaf
6 whole peppercorns
2 whole cloves
4 sprigs parsley
5 tablespoons red wine vinegar
¹/₄ cup fresh lemon juice
¹/₄ cup olive oil
1 teaspoon finely chopped mint

¹/₄ teaspoon hot red pepper flakes
1 cup thinly sliced red onions
2 cups sliced peeled and seeded
    cucumbers
3 plum tomatoes, about ¹/₂ pound,
    cut into cubes
1 tablespoon finely chopped garlic
¹/₄ cup chopped fresh basil leaves
¹/₄ cup chopped parsley
2 endives
1 large bunch watercress, rinsed
    well and tough stems removed

1. Place the pasta in 2 quarts salted boiling water, and cook for about 3 minutes. Do not overcook. Drain, let pasta cool briefly, then cut strands into 3-inch lengths.

2. Remove the beards and barnacles from the mussels. Place them in a large bowl and cover them with cold water. Swirl the mussels about vigorously so that they rub against each other or until they are cleaned. Change the water and repeat the procedure a few times.

3. Place the mussels along with the bay leaf, peppercorns, cloves, parsley sprigs and 2 tablespoons of the vinegar in a large saucepan or pot. Cover tightly and cook over high heat, shaking the pan a bit. Remove the mussels as soon as they open, drain the mussels and reserve about ¹/₄ cup of the juice. Let the mussels cool. Remove the meat from the shells and set aside.

4. Combine the noodles, mussels and all the remaining ingredients, except the endives and watercress, in a large salad bowl. Toss, and blend well. To serve, place a mound of the salad on each chilled plate. Around the periphery radiating away from the center place several endive leaves. Between the leaves, place a small bunch of watercress.

Yield: 4 servings

What I want you to do here, following the same principle exhibited in the pork recipe above, is to eat just a small portion of the lamb—that half pound includes the bone, don't forget—and to be extremely meticulous in trimming away the fat. As for the rest, there's only the 1 tablespoon of olive oil to add anything worth talking about in terms of calories or fat, and that, you'll notice, is poured away, along with any fat rendered from the lamb.

Lamb Chops Provençale Style

4 lean lamb chops, about ¹/₂ pound
    each, with most of the fat
    removed
salt and freshly ground pepper to
    taste
1 tablespoon olive oil
2 teaspoons chopped fresh rosemary
    or 1 teaspoon dried
4 sprigs fresh thyme or 1 teaspoon
    dried

2 tablespoons chopped onion
2 teaspoons finely chopped garlic
1 tablespoon red wine vinegar
2 cups tomatoes, peeled and cut
    into ¹/₂-inch cubes
1 bay leaf
¹/₄ cup pitted black olives
¹/₄ cup pitted green olives
4 tablespoons chopped fresh basil
    leaves or parsley

1. Sprinkle the chops with salt and pepper.

2. Heat the oil in a heavy skillet, preferably cast iron, large enough to hold the chops in one layer. Cook the chops until browned on one side, about 6 minutes. Turn,

sprinkle with the rosemary and thyme and cook for 6 minutes more for rare (longer for medium rare or well done). Remove to a warm platter and keep warm.

3. Pour off most of the fat from the skillet and add the onions and garlic. Cook and stir until wilted. Add the vinegar, tomatoes, bay leaf, black and green olives and salt and pepper to taste. Cook, stir and simmer for about 5 minutes. Add any juices that have accumulated around the lamb chops.

4. Remove the bay leaf and pour the mixture over the lamb chops. Sprinkle with the basil or parsley and serve.

Yield: 4 servings

The Riskiest Fruit

When we drove into Yakima, we couldn't help but notice that this town was a little rough around the edges, a kind of Wild West air suffused the place, and it was obviously proud of it. One of the popular drive-ins is the Lariat Bar.B.Q., where we stopped for a sandwich of baked ham on a hamburger patty topped with melted cheese. At Espinoza's, a Mexican-American bar and grill, we settled into one of the darkest barrooms in the country for a beer, right next to a fellow whose naked, tattooed arms were the size of most normal thighs.

It's in Yakima that fruit-growers have gotten themselves into some high-stakes gambling: Many of them grow cherries, perhaps the riskiest major crop on earth. Each season of the year holds some potential disaster for the cherry. The winter, when it's too cold, can kill the buds and sometimes the trees (and they have taken seven years to mature into commercial producers). If the trees and buds survive the winter, and the glorious blossoms finally begin to emerge, a late frost will take care of that, in short order. But that's not the worst of it. During the cherries' very short harvest time in the summer, the most dread enemy is rain. As the fruit ripens on the tree, its skin is porous. Rain will seep right into the heart of the cherry, force it to expand and then split. Rain can destroy a whole crop.

Fortunately, it doesn't rain much here, only about seven or eight inches a year. The only reason fruit grows abundantly in this region is that water is a gift from the snow-peaked Cascades that sit right on the horizon. And from Gip Redman's cherry orchard, on a day when the sky was unbelievably high and blue, we could see the mountains clearly. Mt. Adams, St. Helens, Mt. Rainier: legendary peaks. First they gave this area its rich volcanic soil. Now, with the help of a sophisticated irrigation system, they supply it with abundant water from the melting snow.

As we walked among the cherry trees, the colors burst around us. There were huge red clusters of Bing cherries ready to be picked and rushed to markets around the country. Between the neat rows of trees lay a carpet of dandelions. But, at the same time, everywhere there were signs of the cherry farmers' struggle. Below many of the trees sat smudge pots to be fired up in the cold weather. Thirty-five feet above us, on towers, were airplane propellers attached to V8 engines. Their job was to bring down warmer air during a frost. And during a rain, they were designed to blow the water off the fruit, with great man-made blasts of wind.

The farmers around here aren't fools. Fragile as those cherries are, when things go right, they bring in a fortune. And because things go wrong so often, they hedge their bets; Yakima County is perhaps the most diversified growing area in the

country. Apples, plums, nectarines, peaches all take advantage of the warm days and the cool nights. Asparagus is grown here, too. And, not surprisingly, given the recent proclivities of the Northwest, grapes are now grown here in tremendous quantity.

Where there were only six wineries 12 years ago, there are now 84. Napa and Sonoma in California have become expensive, of course, and that's one reason the vintners have come here. But it is also true that the area's good climate and soil seem to be very congenial to the wine-maker's craft. Something in the soil seems to make it particularly productive for Riesling, and many wineries have been successful with it. Now there are other wine success stories, too.

When we visited Birchfield Manor, a restaurant and inn in Yakima, we were treated to a fine Cabernet Sauvignon from Woodward Canyon. It was a 1988, young for a rich red wine, but it was smooth anyway. We learned that the wineries here are so young themselves that they have to sell their product fast just to keep the cash flow moving. Fortunately, their wine seems to be more than just drinkable right out of the gate. We wondered if it would age well.

At the Birchfield Manor, the chef was Will Masset, a reserved, former cooking teacher who decided to start cooking in his own restaurant. It's been quite a hit. A readers' survey in a recent issue of *Pacific Northwest* listed it as "Best of the Pacific Northwest." The restaurant is in a large, former home and feels as homey as can be. Will and his wife are antiques buffs and have collected tables and other furnishings during many of their travels. The result is a kind of unmatched but still harmonious decor, with round tables up next to square ones and chairs that might not ordinarily go together standing side by side nevertheless.

We cooked a number of dishes there, the most impressive of which was pork medallions in a fine cherry sauce, served with stuffed zucchini on the side. It was all meant to celebrate the cherries of the region. But I think we were celebrating a bit prematurely.

Just a few days after we visited Yakima, torrential rains hit the valley. Gip Redman lost 85 percent of his crop.

Buying Cherries

The cherry farmers, who've gone through so much worry to produce the fruit, are especially eager to get the cherries to market in the best possible shape. After picking them in the cool morning, they rush them by truck to be cooled further, rapidly bringing the temperature of the fruit down to 35 degrees. The process from orchard to package is usually less than 24 hours, and then they are shipped in containers fitted with polyethylene liners that keep oxygen out and prevent the already ripe cherries from ripening any further.

In the Northwest, 95 percent of the cherries are either Bing or Lambert. When you buy them they should be plump and bright. The color of a fully ripe Bing or Lambert can range from dark mahogany, nearly black, to brilliant red. The Rainier cherry is cream or golden.

Cherries have only an eight-week season, but it is possible to keep them around a lot longer than that. The simplest way is to freeze them. Wash them, place them in a freezer bag and seal it well. They should be good for at least six months. Remove them from the freezer only 30 minutes before serving to maintain their texture.

It is very difficult to execute most cherry recipes without a cherry pitter. There are a great many on the market. Some clamp to the side of a table and pound the pits out of cherry after cherry with great rapidity. Others are simpler, cheaper and slower: little hand-held devices that do one cherry at a time. But since this fruit is so delightful, it really does pay to purchase one pitter or another to be able to enjoy the cherry season in full bloom.

One of the pleasantest and most refreshing uses of cherries is the simple cherry compote. The cherries tend to hold their shape and their character is greatly enhanced, not overwhelmed, by the syrup.

Cherry Compote

$^1/_2$ cup honey
$^1/_2$ cup Beaujolais or light
  Burgundy wine
$^1/_4$ cup sugar

8 orange slices
1 1-inch cinnamon stick
1$^3/_4$ pounds Bing cherries, pitted

1. Combine the honey, wine, sugar, orange slices and cinnamon in a large saucepan. Bring to a boil and reduce to 1$^1/_2$ cups.

2. Add the cherries, bring to a boil and simmer for 5 minutes.

3. Place the cherries and syrup in a bowl and skim off the foam. When the cherries stop steaming put them in the refrigerator to cool. They can be served chilled or warm over ice cream.

Yield: 6 to 8 servings

❦ Clafoutis *is a classic custard dish, often done as a kind of pancake with cherries in it. The version I offer here, though, has the custard in a tart shell.*

Cherry Clafoutis

The Tart Shell

2 cups all-purpose flour

$^{1}/_{4}$ teaspoon salt

1 tablespoon sugar

10 tablespoons very cold butter

$^{1}/_{4}$ cup walnuts, coarsely chopped

2 tablespoons ice water

1. Place the flour, salt and sugar in the container of a food processor. Cut the butter into small pieces and add it to the processor with the walnuts. Blend briefly and add the water.

2. Continue blending just until the pastry pulls away from the sides of the container and starts to form a ball. Using a rolling pin, roll out the dough into a circle 13 inches in diameter. Immediately line a $10^{1}/_{2}$-inch pie tin equipped with a removable bottom with the pastry, trim off the excess dough and put the shell in the refrigerator until ready to use.

The Custard Filling

$^{1}/_{2}$ cup sugar

3 eggs

$^{1}/_{2}$ cup milk

$^{1}/_{2}$ cup heavy cream

$^{1}/_{2}$ teaspoon almond extract

$^{1}/_{2}$ teaspoon pure vanilla extract

$^{1}/_{4}$ cup Cherry Marnier

2 pounds black Bing cherries, pitted

3 tablespoons confectioners' sugar for garnish

1. Preheat oven to 400°.

2. Bake the tart shell for 10 minutes and let it cool.

3. In a bowl combine the sugar and eggs and beat well with a whisk. Add the milk, cream, almond extract, vanilla extract and Cherry Marnier. Blend well. Place the cherries in the bottom of the cooled baked tart shell, arranging them in a tight circular pattern. Pour the custard mixture over the cherries.

4. Place the tart on a cookie sheet and bake for 30 minutes or until set in the center. Remove and, using a small sieve, sprinkle with the confectioners' sugar.

Yield: 6 to 8 servings

  ❧ *A similar effect to the one achieved in the preceding* clafoutis *can be achieved just by using a simple cherry sauce as a topping for any of a countless number of desserts such as custard or ice cream or cake.*

Cherry Sauce for Dessert

²/₃ pound Bing cherries, pitted and coarsely chopped (about 2 cups)

1³/₄ cups late-harvest Riesling

1 teaspoon cornstarch

2 teaspoons water

1. Pour the wine into a saucepan. Add the cherries, bring to a boil and simmer for 5 minutes.

2. Dissolve the cornstarch in the water and blend it into the cherry mixture. Strain the mixture into another saucepan to remove the cherries and set aside.

3. Return the liquid to the heat and reduce by about half. Return the cherries to the sauce and refrigerate.

Yield: about 2 cups

❧ *Cherries have always gone well with crisp poultry, and I could have chosen any number of examples. But the two that follow, very different in execution, make the point.*

Roasted Cornish Hens with Cherries

4 Cornish game hens with giblets, each about $1^{1}/_{4}$ pounds

2 tablespoons vegetable or corn oil

salt and freshly ground pepper to taste

1 large onion, peeled

$^{1}/_{4}$ cup dry sherry

1 tablespoon red wine vinegar

1 tablespoon honey

1 cup fresh or canned chicken broth

1 tablespoon tomato paste

2 cups pitted Bing cherries

1 tablespoon butter

1. Preheat oven to 450°.

2. Place the hens in a shallow heatproof baking dish without crowding. Rub the hens with oil and sprinkle them inside and out with salt and pepper. Cut the onion in half. Place the onion halves, flat side down, around the hens. Arrange the gizzards and the necks around the hens.

3. Place the baking dish on top of the stove over medium-high heat. Turn the hens around in the dish to coat them with the oil. Brown them all over for a few minutes. Arrange the hens on their sides, and bake 15 minutes, basting often.

4. Turn the hens to the other side and continue baking 15 minutes, basting often.

5. Turn the hens, breast side up, and bake about 10 minutes, basting often. Transfer the hens to a heated serving platter. Cover with foil to keep warm.

6. Skim off the fat from the pan liquid. Place the dish on top of the stove and bring the liquid to a boil. Add the sherry and the vinegar and stir to dissolve any brown particles that may cling to the bottom of the pan. Strain the sauce into a saucepan and bring to a boil. Reduce by half. Add the honey, broth and tomato paste. Stir and add any liquid that may have accumulated inside or around the birds. Add the cherries and bring to a boil. Cook about 3 minutes, stirring often. Swirl in the butter and add salt and pepper if necessary. Pour the sauce over the hens and serve.

Yield: 4 servings

An interesting aspect of this dish is that in preparing the duck for cooking, as you'll see from the illustration, most of the fat is removed at the outset. Then the duck is crispened beautifully before the cherry sauce is joined with it. Usually one duck provides two servings but if it is joined by another small course, such as a fish appetizer, it will satisfy four as a main course.

Sautéed Duck with Cherries

1 tablespoon vegetable oil
1 5-pound duck, cut into serving
    pieces (see illustration, page 362)
salt and freshly ground pepper to
    taste
1/4 cup coarsely chopped onion
1/4 cup coarsely chopped carrots
1/4 cup chopped celery
1 clove garlic, sliced
3 sprigs fresh thyme or 1 teaspoon
    dried

1 bay leaf
1 tablespoon arrowroot
2 tablespoons sugar
2 tablespoons white wine vinegar
1 1/2 cups Condensed Duck Broth
    (page 155) or fresh or canned
    chicken broth
2 tablespoons Cherry Marnier
1 tablespoon tomato paste
1 1/2 pounds Bing cherries, pitted

1. Preheat oven to 450°.

2. In an ovenproof skillet large enough to hold all the pieces in one layer heat the oil. Sprinkle the duck with salt and pepper. Sauté the duck, skin side down, over medium heat until the skin is golden brown and crisp, about 7 minutes. Turn and cook on the other side until crispy.

3. Pour off the excess fat and add the onion, carrots, celery, garlic, thyme and bay leaf to the skillet. Place in the oven and bake for 15 minutes.

4. Remove the duck from the skillet and keep it warm on a platter. Return the pan to the stovetop and add the arrowroot, sugar, vinegar, broth, Cherry Marnier and tomato paste. Bring to a boil, stirring to reduce and thicken slightly.

5. Strain the sauce and add the cherries to it. Serve the duck with the cherry sauce spooned over and around it. Accompany it with Buttered Wild Rice (page 367).

Yield: 2 to 4 servings

Cutting Duck into Four Serving Pieces

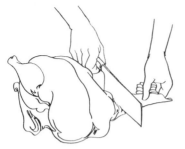

1. Remove tip joint of wing.

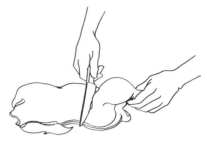

2. Remove leg and thigh in one piece.

3. Begin to cut breast away from bone.

4. Remove breast in one piece.

5. Cut other breast piece.

6. Cut away wing and save for stock if desired.

7. Trim breast of fat.

8. Loosen joint at leg and thigh but do not sever.

9. Serving pieces.

Here's the pork dish we put together with Will Masset at his restaurant in Yakima. He served it with stuffed zucchini and the recipe for that dish follows.

Birchfield Manor's Pork with Cherries

4 pork tenderloin, about ³/₄ pound
    each, trimmed and with excess
    fat removed, each tenderloin cut
    into 4 equal rounds
salt and freshly ground pepper to
    taste
1 tablespoon vegetable oil

1 cup Port
2 cups cherries, pitted
1 teaspoon cornstarch
2 teaspoons water
zest of ¹/₂ lemon
juice of ¹/₂ lemon
2 tablespoons sugar

1. With a mallet pound each pork round to about ¹/₄ inch in thickness. Sprinkle with salt and pepper.

2. In a nonstick pan large enough to hold 8 pieces of pork in one layer heat the oil. Sauté the pork over high heat for about 1¹/₂ minutes on each side. Do not overcook. Remove the pork from the pan, but leave the oil in the pan. Set the pork aside and keep warm. Repeat the procedure for the remaining slices. Set aside and keep warm.

3. Meanwhile, in a medium saucepan bring the Port to a boil and boil for 3 minutes. Add the cherries and simmer for 2 minutes. Dissolve the cornstarch in the water and blend it into the wine. While the wine mixture simmers add the lemon zest and juice. Set aside.

BIRCHFIELD MANOR

4. In a separate pan, larger than the one used to simmer the cherries, cook the sugar over high heat until it caramelizes, turning a light brown. Immediately pour the wine and cherry mixture into the hot sugar. Mix well. Set aside and keep warm.

5. To serve, place 4 pieces of pork on each plate and divide the sauce evenly over each serving. Serve with 2 pieces of stuffed zucchini (recipe follows) per serving, one on each side of the plate.

Yield: 4 servings

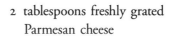

Tomato-Stuffed Zucchini

2 medium zucchini, about 1¹/₄ inches in diameter, ends trimmed
2 tablespoons olive oil
2 tablespoons chopped onion
1 tablespoon finely chopped garlic
4 ripe plum tomatoes, skinned, seeded, cored and coarsely chopped

1 tablespoon tomato paste
salt and freshly ground pepper to taste
2 tablespoons freshly grated Parmesan cheese

1. Preheat oven to 400°.

2. Score the sides of the zucchini with a lemon zester to create a striped effect. Cut each zucchini into four even lengths, about 1¹/₂ inches long. With a melon baller, scoop out the flesh of each section, digging about halfway down.

3. In a small saucepan heat 1 tablespoon of the olive oil and add the onion and garlic. Cook briefly until the onion is wilted. Add the zucchini flesh, tomatoes, tomato paste, salt and pepper. Cook briefly to allow liquid to reduce.

4. Place the zucchini in a baking dish and fill each piece with an even amount of the tomato mixture. Sprinkle with the remaining olive oil. Sprinkle each piece with some Parmesan. Bake 15 minutes or until done. Do not overcook. Serve 2 pieces on each plate as an accompaniment.

Yield: 4 servings

Vegetable Side Dishes, Salads, Sauces and Stocks

Throughout the writing of this book and in the television shows, I frequently found myself referring to side dishes that didn't necessarily fit the theme at hand. I was simply offering them to round out a presentation. Here's a grab bag of them, along with some basic recipes for sauces and stocks that are required time and again.

Buttered Wild Rice

1 cup wild rice
¹/₂ cup finely chopped onions
¹/₂ cup finely chopped celery
2 cups boiling water

salt and freshly ground pepper to
   taste
2 tablespoons butter

1. Place the wild rice, onions, celery, water, salt and pepper to taste and 1 tablespoon of the butter in the top of a double boiler (see Note).

2. Place the pan over boiling water, cover and cook the rice for 1 hour. Fluff the rice with a fork, stirring in the remaining butter.

Yield: 8 small servings

Note: An improvised bain-marie *may be substituted for the double boiler. Place the ingredients in a small kettle or in a large saucepan that will fit inside another utensil containing boiling water. Cover the ingredients tightly and let simmer in the water for 1 hour.*

Spaghetti Squash

1 medium spaghetti squash, about
  2½ pounds
3 tablespoons butter
3 tablespoons chopped chives

salt and freshly ground pepper to
  taste
¼ teaspoon freshly grated nutmeg

1. Preheat oven to 400°.

2. Cut the squash in half lengthwise. Remove the seeds. Place in a roasting pan and add hot water from the tap to a height of 1 inch. Bake for 30 minutes.

3. Using a large heavy metal spoon, scrape out and discard the center section of each half much as you would clean a cantaloupe half. Scoop and scrape out the "spaghetti" strands of the squash, leaving only the shells.

4. Put the strands in a skillet and add the butter, chives, salt and pepper and nutmeg. Heat, tossing gently, until the strands are hot and coated with melted butter. If desired, serve with Fresh Tomato Sauce (page 377).

Yield: 4 to 6 servings

Sautéed Spinach Leaves

$3/4$ pound fresh spinach
2 tablespoons olive oil
$1/4$ teaspoon freshly grated nutmeg

salt and freshly ground pepper to
taste

1. Pick over the spinach leaves and remove the large stems. Wash, drain and remove all the moisture by placing between paper towels and patting dry.

2. In a large nonstick skillet over high heat add 1 tablespoon of the olive oil, half the spinach and half the nutmeg. Add salt and pepper to taste, cook and toss very quickly until the spinach is just wilted. Drain. Repeat the procedure with the remaining ingredients and serve hot.

Yield: 4 servings

Note: The spinach should be served barely cooked.

Fresh Green Peas with Pearl Onions

1 cup pearl onions
$1^1/2$ cups fresh shelled green peas
1 cup finely shredded lettuce
2 tablespoons butter

$1/4$ teaspoon sugar
2 tablespoons water
salt and freshly ground pepper to
taste

1. Peel the onions. To make the job easier, place them in a bowl and pour boiling water over them. Let stand 5 minutes. Drain, cool and peel.

2. Combine all the ingredients in a small heavy casserole with a tight-fitting cover. Bring to a boil and simmer over low heat for 10 minutes.

Yield: 4 servings

⁂ *These days there's a whole industry devoted to making miniature versions of vegetables, most of which are usually sold at specialty food stores. This recipe is meant to take advantage of them.*

Sautéed Baby Vegetables

2 tablespoons olive oil
4 baby zucchini, trimmed
4 baby yellow pattypan squash
4 baby green pattypan squash
2 baby eggplants, trimmed and
　halved lengthwise
4 red or yellow cherry tomatoes
1 tablespoon chopped garlic
1 teaspoon finely chopped jalapeño
　pepper

4 sprigs fresh thyme or 1 teaspoon
　dried
1 bay leaf
salt and freshly ground pepper to
　taste
4 tablespoons coarsely chopped
　fresh basil or Italian flat-leaf
　parsley

1. Heat the oil in a heavy skillet and add the zucchini, squash and eggplant. Sauté, stirring and tossing so that the vegetables cook evenly, about 5 minutes.

2. Add the tomatoes, garlic and jalapeño pepper. Toss to blend.

3. Add the thyme, bay leaf and salt and pepper. Cook, tossing and stirring, about 3 minutes. Add the basil, stir and remove the bay leaf. Serve hot.

Yield: 4 servings

Parslied Baby Carrots

³/₄ pound baby carrots
1 tablespoon butter
2 tablespoons finely chopped
   parsley

salt and freshly ground pepper to
   taste

1. Trim off and discard the ends of the carrots. Scrape them.

2. Place the carrots in a saucepan, cover with water and add salt. Bring to a boil and simmer for 5 minutes, or until tender. Drain.

3. Add the butter, parsley and pepper to taste. Blend well. Serve hot.

Yield: 4 servings

String Beans with Scallions

¹/₂ teaspoon salt
1 pound string beans, trimmed
1 tablespoon olive oil
1 tablespoon butter

2 tablespoons chopped scallions
2 tablespoons chopped fresh
   tarragon or 2 teaspoons dried
freshly ground pepper to taste

1. Bring 2 cups of water to a boil in a saucepan. Add the salt and string beans. Bring the water back to a boil. Simmer for 8 to 10 minutes. The beans should be tender-crisp. Drain.

2. Add the oil and butter to the saucepan. Over the heat add the scallions. Cook briefly. Add the tarragon and pepper and toss to blend. Serve hot.

Yield: 4 servings

Tabbouleh

¹/₂ cup fine bulgur wheat	¹/₃ cup fresh lemon juice
1 cup finely chopped onions	salt and freshly ground pepper to
³/₄ cup finely chopped fresh Italian	taste
parsley	2 tablespoons olive oil
³/₄ cup peeled and seeded chopped	2 tablespoons finely chopped fresh
ripe tomatoes	mint or 1 tablespoon dried
1 teaspoon finely chopped garlic	

1. Place the bulgur wheat in a bowl and cover with cold water. Let soak according to the package instructions. Drain and place in a piece of cheesecloth. Vigorously squeeze out the extra water.

2. Place the bulgur, onions, parsley, tomatoes, garlic, lemon juice and salt and pepper to taste in a bowl. With a fork toss the mixture gently and blend well.

3. Stir in the olive oil and mint before serving.

Yield: 4 servings

Yam Purée

4 yams or sweet potatoes, about 2	2 tablespoons butter
pounds	³/₄ cup milk
salt to taste if desired	

1. Place the yams in a saucepan and add salted water to cover. Bring to a boil and simmer for 30 minutes. Drain and cool.

2. When the yams are cool enough to handle, peel them. Cut the yams into 1-inch cubes. If a food processor is used, process to a medium-coarse texture. Add the butter, process and then add the milk while the machine is running. Process to a fine texture. Serve hot. If the yams are not processed in a food processor, put them through a food mill or ricer. Transfer to a saucepan, add the butter and milk and heat thoroughly, blending well.

Yield: 4 servings

Curried Corn with Red and Green Peppers

4 ears of fresh corn
1 sweet red pepper
1 sweet green pepper
2 tablespoons butter
1/3 cup chopped scallions

1 teaspoon finely chopped garlic
1 teaspoon curry powder
salt to taste
2 tablespoons freshly chopped
   coriander or parsley

1. Scrape the kernels from the corn.

2. Core and remove the seeds from the peppers. Cut the peppers into very thin strips about 1¹/₂ inches long.

3. Heat the butter in a skillet. Add the scallions, garlic and curry powder. Cook, stirring, until the scallions are wilted. Add the corn, peppers and salt to taste. Blend well, cover and cook over medium heat for about 2 minutes. Add the coriander, blend well and serve.

Yield: 4 servings

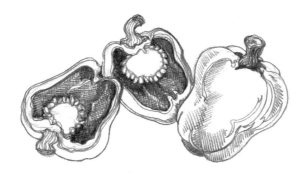

Parslied Cucumbers

2 large firm cucumbers
1 tablespoon butter
4 tablespoons chopped fresh parsley
salt and freshly ground pepper to
taste
juice of 1/2 lemon

1. Trim off the ends of the cucumbers and cut them into 2-inch lengths. Quarter each section lengthwise. With a paring knife partially cut away the green skin if desired. Remove the seeds.

2. In a saucepan cover the cucumbers with water and bring to a boil. Simmer for about 1 minute. Drain.

3. Return the cucumbers to the saucepan. Add the butter, parsley, salt and pepper to taste and the lemon juice. Toss until the butter melts. Serve.

Yield: 4 servings

Cauliflower Mimosa

1 head cauliflower, about 1³/₄
  pounds
salt and freshly ground pepper to
  taste
1/4 cup milk
2 tablespoons butter
1 hard-cooked egg, peeled and
  chopped fine
2 tablespoons finely chopped
  parsley

1. Trim the cauliflower. Break the head into flowerets. Put the pieces in a saucepan and cover with water. Add salt and the milk. Bring to a boil and simmer for 10 minutes, or until tender. Do not overcook. Drain and keep warm.

2. Heat the butter in a nonstick skillet, and add the cauliflower pieces. Toss and stir until the pieces start to color. Add the chopped egg, parsley and salt and pepper to taste. Toss and stir. Serve immediately.

Yield: 4 servings

Mixed Green Salad with
Garlic Croutons and Gorgonzola

2 tablespoons red wine vinegar
1 tablespoon Dijon mustard
1/2 cup crumbled gorgonzola
6 tablespoons vegetable oil
salt and freshly ground pepper to
    taste if desired

10 cups loosely packed bite-size
    pieces of watercress, red leaf
    lettuce, and Belgian endive
Garlic Croutons (page 286)

1. Combine the vinegar, mustard and cheese in a bowl. Blend well. With a wire whisk stir in the oil and salt and pepper to taste.

2. Place the salad greens in a bowl and toss well with the dressing. Serve with croutons.

Yield: 4 to 6 servings

Cucumber and Carrot Salad with Dill

1 seedless cucumber, trimmed and
    peeled
2 large carrots, trimmed and peeled
1/8 teaspoon ground cumin
2 teaspoons finely chopped dill

1 tablespoon white vinegar
salt and freshly ground pepper to
    taste

1. With a vegetable peeler cut large strips of cucumber lengthwise while turning the cucumber. This will yield a curved ribbon. Discard the seeds. Place in a strainer and sprinkle with salt. Let drain for about 10 minutes.

2. Using the same technique, with the peeler make long strips of the carrots while turning them.

3. In a bowl combine the drained cucumber, the carrots, cumin, dill, vinegar and salt and pepper. Toss well and serve immediately.

Yield: 4 servings

Coleslaw

1 head cabbage, about 1 pound
2 medium carrots, about $^{1}/_{3}$ pound,
  trimmed and scraped
2 tablespoons distilled white
  vinegar
1 tablespoon Dijon mustard
1 teaspoon honey

salt and freshly ground pepper to
  taste
$^{1}/_{2}$ cup vegetable oil
2 teaspoons poppy seeds
2 tablespoons finely chopped
  scallions

1. Cut the cabbage into quarters. Cut away and discard the core portions.

2. Process the cabbage in a food processor to any desired degree of fineness. The cabbage can also be chopped with a knife on a flat surface, if desired. Place the cabbage in a mixing bowl.

3. Cut the carrots into $^{1}/_{4}$-inch rounds. Place the carrots in the food processor and process or chop to the desired degree of fineness. Combine the carrots and cabbage.

4. Place the vinegar, mustard, honey and salt and pepper to taste in a bowl and beat until smooth. Beat in the oil. Pour over the cabbage mixture. Add the poppy seeds and the scallions. Blend well and serve.

Yield: 4 servings

Mayonnaise

1 egg yolk
salt and freshly ground white
   pepper to taste
1 tablespoon Dijon mustard

1 tablespoon fresh lemon juice
1 tablespoon white wine vinegar
1 cup vegetable or olive oil or a
   blend of both

1. Place the egg yolk in a bowl and add salt and pepper to taste, the mustard, lemon juice and vinegar. Beat vigorously with a wire whisk or electric beater.

2. Start adding the oil gradually, beating and adding oil until all is used. Taste for seasoning.

3. If the mayonnaise is not used immediately, beat in a tablespoon of water. This will help stabilize the mayonnaise and retard its breakdown when stored in the refrigerator.

Yield: 1 cup

Fresh Tomato Sauce

2 tablespoons butter
1 tablespoon finely chopped shallots
1/4 teaspoon minced chopped garlic
4 ripe plum tomatoes, cored and
   cut into small cubes
1 tablespoon tomato paste
1/2 cup fresh or canned chicken
   broth

1 sprig fresh thyme or
   1/4 teaspoon dried
1 bay leaf
salt and freshly ground pepper to
   taste

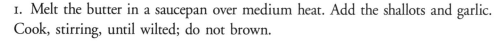

1. Melt the butter in a saucepan over medium heat. Add the shallots and garlic. Cook, stirring, until wilted; do not brown.

2. Stir in the tomatoes, tomato paste, broth, thyme, bay leaf and salt and pepper to taste. Cook, stirring occasionally, for about 10 minutes.

3. Remove the thyme sprig and bay leaf. Place the mixture in a food mill or food processor. Blend to a fine purée. Strain and return the sauce to the pan to warm.

Yield: about 2 cups

Basic Shrimp Stock

shells from 2 pounds raw shrimp
7 cups cold water
6 whole black peppercorns

1 cup coarsely chopped onions
1 cup coarsely chopped celery
1 bay leaf

   Place all the ingredients in a saucepan and bring to a boil. Simmer for about 15 minutes. Strain. The broth, once cooled, can be tightly covered and stored in the refrigerator for several days or frozen for a month or longer.

Yield: 6 cups

Chicken Broth

4 pounds fresh chicken bones
8 cups water
4 whole black peppercorns
1 cup quartered onions
1 cup leek greens, cut coarsely
1/2 cup coarsely chopped carrots
1/2 cup coarsely chopped celery

4 sprigs fresh parsley
1 bay leaf
2 sprigs fresh thyme or 1/2 teaspoon
   dried
1 whole clove
1 garlic clove, cut in half

1. Place the bones in a kettle, add all the remaining ingredients, bring to a boil and simmer, uncovered, for 1 hour. Skim from time to time to remove fat and foam or scum from the top.

2. Strain the broth through a very fine piece of cheesecloth or through a fine mesh strainer into a bowl. Leftover stock can be frozen.

Yield: 6 cups

Afterword: The Studio Set

In my travels, when I meet people who've watched me cook on television, they are frequently curious about the equipment they see me using in the segments taped at the Maryland Public Television studio kitchen. I enjoy responding to their questions because I place a great deal of emphasis on using the best tools. It's always important to have effective equipment if you expect to cook well, and this is especially true on television, where an error can mean shooting the cooking scene over.

Generally speaking, the studio is not the best place to try out unfamiliar equipment. So, for the show, many of the tools I chose were ones I also have at home, often produced in America or France. For instance, I have always liked Le Creuset pots—the enameled iron distributes heat well and the enamel is easy to clean. I particularly like the grill that stretches over two burners of the stove, and that's what I used in a tuna segment. But enameled Le Creuset pans don't brown meat as well as some others will. For browning (and when deglazing is required in the making of a sauce) I prefer stainless steel or cast iron. In the studio I used the pans of anodized aluminum lined with stainless steel produced by All-Clad, an American company. I also turned to some of the excellent French Bourgeat pans, particularly an aluminum nonstick square pan that I used for trout, because it allowed me to cook four fish at one time.

Some years back, Sabatier, a French-made knife, seemed to have fallen behind the fine Wusthof and Henckel products. But I was happy to discover that the new French high-carbon steel knives were now on a par with the others, and it's the Sabatier I used this time. High-carbon steel is by far the best material for knives because it takes an edge better than stainless steel will and won't rust the way the old carbon-steel blades do. In a departure from my practices in the past, I've started to use an electric knife sharpener—the Chef's Choice. I resisted these machines for a long time because those made for the home kitchen couldn't come close to what I can do manually with a good stone. But this one is successful.

My favorite gadget for TV, as well as home use, is Sunbeam's Oskar Jr. chopper/grinder. This is a small version of a food processor with a powerful motor that makes it extremely valuable for blending a small amount of sauce, chopping parsley or making bread crumbs (for larger chores, of course, I used a standard food processor). One of the most noticeable parts of the kitchen is the work surface; I chose Corian this time because it is smooth, looks good and cleans easily.

Another especially striking item on the set is the large blue enameled stove with brass fittings. That's a Morice; it's a French import. I liked it for its looks and sense of solidity; you close its oven and it feels like a safe door is shutting. One of the burners on the range was designed to produce more heat than the others and thus could do things like bring a pot of water to the boil more quickly. In the center there's a flat cooking area that is hotter in the middle than at the periphery so that you can adjust the heat under a saucepan with great precision simply by moving the pan. (Behind the scenes, we had the more familiar Garland, a restaurant range that many serious home cooks have taken to over the years; at home, my stove is a Wolf and they are very similar.)

A piece of equipment that provokes some sentimental feelings in me every time is the KitchenAid mixer, still the best of the mixers in my opinion. When my wife, Betty, and I first got married more than 40 years ago we bought a KitchenAid. It's still working. Tools, like relationships, ought to last.

Index

adobo seasoning, 287
aïoli sauce, 221–2
almonds, pompano with, 147
anchovy paste, pasta with vegetables, capers and, 208
angel hair pasta, mussel salad with, 347–8
apples, pork tenderloin with, 105
aromatic rice, 190
arroz con pollo, 27–8
artichokes, 230–2
    grilled salmon with, 239–40
    preparation for poaching, 243
    purchasing, 232
    stuffed, 240–2
    vinaigrette, 242
arugula
    Cheddar tart with, 203–4
    salad, with tomatoes, 225
asparagus, fettuccine with blue cheese and, 209
avocado, shrimp with sweet red pepper and, 288

bacalaitos fritos, 31
barbecue sauce, honey
    for Cornish hens, 100–1
    for swordfish, 102–3
beans
    dried, to cook, 29
    kidney, and red pepper salad, 29
    rice and, 28

beans *(continued)*
    string, with scallions, 371
béarnaise sauce, 10–11
beef, 5–9
    braised, with red wine, 12–13
    brochettes, with red peppers and coriander, 14–15
    calves' feet soup, 116
    chopped
        broiled, with capers, 15–16
        with goat cheese, 16
        meat loaf with herbs, 17–18
    fillet of, roast, with Madeira mushroom sauce, 20
    pot roast and oxtail in red wine, 18–19
    with red and green peppers, 106
    steak
        béarnaise sauce for, 10–11
        with green peppercorns, 333–4
        skirt steak with warm lentil salad, 302
    tongue, with mustard sauce and lentil salad, 300–1
blue cheese
    fettuccine with asparagus and, 209
    sauce, 205
bread, honey walnut, 103–4
brioches, raisin, 46
brochettes
    beef, with red peppers and coriander, 14–15
    lamb, marinated with honey, 99

brochettes *(continued)*
    shrimp, with orange butter sauce, 315–16
broth
    chicken, 378
    duck, condensed, 155
    fish, 285
bull's foot soup, 116
butter, 344
    sauce
        herbed, 64–5
        orange, 315–16

cabbage slaw, 376
Cajun cooking, 53–7
    cast-iron cookware for, 58
    catfish, fried, 59–60
    chicken and sausage gumbo, 69
    crawfish *étouffée à la Creole*, 61–2
    eggplant pirogues, 70–1
    oysters and clams on the half shell
        cocktail sauce for, 67
        mignonette sauce for, 66
    pork jambalaya, 68–9
    potato salad, 67–8
    shrimp
        barbecued, 62
        and crab meat salad with jalapeño pepper,
            73
        Creole, 74
        fried, with squid, 65–6
        grilled, with herbed butter sauce, 64–5
        gumbo, 75–6
        with yogurt and Tabasco sauce, 72
calves' feet soup, 116
caper(s)
    pasta with vegetables, anchovy paste and, 208
    sauce, pork cutlets with, 133–4
carrot(s)
    baby, parslied, 371
    and cucumber salad with dill, 375
    potatoes mashed with, 173
Casita Blanca, 23–4

casserole, macaroni, with fresh herbs and
        Cheddar, 206–7
cast–iron cookware, 58
catfish, fried, 59–60
cattle ranching, 5–9
cauliflower mimosa, 374
cayenne, 143
Champagne sauce, 273
Cheddar cheese, 199–201
    macaroni casserole with fresh herbs and,
        206–7
    tart, with arugula, 203–4
cheese, 199–201
    blue
        fettuccine with asparagus and, 209
        sauce, 205
    Cheddar
        macaroni casserole with fresh herbs and,
            206–7
        tart, with arugula, 203–4
    feta, salmon baked with coriander and, 334–5
    goat, chopped steak with, 16
    gorgonzola, mixed green salad with, 375
    Gruyère, baked sliced potatoes with, 168
    Parmesan
        baked mashed potatoes with, 171–2
        sauce, ziti with, 207
    purchasing, 202
cheesecake, strawberry, 237–8
cherry(ies), 353–5
    clafoutis, 358–9
    compote, 357
    Cornish hens with, 360
    duck, sautéed, with, 361
    pork with, 363–4
    purchasing, 356
    sauce, 359
chicken
    breasts
        with blue cheese sauce, 205
        breaded, 43
        broiled, with grapefruit, 318
    broth, 378

chicken *(continued)*
    curried, 117
    fajitas, 47–8
    gumbo, with sausage, 69
    with rice, 27–8
    strips, with garlic butter, 291
children, cooking with, 37–9
    breaded chicken breasts, 43
    chicken fajitas, 47–8
    crepes with strawberry filling and raspberry
        sauce, 41–2
    Diane's pancake, 45
    raisin brioches, 46
    safety precautions, 40
    salmon lasagne, 48–9
chili sauce mayonnaise, 89
citrus fruit, 309–12
    grapefruit
        broiled chicken breasts with, 318
        trout sautéed with, 181–2
    lemon
        boiled potatoes with, 172
        tuna broiled with, 217
    orange
        butter sauce, 315–16
        jalapeño relish, 313–14
        pie, with pistachio crust, 314–15
        sauce, 320
        vinaigrette, 317
clafoutis, cherry, 358–9
clams on the half shell
    cocktail sauce for, 67
    mignonette sauce for, 66
cocktail sauce, 67
codfish fritters, 31
coleslaw, 376
compote
    cherry, 357
    honey-onion, 98
coriander, 282
    salmon baked with feta cheese and,
        334–5
    vegetable soup with turkey and, 260

corn
    and ancho chili pudding, 253
    curried, with red and green peppers, 373
    salad, with mustard vinaigrette, 84–5
    turkey and
        rolled, 252–3
        steaks, with basil, 254
Cornish hens
    barbecued, 100–1
    roasted, with cherries, 360
    sautéed, with olives, 331–2
cornmeal with okra, 114
coulis, red pepper, 346
crab(s), 79–81
    cakes, potato, with *crème fraîche*, 165
    Dungeness, 265–6
    and ham, on toast, 86–7
    omelettes, with spicy mayonnaise, 88–9
    salad, with shrimp and jalapeño pepper, 73
    salmon *en papillote* with, 275–6
    soft-shell, 82
        Creole, 144
        and pasta à la Giobbi, 85–6
        with salsa and corn salad, 83–4
crawfish *étouffée à la Creole*, 61–2
crème fraîche, grilled scallion, 165
Creole cooking, 137–42
    cayenne in, 143
    Dover sole *meunière*, 153
    duck breasts, grilled, with pepper jelly glaze,
        154–5
    frogs' legs
        concassé, 149–50
        Provençale, 150–1
    oysters Rockefeller, 148–9
    pompano *amandine*, 147
    salmon, steamed, with yogurt and coriander
        sauce, 157
    scallops with sweet peppers and snow peas,
        156
    seafood seasoning, 145
    soft-shell crabs with Creole sauce, 144
    Worcestershire sauce, homemade, 146

crepes with strawberry filling and raspberry
    sauce, 41–2
croutons, garlic, 286
crustaceans. *See* crab(s); lobster
cucumber(s)
    and carrot salad with dill, 375
    parslied, 374
curry, chicken, 117

deglazing, 326
desserts
    cherry sauce for, 359
    crepes with strawberry filling and raspberry
        sauce, 41–2
    French plum tart, 44–5
    frozen
        pineapple sorbet, 290
        strawberry sorbet, 235
    pineapple and kiwi flan, 120
    rice pudding, 195–6
    strawberry cheesecake, 237–8
Diane's pancake, 45
Disney World, 37–8
Dover sole *meunière*, 153
dressing, pork chops with, 127–8
duck
    breasts, grilled, with pepper jelly glaze,
        154–5
    broth, condensed, 155
    Muscovy, 329–30
    sautéed, with cherries, 361

eggplant
    pirogues, 70–1
    ratatouille, 219–20
eggs: cold crab meat omelettes with spicy
        mayonnaise, 88
escabèche, 222–3

fajitas, chicken, 47–8
feta cheese, salmon baked with coriander and,
        334–5

fettuccine with blue cheese and asparagus,
        209
figs, honeyed, 97
fish, 213–16
    broth, 285
    codfish fritters, 31
    Dover sole *meunière*, 153
    grouper, sautéed, with orange-jalapeño relish,
        313–14
    mahimahi, sautéed, 118–19
    monkfish stew, 218
    pompano amandine, 147
    salmon
        baked, with feta cheese and coriander,
            334–5
        cakes Pojarski, 274–5
        grilled, with artichoke sauce, 239–40
        lasagne, 48–9
        en papillote, with crab, 275–6
        salad, with orange vinaigrette, 317
        sautéed, with honey-onion compote, 98
        smoked, *orecchiette* with, 332–3
        steamed, with green vinaigrette, 271
        steamed, with yogurt and coriander sauce,
            156
        yogurt mousse, with Champagne sauce,
            272–3
    sole, rolled fillets *à la nage*, 336–7
    steamed, 113–14
    stew à la Puerto Rico, 284–5
    swordfish
        broiled, with herbs and ginger, 223
        escabèche, 222–3
    trout, pan-fried, with lentils, 299–300
    tuna
        broiled, in lemon marinade, 217
        grilled, with tomato and arugula salad,
            224–5
flan, pineapple and kiwi, 120
fritters, codfish, 31
frogs' legs
    concassé, 149–50
    Provençale, 150–1

fruit
  cherry(ies)
    clafoutis, 358–9
    compote, 357
    Cornish hens with, 360
    duck, sautéed, with, 361
    pork with, 363–4
    purchasing, 356
    sauce, 359
  citrus. *See* citrus fruit
  figs, honeyed, 97
  melon soup with passion fruit sorbet,
    151–2
  pineapple
    and kiwi flan, 120
    with passion fruit, 289
    sorbet, 290
  plums
    pork medallions sautéed with, 130–1
    tart, French, 44–5
  strawberry(ies)
    cheesecake, 237–8
    filling, 42
    in a purse, 233–4
    Romanoff, 236
    sorbet, 235
fungi, 114

garlic
  butter, chicken strips with, 291
  croutons, 286
  sautéed potatoes with, 170
goat cheese, chopped steak with, 16
gorgonzola, mixed green salad with,
  275
Grand Marnier soufflé, 319
grapefruit
  broiled chicken breasts with, 318
  trout sautéed with, 181–2
grouper, sautéed, with orange-jalapeño relish,
  313–14
Gruyère, baked sliced potatoes with, 168

gumbo
  chicken and sausage, 69
  shrimp, 75–6

ham
  and crabmeat on toast, 86–7
  prosciutto, 324–5
hamburgers
  broiled, with capers, 15–16
  with goat cheese, 16
hazelnut or hickory nut pie crust, 203
honey, 93–6
  barbeque sauce
    for Cornish hens, 100
    for swordfish, 102–3
  beef with peppers and, 106
  figs with, 97
  marinade for meats, 99
  and onion compote, sautéed salmon with, 98
  pork tenderloin with apples and, 105
  walnut bread, 103–4
horseradish sauce, 184

jambalaya, pork, 68–9

kiwi and pineapple flan, 120

lamb
  brochette of, marinated with honey, 99
  chops, Provençale style, 348–9
  goat water stew, 115
  medallions of, with shallot sauce and roast leg
    of, with thyme, 165–6
lasagne
  salmon, 48–9
  with turkey and tomato sauce, 255–6
lemon
  boiled potatoes with, 172
  tuna broiled with, 217

lentils, 295–8
    with balsamic vinegar, 304
    pan-fried trout with, 299–300
    salad, 301
        warm, 302
    soup, 305
    sprouts, 298
lobster, 216
    with aïoli sauce, 221–2
    with *mojita* sauce, 283-4
    with *ratatouille* and sautéed mushrooms,
        219–20

macaroni casserole with fresh herbs and Cheddar,
    206–7
Madeira mushroom sauce, 20
mahimahi, sautéed, 118–19
margarine, 344
marinades
    for beef, 12
    for chicken, 47
    honey, 99
    for pork, 128
    for tuna, 217
mayonnaise, 377
    chili sauce, 89
meat loaf with herbs, 17–18
melon soup with passion fruit sorbet, 151–2
mignonette sauce, 66
mofongo, 32
    food processor method, 33
mojita sauce, 283
monkfish stew, 218
mousse, salmon yogurt, with Champagne sauce,
    272–3
Moscovy duck, 329–30
mushroom(s)
    sauce, Madeira, 20
    sautéed, 219–20
mussel(s)
    rice pilaf with, 193–4
    salad with angel hair pasta, 347–8

mustard
    sauce
        beef tongue with, 300–1
        pork medallions with, 129–30
        turkey breast with, 259
    vinaigrette, 84–5

nuts
    almonds, pompano with, 147
    pie crusts
        hazelnut, 203
        pistachio, 314–15
    walnut bread, 103–4

octopus salad, 30
okra, 111
    with cornmeal, 114
olives, sautéed Cornish hens with, 331–2
omelettes, crab meat, with spicy mayonnaise, 88–9
onion(s)
    and honey compote, sautéed salmon with, 98
    pearl, peas with, 369
orange
    butter sauce, 315–16
    jalapeño relish, 313–14
    pie, with pistachio crust, 314–15
    sauce, 320
    vinaigrette, 317
orecchiette and smoked salmon, 332–3
oxtail and pot roast in red wine, 18–19
oysters
    on the half shell
        cocktail sauce for, 67
        mignonette sauce for, 66
    Rockefeller, 148–9

pancake, Diane's, 45
Parmesan cheese
    baked mashed potatoes with, 171–2
    sauce, ziti with, 207

parsley
    cucumbers with, 374
    potatoes with, 172
passion fruit
    pineapple with, 289
    sorbet, 151–2
pasta
    angel hair, mussel salad with, 347–8
    fettuccine with blue cheese and asparagus, 209
    lasagne
        salmon, 48–9
        with turkey and tomato sauce, 255–6
    macaroni casserole with fresh herbs and
        Cheddar, 206–7
    orecchiette and smoked salmon, 332–3
    soft-shell crabs and, à la Giobbi, 85–6
    with vegetables, capers and anchovy paste
        sauce, 208
    ziti with creamy Parmesan sauce, 207
pastry
    phyllo
        strawberries in, 233–4
        vegetable strudel, 345–6
    for tart shells, 44, 358
peas with pearl onions, 369
peppers
    hot
        cayenne, 143
        corn and ancho chili pudding, 253
        orange-jalapeño relish, 313–14
        shrimp and crab meat salad with jalapeño, 73
    sweet
        beef with, 106
        beef brochettes with coriander and, 14–15
        coulis, 346–7
        curried corn with, 373
        and kidney bean salad, 29
        mojita, 283
        pork chops with, 132–3
        ratatouille, 219–20
        scallops with snow peas and, 156
        shrimp with avocado and, 288
        swordfish with, 222–3

phyllo pastry
    strawberries in, 233–4
    vegetable strudel, 345–6
pie. *See also* tarts
    orange, with pistachio crust, 314–15
pilaf, rice
    basic, 192
    with mussels, 193–4
pineapple, 281
    and kiwi flan, 120
    with passion fruit, 289
    sorbet, 290
pine nut and spinach sauce, 49
pirogues, eggplant, 70–1
pistachio pie crust, 314–15
plantains
    deep-fried, 26
    mofongo, 32
        food processor method, 33
    sautéed ripe, 34
plums
    pork medallions sautéed with, 130–1
    tart, 44–5
pollo, arroz con, 27–8
pompano *amandine*, 147
pork, 123–5
    burgers, Oriental style, 131–2
    with cherries, 363–4
    chops
        with dressing, 127–8
        with peppers, 132–3
    cutlets, with caper sauce, 133–4
    jambalaya, 68–9
    leaner, 126
    medallions
        grilled, with herb marinade, 128–9
        with mustard sauce, 129–30
        sautéed with plums, 130–1
    roast pig, 279–81
    shoulder, barbecued, 286–7
    tenderloin, with apples, 105
potato(es), 161–4
    baked sliced, with Gruyère cheese, 168

potato(es) *(continued)*
    boiled, with lemon, 172
    cakes, 169
        crab, with *crème fraîche*, 165
    mashed
        baked with Parmesan cheese, 171–2
        with carrots, 173
    parslied, 172
    salad, Cajun, 67–8
    sautéed with garlic, 170
    tiny diced, 170–1
pot roast and oxtail in red wine,
        18–19
prosciutto, 324–5
pudding
    corn and ancho chili, 253
    rice, 195–6
Puerto Rican cooking, 23–5, 279–81
    adobo seasoning, 287
    arroz con pollo, 27–8
    beans
        dried, 29
        kidney, and sweet pepper salad, 29
        rice and, 28
    chicken strips in garlic butter, 291
    codfish fritters, 31
    coriander in, 282
    fish stew, 284–5
    lobster with *mojita* sauce, 283–4
    mofongo, 32
        food processor method, 33
    octopus salad, 30
    pineapple
        with passion fruit, 289
        sorbet, 290
    pork shoulder, barbecued, 286–7
    sautéed ripe plantains, 34
    shrimp with avocado and sweet red pepper,
        288
    tostones, 26

quail, braised stuffed, 327–8

raisin brioches, 46
ranching, 5–9
raspberry sauce, 42
ratatouille, 219–20
relish
    orange-jalapeño, 313–14
    tomato, 253
rice, 187–9
    aromatic, 190
    and beans, 28
    chicken with, 27–8
    creamy, pan-roasted shrimp with, 191–2
    Creole, 195
    pilaf
        basic, 192
        with mussels, 193–4
    pudding, 195–6
    wild, buttered, 367
Royal Lee tangerines, 312

safety precautions for cooking with children, 40
salad
    coleslaw, 376
    corn, with mustard vinaigrette, 84–5
    cucumber and carrot, with dill, 375
    kidney bean and red pepper, 29
    lentil, 301
        warm, 302
    mixed green, 375
    mussel, with angel hair pasta, 347–8
    octopus, 30
    potato, Cajun, 67–8
    salmon, with orange vinaigrette, 317
    shrimp and crab meat, with jalapeño pepper,
        73
    tabbouleh, 372
    tomato and arugula, 225
salmon, 263–70
    baked, with feta cheese and coriander, 334–5
    cakes Pojarski, 274–5
    grilled, with artichoke sauce, 239–40
    lasagne, 48–9

salmon *(continued)*
  en papillote, with crab, 275–6
  salad, with orange vinaigrette, 317
  sautéed, with honey-onion compote, 98
  smoked, *orecchiette* with, 332–3
  steamed
    with green vinaigrette, 271
    with yogurt and coriander sauce, 156
  yogurt mousse, with Champagne sauce, 272–3
salsa, tomato
  green, 84
  red, 84
sauce
  aïoli, 221–2
  artichoke, 239–40
  barbecue
    for Cornish hens, 100
    for swordfish, 102–3
  béarnaise, 10–11
  butter
    herbed, 64–5
    orange, 315–16
  caper, 133–4
  Champagne, 273
  cheese
    blue, 205
    Parmesan, 207
  cherry, 359
  cocktail, 67
  Creole, 145–6
  horseradish, 184
  mignonette, 66
  mojita, 283
  mushroom Madeira, 20
  mustard
    for beef tongue, 300–1
    for pork medallions, 129–30
    for turkey breast, 259
  orange, 320
    butter, 315–16
  pine nut spinach, 49
  raspberry, 42
  shallot, 303

sauce *(continued)*
  tomato, 255
    fresh, 377
  Worcestershire, homemade, 146
  yogurt and coriander, 156
sausage and chicken gumbo, 69
scallions
  grilled, *crème fraîche* with, 165–6
  string beans with, 371
scallops with peppers and snow peas, 156
seafood. *See also* fish; shellfish
  Creole seasoning for, 145
  octopus salad, 30
shallot sauce, 303
shellfish, 216; *see also* shrimp
  clams on half shell, sauces for, 66, 67
  crab(s)
    cakes, potato, with *crème fraîche*, 165
    and ham, on toast, 86–7
    omelettes, with spicy mayonnaise, 88–9
    salad, with shrimp and jalapeño pepper, 73
    salmon *en papillote* with, 275–6
    soft-shell, 82–6, 144
  crawfish *étouffée à la Creole*, 61–2
  lobster
    with aïoli sauce, 221–2
    with *ratatouille* and sautéed mushrooms,
      219–20
  oysters
    on half shell, sauces for, 66, 67
    Rockefeller, 148–9
shrimp
  with avocado and sweet red pepper, 288
  barbecued, 62–3
  brochettes, with orange butter sauce, 315–16
  Creole, 74
  fried, with squid, 65–6
  grilled, with herbed butter sauce, 64
  gumbo, 75–6
  pan-roasted, with creamy rice, 191–2
  salad, with crab meat and jalapeño pepper, 73
  stock, 378
  with yogurt and Tabasco sauce, 72

snow peas, scallops with peppers and, 156
sole
　　Dover, *meunière*, 153
　　rolled fillets of, *à la nage*, 336–7
sorbet
　　passion fruit, 151–2
　　pineapple, 290
　　strawberry, 235
soufflés, Grand Marnier, 319
soup
　　bull's foot, 116
　　lentil, 305
　　melon, with passion fruit sorbet, 151–2
　　vegetable, with turkey and coriander, 260
spa cuisine, 341–3
　　butter in, 344
　　lamb chops Provençale style, 348–9
　　mussel salad with angel hair pasta, 347–8
　　vegetable strudel, 345–6
spaghetti squash, 368
spinach
　　and pine nut sauce, 49
　　sautéed, 369
sprouts, lentil, 298
squash. *See also* zucchini
　　spaghetti, 368
squid, fried, with shrimp, 65–6
stew
　　fish
　　　　à la Puerto Rico, 284–5
　　　　monkfish, 218
　　goat water, 115
stock. *See also* broth
　　shrimp, 378
strawberry(ies), 229–30
　　cheesecake, 237–8
　　filling, crepes with, 42
　　purchasing, 232
　　in a purse, 233–4
　　Romanoff, 236
　　sorbet, 235
string beans with scallions, 371
strudel, vegetable, 345–6

sweet potato purée, 372
swordfish
　　broiled, with herbs and ginger, 223
　　escabèche, 222–3
　　honey-barbecued, 102–3

Tabasco sauce, 54
　　shrimp with yogurt and, 72
tabbouleh, 372
tangerines, 312
tarts
　　Cheddar, with arugula, 203–4
　　cherry *clafoutis*, 358–9
　　plum, 44–5
tomato(es)
　　relish, 253
　　salad, with arugula, 225
　　salsa
　　　　green, 84
　　　　red, 84
　　sauce, 255
　　　　fresh, 377
　　　　mojita, 283
　　zucchini stuffed with, 364
tostones, 26
trout, 177–9
　　buying and handling, 180
　　with ginger stuffing, 182–3
　　pan-fried, with lentils, 299–300
　　sautéed, with grapefruit, 181–2
　　smoked, with horseradish sauce, 184
tuna
　　broiled, in lemon marinade, 217
　　grilled, with tomato and arugula salad, 224–5
turkey, 245–51
　　breast
　　　　with mustard sauce, 259
　　　　roast, 257
　　lasagne with, and tomato sauce, 255–6
　　rolled, with corn, 252–3
　　scallopine à la Bolognese, 258

turkey *(continued)*
    steaks, with fresh corn and basil, 254
    vegetable soup with coriander and,
        260

vegetable(s). *See also* peppers; tomato
    artichokes, 232
        grilled salmon with, 239–40
        preparation for poaching, 243
        stuffed, 240–2
        vinaigrette, 242
    arugula
        Cheddar tart with, 203–4
        salad, with tomatoes, 225
    asparagus, fettuccine with blue cheese and,
        209
    avocado, shrimp with sweet red pepper and,
        288
    baby, sautéed, 370
    beans, dried
        to cook, 29
        kidney, and red pepper salad, 29
        rice and, 28
    carrot(s)
        baby, parslied, 371
        and cucumber salad with dill, 375
        potatoes mashed with, 173
    cauliflower mimosa, 374
    corn
        and ancho chili pudding, 253
        curried, with red and green peppers,
        373
        salad, with mustard vinaigrette, 84–5
        turkey and, 252–4
    cucumbers
        and carrot salad with dill, 375
        parslied, 374
    lentils, 298
        with balsamic vinegar, 304
        pan-fried trout with, 299–300
        salad, 301–2
        soup, 305

vegetable(s) *(continued)*
    okra, 111
        with cornmeal, 114
    pasta with capers, anchovy paste and,
        208
    peas, with pearl onions, 369
    ratatouille, 219–20
    soup, with turkey and coriander, 260
    spaghetti squash, 368
    spinach, sautéed, 369
    string beans with scallions, 371
    strudel, 345–6
    zucchini
        in meat loaf with herbs, 18
        tomato-stuffed, 364
vinaigrette
    for artichokes, 242
    green, steamed salmon with, 271
    mustard, 84–5
    orange, 317

walnut honey bread, 103–4
West Indian cooking, 109–12
    bull's foot soup, 116
    chicken, curried, 117
    fish, steamed, 113–14
    fungi, 114
    goat water stew, 115
    mahimahi, sautéed, 118
    okra, 111
    pineapple and kiwi flan, 120
wild rice, buttered, 367
wine, cooking with, 323–4, 326
    braised beef, 12–13
    Cornish hens, sautéed, with olives,
        331–2
    Muscovy duck, 329–30
    orecchiette with smoked salmon, 332–3
    pot roast and oxtail, 18–19
    quail, braised stuffed, 327–8
    salmon fillets baked with feta cheese and
        coriander, 334–5

wine, cooking with *(continued)*
    sole, rolled fillets of, *à la nage*, 336–7
    steak with green peppercorns, 333–4
Worcestershire sauce, homemade, 146

yam purée, 372
yeast breads
    honey walnut, 103–4
    raisin brioche, 46

yogurt
    and coriander sauce, 156
    salmon mousse with Champagne sauce, 272–3

ziti with creamy Parmesan sauce, 207
zucchini
    in meat loaf with herbs, 18
    ratatouille, 219–20
    tomato-stuffed, 364

A NOTE ABOUT THE AUTHOR

Pierre Franey was born in St. Vinnemer, France (Burgundy), in 1921 and did a classical restaurant apprenticeship as a chef in Paris, beginning at the age of thirteen. He came to America for the World's Fair in New York in the late 1930s as a teenager to work in the restaurant of the French Pavilion. He fought in the American army in World War II. Afterward, he went to work in Le Pavillon, the magnificent restaurant that had evolved out of the World's Fair. Soon he was executive chef of this, the finest French restaurant in America. He was also executive chef at La Côte Basque, which opened in 1957. He left in 1960 and then served as a food consultant, especially helping Craig Claiborne revolutionize food journalism and food tastes, collaborating with him on several books. Pierre in the 1970s became a columnist for *The New York Times*, creating the hugely successful "60-Minute Gourmet." The column turned into two best-selling books in 1979 and 1981 (and other books as well). He has made two public-television series, "Cuisine Rapide" and "Pierre Franey's Cooking in America"; a third show will debut in summer 1994 ("Pierre Franey's Cooking in France");—Knopf will publish the tie-in book). He will continue to write feature stories for the *Times* with Bryan Miller. He lives primarily in East Hampton, New York, but maintains an apartment in Manhattan. He travels extensively because of his commitment to various charities, including the March of Dimes and Meals on Wheels. He is truly beloved by his peers.

A N O T E O N T H E T Y P E

The typeface used in this book is Adobe Garamond. Known for their clean appearance, elegance, and remarkable legibility, Garamond typefaces are named after and based on the lovely classical designs of Claude Garamond, the foremost type designer in France in the sixteenth century. Over many centuries, Garamond's types have served as models for many other type designers.

Design and composition by The Sarabande Press

Illustrations by Lauren Jarrett

Printed and bound by R. R. Donnelley & Sons, Harrisonburg, Virginia